INVENTORY 98

INVENTORY 1985

St. Louis Community College

Forest Park
Florissant Valley
Meramec

Instructional Resources
St. Louis, Missouri

Classical Greece

Tragic actor, masked, as Heracles. Terracotta bust, 3rd century B.C.
American School of Classical Studies at Athens

MASTERWORKS OF WORLD DRAMA

CLASSICAL GREECE

Anthony Caputi

CORNELL UNIVERSITY

D. C. HEATH AND COMPANY

CONTENTS

Acknowledgements

THE ORESTEIA (*Agamemnon, The Choephoroe, The Eumenides*) by Aeschylus. Translated by Sir John Tersidder Sheppard and used with his permission.

OEDIPUS REX by Sophocles. Translated by Albert S. Cook; copyright 1948, 1957, by Albert S. Cook and used with his permission.

THE TROJAN WOMEN by Euripides. From *Three Greek Plays,* translated and with Introductions by Edith Hamilton. By permission of W. W. Norton & Company, Inc. Copyright 1937 by W. W. Norton & Company, Inc.; copyright renewed 1965 by Doris Fielding Reid.

THE BACCHAE by Euripides. Translated by Margaret Kinmont Tennant; reprinted by permission of Methuen & Company, Ltd.

LYSISTRATA by Aristophanes. An English Version by Dudley Fitts, copyright, 1954, by Harcourt, Brace & World, Inc.; © 1962 by Dudley Fitts. Reprinted by permission of the publishers and Faber & Faber, Ltd.

CAUTION: Professionals and amateurs are hereby warned that this play, being fully protected under the copyright laws of the United States of America, the British Empire, including the Dominion of Canada, and all other countries which are signatories to the Universal Copyright Convention and the International Copyright Union, is subject to royalty. All rights, including professional, amateur, motion picture, recitation, lecturing, public reading, radio broadcasting, television, and the rights of translation into foreign languages are strictly reserved. Inquiries on professional rights should be addressed to Lucy Kroll Agency, 119 West 57th Street, New York 19, New York; inquiries on amateur and translation rights should be addressed to Harcourt, Brace & World, Inc.; 757 Third Avenue, New York, N.Y. 10017.

*The drawings on pages xxiv and 95 are
by* PETER KAHN, *Cornell University.*

Classical Greece

Clay copy of actual comic stage-mask from the Athenian Agora,
3rd century A.D. By this time Greece had become part of
the Roman Empire. *American School of Classical Studies at Athens*

THE DRAMA OF
Classical Greece

THE DRAMATIC FESTIVALS One of the most provocative facts about the development of drama is that at its sources it was always associated with religion. Wherever we look—whether at primitive cultures in Africa, Australia, or the Americas, at the early Greeks, or at the Christians of the Middle Ages—we find that drama invariably grew out of ceremonies designed to solve practical problems by putting the worshipper in rapport with the forces that controlled him. By the time plays as we know them today had emerged from any one of these traditions, of course, they were no longer expected to increase plant and animal food or to promote fertility, though many of them still served to teach the lore of religion through reenactments of religious story. Their connection with a religious past is best seen in the fact that they continued to dramatize the great issues of life. What is the more remarkable, moreover, is that this purpose has persisted, through dozens of centuries and scores of traditions. Our word "drama" derives from an ancient Dorian word meaning "doing" or "action." In general we understand "drama" to mean that mode of expression which typically works through actions, through the language of actors doing and saying things. At its best drama has the power to deepen and enrich our relations with our world, a power rather like that presumably produced when its function was religious.

In Greece the origins of drama trace to the worship of Dionysus, a relatively late and rather sensational god in the story of that civilization. Sometimes known as the "divine young man" or Bacchus, Dionysus was not one of the gods found in Homer, but was apparently imported from Thrace in the eighth century B.C. Typically, a myth was invented to account for his coming. In its most popular version, Zeus had become enamored of Semele, the daughter of the King of Thebes. At her request that he come to her in all his heavenly splendor, Zeus appeared to her as a tower of fire and consumed her. The product of this ecstatic union was Dionysus, whom Zeus rescued from the flames and encased in his thigh to protect him from his vengeful wife, Hera. In time, the baby was born again and raised by nymphs on Mount Nysa; when he reached maturity, he began to wander, taking the grape to distant lands and instructing people in its cultivation.

Dionysus was chiefly worshipped, accordingly, for his powers to produce fruitfulness, abundance, health, and that natural consequence of abundant wine, exhilaration or ecstasy. Part of the cult celebrated him with revel songs, wild, joyous processions, and spirited ceremonies designed to win his blessing for some phase of wine production. But he was also worshipped for his knowledge of suffering, death, and resurrection, and for this worship there were solemn and stately ceremonies, some of which, it is thought, contained reenactments of parts of the myth of his birth. As the cult spread in Greece, several types of ceremonial performance apparently spread with it or developed out of it. One such was the *dithyramb,* a choral song that celebrated events from the myth; by the sixth century it had achieved the form in which it was subsequently sung and danced by choruses of fifty men or boys at the great dramatic festivals of the classical period. Among the other forms to develop, tragedy and comedy were the most important. As they evolved, gradually passing from religious exercise to secular art-work, the customs governing their presentation also evolved, until by the last quarter of the sixth century three key festivals in honor of Dionysus had been firmly established.

The dramatic festivals in Greece were always conducted under the auspices of the state. State officers selected the plays to be shown, delegated the responsibility for their production to certain citizens, arranged for the necessary processions and civic ceremonies, and themselves took prominent parts in many of these events. In addition, the state paid the leading actors assigned to the playwrights and controlled by special laws the behavior of citizens during festival time. A time of festival was a sacred time. The courts and businesses were closed; certain legal practices, such as restraining a debtor, were suspended; physical violence became a capital offence. The events began at sunrise with processions culminating in sacrifices and ceremonies calculated to purify the theater; as the sun rose, the crowd, bedecked with ivy and armed with cushions and lunches, settled down to watch the day's program. It lasted all day.

The Rural Dionysia, sometimes called the Lesser Dionysia or the Dionysia of the Fields, were held in a number of the country districts in Attica at the completion of the harvest in December, and, like all "Dionysia" were festivals honoring Dionysus. Originally simple folk festivals something like May Day celebrations, they gradually grew in popularity and borrowed features from the great festivals in Athens. They are important in the history of Greek drama chiefly because they provided occasions for the production of old plays, which, by custom, were shown only once in Athens until well into the fourth century; in this way the Rural Dionysia kept many masterpieces before the public. A more important festival was the Lenaea, which was celebrated in a sacred precinct near the market place in Athens in January. Comprising several kinds of events, the Lenaea was chiefly associated, in the fifth century, with the production of comedies: sometime after 450 B.C. it provided a contest for comic actors, and throughout the century it attracted the superior writers of comedy, while it could attract only the young and inferior tragic writers.

But the dramatic festival of most importance to Greek drama was by all odds the City or Great Dionysia. Dedicated to Dionysus Eleuthereus, that is, to Dionysus as represented in this case by an ancient statue from the town of

Eleutherae, it was celebrated in March in anticipation of the planting, and it embraced a period of five or six days. Among its many events were the contests in tragedy and comedy that pitted the greatest dramatists of antiquity against each other in what was easily the most important of all the theaters of antiquity, the Theater of Dionysus Eleuthereus in Athens, still to be seen on the southeastern slope of the Acropolis. Despite its importance, the early history of the City Dionysia is now all but lost to us. It was apparently instituted toward the middle of the sixth century, probably during the reign of the benevolent tyrant Peisistratus (c.600–527 B.C.); our earliest secure information is that it offered the first contest for tragic poets in 534 B.C., when the prize was won by Thespis (fl.550–520 B.C.). An actor-playwright from Icaria, a village near Marathon, Thespis is traditionally thought to have journeyed from village to village in Attica, presenting plays from a cart, and in the course of his long career to have made a number of crucial contributions to dramatic art. Among other things, he is credited with having first separated an actor from the chorus, in this way making dramatized dialogue possible. In any event, his position at the beginning of the story of Greek drama has earned him the title the father of the drama. After his time, fortunately, and particularly during the great century of Aeschylus, Sophocles, Euripides, and Aristophanes, our records for the festivals are much fuller.

During the classical period the City Dionysia typically opened on the first day with a magnificent procession which brought the image of Dionysus to the theater. The order of march included state officials, priests of Dionysus, certain young men known as *epheboi* who escorted the figure of the god, young girls, the performers in the plays to be produced, and the animals for sacrifice, including the bull associated with the god. Throughout the day there was feasting, sports, and revelry; then toward evening the playwrights and their actors and staffs went to a kind of sacred music hall near the theater called the Odeon, where they introduced themselves and their plays to the audience in an event known as the *proagon,* which means "before the contest." There is a touching story of Sophocles' appearance for this event in 406 B.C., when, himself a very old man, he came dressed in black to tell the spectators that Euripides was dead. On the second day the processions continued and ten dithyrambic choruses from various localities in Attica competed for a prize. Then the dramatic contests took place during the next three days. During the fifth century the typical schedule for each of these days consisted of three tragedies and a satyr play by one writer and a comedy by a second. With the completion of the competition, the judges met on the sixth day to determine the winners and honor them: all the victors were crowned with ivy; the tragic playwright received the traditional goat; the comic playwright a jug of wine and a basket of figs; both received a sum of money from the state.

The history of these festivals tells a story of gradual change, understandable error, and phenomenal achievement. The practice by which plays were presented only once was gradually modified in the fourth century as old tragedies were introduced either in place of the satyr play or as curtain raisers to the newer competition; in the second half of that century an old comedy was used to introduce the new ones. Gradually, contests for actors, first for the tragedians and then for the comedians, were added to the format. The decisions reached in various of the competitions suggest that occasionally mistakes were made: we hear of bribery and know that feeling ran very high; but we can only assume that the play with which Philocles defeated Sophocles' *Oedipus Rex* was not its equal: we cannot know for certain. Despite their strangeness to our eyes and their inherent problems, the dramatic festivals in Greece provided a system that nurtured a period of unparalleled excellence in the drama.

THE PHYSICAL THEATER   As the dramatic festivals and the dramatic forms developed and achieved distinction, physical theaters were developed to serve them. Actually no two Greek theaters were exactly the same: since they were built on hillsides, they invariably differed in shape and size; and since in time they were gradually rebuilt and remodelled, some of the extant examples understandably conform to earlier models, some to later. Yet the quite abundant evidence of the ruins suggests that, despite the variety, one general idea for a physical theater dominated in ancient Greece. In its earliest period the theater, too, was an aspect of wholly religious celebrations in honor of Dionysus. At these celebrations the worshippers presumably gathered and seated themselves on a hillside around a flat place, perhaps a threshing floor, to watch the ceremonies and dancing and to listen to the revel songs. In time wooden seats were built on the semi-circle of the hillside and a two-part theater was born consisting of a *theatron,* or viewing place, and an *orchestra,* or flat, circular dancing place. At some point, moreover, an altar, or *thymele,* was placed in the center or on the edge of the circle of the *orchestra,* and seats of honor for priests and officials were placed around the perimeter. This two-part theater apparently existed for many decades.

During the first half of the fifth century the next important step in construction was taken when a long, low building called the scene-building, or *skene,* was erected along the open side of the *orchestra,* facing the banks of seats. Because the ruins relating to this part of the theater are highly disordered and fragmentary, however, the exact character of the *skene* is one of the most vexing questions in this field of research. It is clear that it was a long building, perhaps as long as one hundred feet, and that in its earliest form it was probably a one-story structure made of wood; but it is hard to go beyond these general statements. Most scholars now contend that in the fifth century it had either no "stage" or a very low, shallow one along the side facing the *orchestra,* that it probably had three doors on that side, and that it may have had wings to define the ends of the low platform or playing area, which because of its position in front of the *skene* became known as the *proskenion.*

In any event, by the second quarter of the fifth century the normal Greek theater was a three-part wooden structure consisting of a *theatron,* an *orchestra,* and a *skene.* It was usually large: the theater of Dionysus Eleuthereus in Athens held 14,000 spectators and had an *orchestra* sixty feet in diameter, and, of course, it was uncovered. Each morning during festival time the crowds filed in through the *paradoi,* the passageways between the *theatron* and the ends of the *skene,* to take their seats in the sun. The question of where the action of the plays was located—whether the actors were limited to the *proskenion* while the chorus was limited to the *orchestra,* or whether the actors could move freely from one area to another—has never been resolved. But it is clear that the *skene* was used both as dressing rooms for the actors and as a scene-backing.

In time these large, but quite simple wooden theaters were rebuilt in stone: the theater of Dionysus Eleuthereus was rebuilt in the second half of the fifth century. The only extant structure which closely resembles the normal type at this important stage of its evolution, however, is the theater of Epidaurus (*c.*350 B.C.); in the others changes continued to be introduced and embellishments added. The theater of Dionysus Eleuthereus was again remodelled under Lycurgus (*c.*300 B.C.), again in late Hellenistic times, and was entirely reconstructed in Roman times when the Emperor Nero visited Athens in 67 A.D. Sometime in the second century B.C. the earlier *proskenion* gave way to a raised platform some thirteen feet high, and the *skene* developed a second story; during the last period of construction it was patterned after the Roman theater, which gave it the semi-circular *orchestra* that is to be viewed in Athens today.

The influence of this structure on the plays written for it was tremendous. Such obvious facts as that Greek plays were written to be performed in a huge structure under an open sky explain to some extent why they were composed on relatively bold, broad, simple lines: the intricacy of action and psychological interest to be found in later traditions would have been difficult, if not impossible, to communicate under these conditions. The further fact that they were staged in a physical setting that made getting people on and off stage difficult clarifies why the chorus usually remained in the *orchestra* once it had entered, why single scenes were constructed in terms of single character-groupings, and why, more generally, the action was usually limited to a single place, a single day, and a single cluster of events, in other words, limited to the celebrated unities made so much of by later critics. This was a theater that required a stylized, distinctly larger-than-life mode of production; its size, shape, acoustical conditions, and arrangement encouraged a certain bigness in all things.

THE PERFORMERS AND CONVENTIONS OF PRODUCTION

Despite the haziness of its formative years, we know that Greek drama began as choral performances of various kinds and passed through several phases before developing the forms now known as tragedy, comedy, and the satyr play. During the pre-dramatic, choral period, the choruses were quite large, including, if we can judge from the later dithyrambic chorus, as many as fifty members, characteristically dressed as satyrs, animals, or revellers. In time, their character and costumes were adjusted to the needs of particular plays and their number was gradually reduced: in the first half of the fifth century Aeschylus lowered the number for the tragic chorus to twelve and Sophocles fixed it at fifteen, while the comic writers stabilized the comic chorus at twenty-four. By this time, moreover, the preparation and use of choruses were governed by reasonably firm conventions. Once the state officials had selected the playwrights and plays to compete in a festival, they next selected a number of wealthy citizens to serve as *choregi* and assigned them to the playwrights. The *choregus* was responsible both for those expenses of production not defrayed by the state, and for the chorus, for which he usually hired a chorus-trainer. Some *choregi* warmed to this task enthusiastically: Demosthenes boasted of the money he had spent on gold crowns for his chorus; but others were apparently moved neither by the honor nor by the prize awarded to the *choregi* associated with the winning playwrights, and some very probably marred their playwrights' chances of success with bad taste and stinginess.

In performance the chorus usually made its first entrance by way of the *parodoi,* the passageways between the *skene* and the *theatron,* singing its first ode, known appropriately as the *parodos.* Everything that precedes this *parodos* in a Greek play is called the prologue. Once in the *orchestra,* the choral members were drawn up in a military formation, in variations of which they then executed their dances and spoke or sang their parts. Of the dancing we know very little beyond that it was intricate and accompanied by a flute. For the most part the songs were the odes called *stasima* (from *stasis,* meaning "stand"), which were used to mark the breaks between the acted scenes, or episodes, and the performance of a *stasimon* of any length also involved dancing and movement. In addition to the odes, sometimes the chorus also sang passages of lyrical dialogue with one or more of the actors in an ensemble piece, typically a joint lamentation known as a *kommos.* When the chorus had completed its part with a final *stasimon,* they exited— hence the last scene was called the *exodos.* Like the dancing, unfortunately, we also know very little of choral singing. Apparently, it too was accompanied by a flute; and the single extant musical fragment, for an ode from Euripides' *Orestes* 408 B.C.), suggests that it was something like our plain chant. But generalization here is dangerous: though the total contribution of the chorus to Greek play production obviously was important, it is safest not to try to visualize it too precisely.

Some measure of visualization is possible and desirable, however, in matters of physical appearance. Apparently all choral members wore masks and some light form of footwear to facilitate their dancing. In the fifth century, the comic choruses still wore padded, grotesque costumes and, sometimes, animal costumes; and the satyr chorus was still to be seen in the satyr play. By the time of Aeschylus, however, the tragic choruses usually dressed in roughly contemporary costumes, as do the elders, maidens, or military groups that we meet in most extant plays. The one notable departure from this usage in Aeschylus' chorus of Furies in *The Eumenides* (458 B.C.)—it is said that this chorus caused strong men to faint and women to miscarry—merely indicates that the tragic playwrights had considerable freedom in these matters, as they had in others. Certainly this freedom is to be met in their practice of occasionally assigning spoken lines and passages to be delivered in recitative to the chorus or to individual members of it; frequently the leader of the chorus, or *coryphaeus* (he was earlier called the *choregus*), had sufficient spoken lines to be considered an additional actor.

Throughout the fifth century, the chorus defined by these conventions persisted as an element of first importance in Greek plays, and this despite the fact that its use gradually declined as playwrights increasingly favored represented action over lyrical accompaniment and commentary. Whereas fairly early in the century Aeschylus had given as many as two-thirds of the lines of *The Suppliants* (466 B.C.) to the chorus, toward the end Euripides sometimes relegated only about one-ninth of the lines to it. The actors, on the other hand, trace a different but related story in that their prominence naturally increased as the choral element declined. The decisive step from a wholly choral performance to one involving characters exchanging lines of dialogue had first been taken by Thespis sometime in the sixth century when he added the first actor to the chorus; with this crucial innovation, it is said, he invented tragedy. Known as the *hypocrites,* or "answerer," this first actor served to answer the chorus or *coryphaeus,* or, perhaps, to comment on the choral recitation; and during the earliest period the playwright himself always filled the role. In the fifth century the second and third actors brought with them the development of the dramatic forms with which Greek drama achieved its greatness. Early in the century Aeschylus, who had himself served as the *hypocrites* in his now lost one-actor plays, added the second actor to create the two-actor tragedy exemplified in *The Persians* (472 B.C.), *Seven Against Thebes* (467 B.C.), and *The Suppliants* (466 B.C.). Later, Sophocles added the third actor to create the form of the other extant tragedies. Although we know less of the development of comedy in this respect, it seems to have stabilized itself relatively early in its history in a four-actor form.

With these changes and the rapid increase in the actor's prominence, the responsibility for his contribution passed, understandably, from the playwright to a group of highly trained professionals whose range of accomplishments was staggering. Since they were limited in number to three to a play, at most four, they were forced to considerable doubling of parts; since, moreover, they played both men's and women's roles, they had to manage in the extremely large theaters in which they performed remarkable feats of voice control and projection. In addition, as we have seen, they were always expected to be expert singers and dancers. In the face of such demands a corps of quite brilliant performers, with individuals specializing either as tragedians or comedians, developed in the course of the fifth century and became known as the Artists of Dionysus. These actors were at all times held to the highest standards of performance. We hear that Greek audiences sometimes threw cushions and stones to express their disapproval and that on one occasion an actor named Aeschines nearly lost his life in such a barrage. But actors were also held in high esteem by their countrymen and generously rewarded for real achievement. Towards the middle of the century prizes were instituted for the tragic and comic protagonists (the leading actors), while certain other civic privileges, such as exemption from military service, were commonplace. Occasionally, actors were even selected for diplomatic missions and other official activities that carried with them considerable honor.

On the whole the system by which actors were trained and used worked superbly. Although it has seemed to some that the limitation in number of actors imposed needless difficulties on everyone, the practice had the singular advantage of insuring that performances in all roles would be first-rate. Moreover, doubling was really a rather easy matter with the help of full masks and complete but simple costume changes. By the fifth century the actor always wore a mask appropriate to the character he was portraying. Typically, it was larger-than-life and stylized so that the character type depicted could easily be identified at a distance, and it may have had a contrivance built into the mouthpiece to aid in voice projection. In the matter of costume they usually wore roughly contemporary clothes appropriate to their characters and on their feet a high, but light shoe to allow them to move nimbly—not the thick-soled boot associated with the later platform stage of Hellenistic times. With these aids, a complete change in appearance was possible in a very short time, and great flexibility within a small group of players was managed. The acting style of these performers, of course, was probably quite remote from anything we know from the relatively realistic players of our time. The size of the theater, the masks, the continuous presence of the chorus, the great attention given to delivery—all these elements suggest a rather formal, conventionalized style of playing by which the emphasis typically went to largeness, clarity, and eloquence of effect.

Certainly a formal style of acting stressing clarity of delivery and boldness of theatrical effect would have been consistent with what we know about other aspects of play production in Greece. Only minimal attempts were made, for example, to provide anything like particularized scenery for a play. Before the *skene* had appeared, the scene was either unlocalized or only vaguely localized, as in Aeschylus' early extant plays. Once the *skene* was introduced, however, it became the principal scenic element, serving as whatever building was needed by the play and making certain simple scenic differentiations possible. The roof of the building provided a secondary area for such scenes as the Watchman's at the beginning of the *Agamemnon,* or for ascents or descents, when they were called for; the area immediately in front of the *skene* and flanked by its wings—the *proskenion*—was distinguished from the *orchestra* as a primary playing area; and the three doors in the front wall of the *skene* were used for entrances and exits and for distinguishing the interior places not seen by the audience. In time the practice of painting the panels between these doors produced the first significant attempts at painted scenery.

Unfortunately, the history of scene-painting in Greece is, like so much else, obscure. Aristotle credits Sophocles with its invention, while Vitruvius, a Roman writer on architecture in the first century B.C., says that Agatharchos of Samos "made a scene" for a production of a play by Aeschylus. Both accounts, it is clear, put the development of this art in the second quarter of the fifth century. Yet whatever the precise time of its development, scene-painting seems never to have involved more than representations on the panels between the doors of stylized locales that suggested the type of play being performed—tragedy, comedy, or satyr play—and the play's general location—in a city, on a rocky island, before a grove, etc.; in so large a theater, apparently, realistic detail would have been to no avail. At some point, moreover, perhaps in the fifth century, these painted panels were complemented by three-sided columns mounted somewhere in front of the *skene* and called *periaktoi*. On the three faces of this device three simple scenes were painted; and as it was turned, a different scene came into view, indicating a change of locale. Indeed, sometimes the *periaktoi* were also used to depict interiors or to locate characters in the world of the dead or in the act of swimming.

Like these methods for handling scenery, the properties and machines used were also relatively simple. Objects crucial to the action, such as images of the gods, small altars, Philoctetes' bow, or the crimson tapestry in the *Agamemnon,* were simply introduced. But there is no evidence that secondary properties, properties by which a world in detail might be established, were ever used; and, in fact, the only events in plays for which something like scenic extravagance was permitted were arrivals by chariot, like that of Agamemnon and his entourage, and then, apparently, horses and chariots were driven right into the *orchestra.* The machines, on the other hand, served largely to embellish the production in perfectly obvious ways. There were devices for imitating lightning and the sound of thunder and in the last half of the fifth century a crane for raising actors from the ground to the second story or roof of the *skene.* Best illustrative of the purpose of most of this apparatus to suggest rather than to imitate in any literal way was the *eccyclema,* a low platform on wheels that could be pushed through one of the doors of the *skene* and that was used to display the bodies of characters who had been killed offstage or to represent tableaux or still-life scenes of action that were taking place or that had taken place inside the building. The artificiality involved in its use points again to the degree of stylization and abstractness implied by most of the conventions of Greek play production. It is particularly important for people accustomed as we are to the realist tradition to remind ourselves continuously that this was a dramaturgy geared to a vast, outdoor theater.

GREEK TRAGEDY   The story of dramatic production in Greece is ultimately inseparable from the history of the dramatic forms for which production techniques were developed; indeed it is frequently impossible to say which came first: the theater practice or the modification in tragedy or comedy for which it proved useful. Our earliest historian of the development of tragedy and comedy in Greece is Aristotle, and in Book IV of the *Poetics* he tells us:

> Tragedy—as also Comedy—was at first mere improvisation. The one originated with the authors of the Dithyramb, the other with those of the phallic songs, which are still in use in many of our cities. Tragedy advanced by slow degrees; each new element that showed itself was in turn developed. Having passed through many changes, it found its natural form, and there it stopped.
> Aeschylus first introduced a second actor; he diminished the importance of the chorus, and assigned the leading part to the dialogue. Sophocles raised the number of actors to three, and added scene-painting. Moreover, it was not till late that the short plot was discarded for one of greater compass, and the grotesque diction of the earlier satyric form for the stately manner of tragedy [Butcher's translation].

Despite its very great importance, this account is not without difficulties. It seems likely that tragedy began with "mere improvisation" and we can scarcely dispute that in its early stages it owed something to the "authors of the Dithyramb" and "satyric form." But we must realize that the "Dithyramb" and "satyric form" alluded to probably have relatively little to do with the dithyrambs of the fifth century or with the satyr play; in fact, we know little of the earlier forms from which tragedy evolved, except that they were at first improvisatory. At best we can assume that tragedy grew out of the forms of the choral performances honoring Dionysus that even at the beginning of the development were solemn and sorrowful, and that gradually it accumulated dramatic content. The word *"tragodia,"* meaning "goat-song," suggests that in its initial phase it may have used a goat-chorus.

Beyond this earliest period, however, Aristotle's account is very helpful for it marks clearly the principal stages of tragedy as it passed from one-actor to two-actor to three-actor forms. The period initiated by Thespis when he added the first actor was brought to a close by Aeschylus when he added the second actor and diminished the importance of the chorus by reducing its size. The implications of the second actor for developments in dialogue and for representing conflict were immense. For the first time the force opposing the hero could receive extended treatment in the hero's presence, with the result that conflict could be more clearly and more dramatically presented. Moreover, the hero himself could be more fully developed simply because he could be on stage more often than he had been in one-actor plays. Inevitably, then, two-actor tragedy was a more supple and more subtle form than its predecessor, though it continued to give great prominence to the chorus. Each of the three extant two-actor tragedies contains passages of intricate choral work, which, far from burdening these plays, are the principal source of the lyricism so important in them. Despite Aristotle's implication that two-actor tragedy is but a step on the way to tragedy's "natural form," Aeschylus' *The Suppliants, The Persians,* and *Seven Against Thebes* show that it was in its own right a finished form of a high artistic order, one rather slower and less dramatic than later forms, but brilliantly designed to speak in its own way.

Aeschylus' contributions to tragedy did not end with the invention and perfection of the two-actor form: he is also credited with the invention of the tragic trilogy, by which three related tragedies were presented as a unit. Actually, these units are sometimes called tetralogies because they included, in addition to the three tragedies, a satyr play; but "trilogy" is the more frequent term because only the tragedies were always unified in some way. Since we have only one extant trilogy, *The Oresteia* (458 B.C.)—it is difficult to know by what principles this unity was typically achieved and how close a relationship the member plays typically had. The three plays of *The Oresteia,* as it happens, are very closely linked, but the evidence of titles from other trilogies suggests that a rather looser unity was possible. Aeschylus' trilogy on the house of Laius (467 B.C), comprising a *Laius,* an *Oedipus,* and *Seven Against Thebes,* for example, suggests a total pattern much less tightly knit than that of *The Oresteia.* Such units, it should be noticed, are to be carefully distinguished from single plays written at different times, though dealing with the same saga or legend.

During the same period that saw the development of the trilogy, Sophocles invented the three-actor form to take Greek tragedy still farther from the choral performances with which it had begun. With the addition of the third actor, the opportunities for dramatization increased and the role of the chorus proportionately declined, with the consequence that the number of important participating characters could be enlarged and their relationships treated in greater complexity. The resulting tragic form, embodied in all but three of the extant tragedies, exemplifies the greatest achievement in Greek drama. Sophocles' other technical contributions to tragedy include his discovery, or re-discovery, of the single play, which, however, continued to be submitted in groups of threes. Although the single play had existed before Aeschylus perfected the idea of the trilogy, it was then predominantly choral and characterized by what Aristotle called the short plot. To Sophocles, accordingly, goes the credit for the more elaborately dramatic, more ample linear structure of his best plays, as well as his enlargement of the chorus from twelve to fifteen members, at which number it remained fixed, and his possible invention of scene-painting.

The story of the formal development of Greek tragedy from the choral performances of the pre-dramatic era to its status when Sophocles wrote *Oedipus Rex* (*c.*429 B.C.) centers, then, on the gradual addition of actors, the gradual decline of the chorus, and the gradual movement from one kind of single play into the trilogy, and then to a second, more ample kind of single play. It traces a growth from a highly choral, lyrical, relatively static form to an increasingly more dramatic one; from what has been called a vertical drama, a kind of drama involving great development in depth but relatively little movement in time, to a horizontal or linear drama. Fairly early in the story, the playwrights had apparently abandoned the practice of retelling only the myths related to Dionysus. Although it is thought that in the fifth century these myths continued to furnish the subject matter for the dithyrambs, certainly by the time of Aeschylus playwrights were ranging freely through Greek legend and history for their actions. The tragic form that finally crystallized in the second half of the fifth century persisted without serious modification for some centuries, though none of the later tragedies are extant.

GREEK COMEDY   Greek comedy apparently developed later than tragedy and achieved in the fifth century only one of its distinctive forms in antiquity. Its early history is highly problematical. The word *"comodia,"* or *"comus-*song," refers it to the revel songs sung to honor Dionysus, and Aristotle's mention of "phallic songs" supports that theory of origins. But it is difficult to go beyond the very general hypothesis that comedy evolved from the gay, extravagant, rather obscene festive rituals illustrated in abundant vase paintings. On the one hand we have the rich, if always fragmentary, evidence of the phallic and revel songs, and on the other the fully developed comic forms of the fifth century known as Old Comedy. Although it is possible to discover numerous correspondences between the one and the other, it has so far been impossible to trace a clear line of development.

The early history of Greek comedy, accordingly, is best viewed rather tentatively, as a process by which the form that we now recognize as Old Comedy gradually grew out of certain, perhaps numerous, antecedents of the sort that we know something about from the *comus,* the lampoon, the beast mummeries, and the satyr play. The beast mummeries were short, ribald entertainments in which the participants dressed as animals, a convention which perhaps survived in the animal choruses in plays like *The Wasps* (422 B.C.) and *The Birds* (414 B.C.). The lampoon consisted of short, comic, rather scurrilous addresses that were usually directed at crowds in public places, and it could well have contributed something to the direct addresses of the comic chorus. The *comus,* on the other hand, was a kind of masquerade in which performers dressed in extravagant costumes, sometimes as animals, and danced and sang. In its fully developed form it was a kind of processional, largely choral entertainment: the chorus went from house to house or circulated in the theater, singing, dancing, and giving satiric speeches, though seldom engaging in anything more dramatic than comic arguments between different parts of the chorus. Because of its relation to the word "comedy" and its many points of contact with Old Comedy, the *comus* is usually cited as the most likely of the possible antecedents.

The satyr play, of course, was not an antecedent, but the form roughly contemporary to Old Comedy that was used to conclude the tragic trilogy. It has interest and relevance here because it probably had a development analogous to that of Old Comedy, but arrested at a point rather prior to that to which Aristophanes took Old Comedy. The satyr play, too, evidently began as a kind of phallic mummery in which the performers represented the half-men, half-goats called satyrs. In its fully developed form these satyrs made up the chorus that was led by Silenus, an old, often drunken leader of the satyrs, no less outrageous in sexual matters than they. To these stock characters were added certain free characters drawn from legend and tragic story, and together, fitted out with their grotesque masks, tightfitting costumes, animal skins, and prop phalluses, they typically engaged in a preposterous burlesque of some legendary situation. Our only complete satyr play is the *Cyclops* (*c.*423 B.C.) of Euripides.

Taken together, these forms give us some idea of the revel songs and semi-dramatic forms which probably affected the evolution of Greek comedy. Although they settle nothing precisely, they illuminate Old Comedy's basis in merrymaking and its pervasive emphasis on exorcism, satire, and sex; certainly they go far toward explaining the peculiar hilarity and exuberance of the form. Beyond the ghosts of such forms, however, we know very little. Apparently, Old Comedy did not develop before the beginning of the fifth century, though it probably existed as early as 486 B.C. During the period of its emergence names like Chionides (*fl.*460 B.C.), Magnes (*c.*500–430 B.C.), and Crates (*fl.*450–424 B.C.) occur, each of whom evidently added something to the form; but before the appearance of Aristophanes the record is very fragmentary. In the last quarter of the century the perfected form of Old Comedy is richly illustrated by nine of Aristophanes' eleven extant plays.

In form Old Comedy differed markedly from Greek tragedy. To begin with, it gave greater prominence to the chorus and put it to uses not to be met in tragedy. The most important of these proceed from two of the oldest and most distinctive features of the form, the *parabasis* and the *agon*. Present in the oldest plays, but the first to disappear, the *parabasis* means "a coming forward" and consists of a long address which the chorus directed at the audience; sometimes satiric, sometimes lyrical, it was frequently used as a device for attempting to prevail on the judges, but more typically as a commentary on the subject of the play. The *agon* is essentially a comic debate or combat, and it typically pitted two semi-choruses (the comic chorus of twenty-four divided into two groups of twelve) against each other, or opposed two actors supported by semi-choruses. The *agon* was usually fairly formal, though it sometimes abounded in abusive and scurrilous language, and usually not more than one is found in a play, though this was by no means a hard and fast rule.

The second principal way in which Old Comedy differed from Greek tragedy, is that it was governed by relatively few strict conventions: its structure was more variable than that of tragedy and so loose as to suggest, mistakenly, a kind of heedlessness. Although the same parts appear—the prologue, *parodos,* episodes, *stasima,* and *exodus,* as well as the *parabasis* and *agon*—they impose only the slightest sense of a conventional development on the structure; and the episodes or scenes of dialogue in the latter portion of the play—appropriately called the "illustrative episodes"—are frequently so little related to each other as to be almost interchangeable. The air of disjointed extravagance to be met in this structure, moreover, is supported by other standard features of Old Comedy. The comic chorus was normally dressed in grotesque costumes, with padded stomachs and behinds, prop phalluses, and highly stylized masks, and the characters were regularly burlesque figures impersonated by actors who specialized in the comedic style. Furthermore, the typical subjects of Old Comedy—fantasy, burlesque of legend, and politics— lent themselves readily to an exaggerated style of treatment that was utterly consonant with the hilarity and outrageousness of the form. The danger to our understanding of Old Comedy is that this looseness of structure and seeming wildness in the treatment of details can be too easily dismissed as carelessness or shoddiness of workmanship; actually it is integral to the spirit of Old Comedy, even necessary to the raucous vitality and exuberance so characteristic of it.

It is one of the freaks of dramatic history that, despite the many obscurities in the story of Old Comedy, we can say with considerable accuracy that it ended abruptly in, or shortly after, 404 B.C., the year in which Athens went down in defeat to Sparta. That catastrophe seems to have entailed a loss of energy or verve that had been crucial to the form, and shortly thereafter, even in the last two extant plays of Aristophanes, *The Ecclesiazusae* (*c.*39 B.C.) and the *Plutus* (388 B.C.), a less indecent, more subdued form known as Middle Comedy emerged. Although our only two extant examples of Middle Comedy are these last plays by Aristophanes, it was apparently a very vigorous form. A certain Athenaeus lists the authors of upwards of eight hundred plays, all of which would have been Middle Comedies, and all the other Middle Comedy writers who are remembered wrote more than two hundred and fifty plays apiece. From our fragmentary evidence of this work we can infer that the principal differences between it and Old Comedy were that in Middle Comedy the chorus was far less prominent and the action was more intricately and carefully worked out. This emphasis on action perhaps explains Middle Comedy's greater attention to society as it actually was. As love and the relations between the sexes became the center of focus, for example, the sheltered and undramatic position of respectable women in the Greek society of the time led to the introduction of prostitutes as prominent characters. The typical frame- work for relationships was built on the family, and relatively commonplace domestic problems became the source of complications. Although the break with the fantasy and indifference to verisimilitude so characteristic of Old Comedy was yet by no means complete, the break with its joyousness was: Middle Comedy was by comparison polite and moderate. Altogether, it lasted for some- thing less then one hundred years; although we have no single date or event to mark it, apparently its demise was concurrent with the collapse of the Mace- donian empire in the last quarter of the fourth century.

By the late fourth century still another comic type called New Comedy had defined itself, and with its appearance the transition from Old Comedy to a comic form relatively familiar to us was completed. In New Comedy the chorus was further divested of its traditional functions: its expository role was taken over by a

Prologue; its interpretive and lyrical functions were abandoned; its new purpose was for the most part to divert the audience between the acts. In New Comedy, moreover, interest was centered in carefully constructed actions dealing typically with the problems of lovers and always concluding with a happy ending, and the world of the plays was limited to people of leisure, a society in which values were relatively clear and in which fixed character types appeared with regularity. The miserly father, the knavish slave, the loyal slave, the courtesan, the young lover, the boor, the parasite—these were the stock characters in actions scrupulously constructed to give an illusion of everyday reality and executed with a high degree of polish and urbanity. With New Comedy emerged the five-act structure and what was many centuries later to be called the Comedy of Manners.

New Comedy flourished for more than one hundred and fifty years and produced a great many plays, though again, unfortunately, we have scarcely more than fragments. Its leading exponent was Menander of Athens (c.342–291 B.C.), a man whose fame in antiquity was surpassed only by that of Homer and Virgil. Of Menander's more than one hundred plays, we have one complete work, the recently discovered *The Grouch* (316 B.C.), and substantial fragments of three others, but we also know considerable about nine others from the adaptations made of them by the Roman dramatists, Plautus and Terence. Menander's excellence as a comic writer apparently rested in his great skill in constructing the kind of tightly knit action that has since been the staple of this kind of comedy, the familiar love escapade in which the boy wins the girl, loses the girl, and then, invariably, wins the girl. The formula is now commonplace, and it all began here, seasoned with elegance and delicate sentiment. Menander was so skillful at handling the intricate complications by which he tied these actions into knots that when Roman comic writers turned to Greece for plays to imitate and adapt—and they turned almost nowhere else—they most frequently drew on him.

By the time of New Comedy, of course, the total picture of Greek drama had undergone considerable change. In the theater the low platform in front of the *skene* had been replaced by a high stage; the front of the *skene* had come to represent two houses before which all the action took place; and the *parodoi* had been all but eliminated as the *theatron* and *skene* began to merge. Meantime, the tragic actors had added the thick-soled boot and elongated headdress to their costume to increase their stature, and the circular *orchestra* had been abbreviated to a rough semi-circle. Finally, as if to underscore that the drama no longer had any relationship to its religious origins, the altar to Dionysus disappeared.

This Hellenistic theater was in all respects consistent with its age: cosmopolitan, sophisticated, technically superb, but notably jaded and artificial. Plays continued to be written for it until as late as the second century A.D. and continued to be produced in the theater of Dionysus Eleuthereus in Athens until as late as the fifth century A.D. But Greek tragedy had largely died by the end of the fourth century B.C., and comedy had become rather thin by the end of the third. Through these centuries of decline certain minor comic forms persisted, which, with the rise of the Roman drama, made inroads into that culture and theater; indeed, the Greek mime and the crude farces popular in the Greek colonies in Italy undoubtedly proved to be the hardiest of all the dramatic forms in antiquity. But these forms are properly part of the story of the drama on which they exerted a more telling influence, the Roman drama.

Bibliography

Allen, J. T., *Stage Antiquities of the Greeks and Romans and Their Influence,* New York, 1927.

Arnott, Peter D., *Greek Scenic Conventions in the Fifth Century, B.C.,* Oxford, 1962.

————, *An Introduction to the Greek Theatre,* London, 1959.

Barnett, Lionel D., *The Greek Drama,* 4th ed., London, 1922.

Bieber, Margarete, *The History of the Greek and Roman Theater,* 2nd ed., Princeton, N.J., 1961.

Cornford, Francis M., *The Origin of Attic Comedy,* London, 1914.

Flickinger, R. C., *The Greek Theatre and Its Drama,* 4th ed., Chicago, 1936.

Gaster, Theodor, *Thespis; Ritual, Myth and Drama in the Ancient Near East,* New York, 1950.

Greene, William C., *Moira: Fate, Good, and Evil in Greek Thought,* Cambridge, Mass., 1944.

Haigh, A. E., *The Attic Theatre,* Oxford, 1898.

————, *The Tragic Drama of the Greeks,* Oxford, 1896.

Hamilton, Edith, *The Greek Way,* New York, 1952.

Harsh, Philip W., *A Handbook of Classical Drama,* Stanford, Calif., 1944.

Kitto, H. D. F., *Greek Tragedy,* 2nd ed., London, 1950.

Jaeger, Werner, *Paideia: The Ideals of Greek Culture,* tr. Gilbert Highet, 3 vols., New York, 1939–44.

Lattimore, Richard, *The Poetry of Greek Tragedy,* Baltimore, 1958.

Lever, Katherine, *The Art of Greek Comedy,* London, 1956.

Little, A. M. G., *Myth and Society in Attic Drama,* New York, 1942.

Lucas, D. W., *The Greek Tragic Poets: Their Contribution to Western Life and Thought,* London, 1950.

Norwood, Gilbert, *Greek Tragedy,* 2nd ed., London, 1928.

Pickard-Cambridge, A. W., *Dithyramb, Tragedy and Comedy,* Oxford, 1927.

————, *The Dramatic Festivals of Athens,* Oxford, 1953.

————, *The Theatre of Dionysus in Athens,* Oxford, 1946.

Webster, T. B. L., *Greek Theatre Production,* London, 1956.

A glossary of Greek gods and goddesses appears at the end of the book.

Theater at Epidaurus

Aeschylus

Aeschylus (525–456 B.C.) was the eldest of the important Greek
writers of tragedy in the fifth century and the first to take tragic
expression to the exalted position it enjoyed during the Periclean Age.
He is credited by Aristotle with having invented the two-actor form;
certainly he perfected it in plays like THE PERSIANS *(472 B.C.).*
In addition, he reduced the size of the tragic chorus from fifty
(e.g. THE SUPPLIANTS*) to twelve (e.g.* PROMETHEUS BOUND*) and*
invented and perfected the tragic trilogy (e.g. THE ORESTEIA*).*
Altogether, Aeschylus wrote about ninety plays and won thirteen
prizes. He was the master of the highly lyrical, slow-moving, massive
structure that is perhaps best exemplified in the AGAMEMNON, *the*
first play in the trilogy dealing with the curse on the house of Atreus.

Chronology

525 B.C. Born at Eleusis, near Athens, the son of Euphorion, of a noble Athenian family.

c.500 First entered the contest for tragedy.

490 Fought at Marathon against the Persians; later cited this fact in his epitaph.

484 Won his first prize.

480 Probably fought at Salamis against the Persians.

476 Visited Sicily (he made several trips) and wrote the lost *Women of Aetna* to honor the tyrant Hiero.

472 Produced *The Persians* with two other tragedies (the lost *Phineus* and *Glaucus*) with which it had no connection.

467 Produced his trilogy on the Oedipus legend, consisting of the lost *Laius* and *Oedipus* and the extant *Seven Against Thebes*.

466 Probable year of *The Suppliants,* the first play in a trilogy which also included the lost *Egyptians* and *Danaïds*.

c.460 Possible, but highly conjectural year for *Prometheus Bound,* a play in a trilogy which also included the lost *Prometheus Unbound* and *Prometheus The Firebringer*.

458 Produced *The Oresteia*.

456 Died in Gela, Sicily.

Selected Bibliography

Anderson, F. M. B., "The Character of Clytemnestra in the *Choephoroe* and the *Eumenides* of Aeschylus," *American Journal of Philology,* LIII (1932), 301–19.

Bodkin, Maude, *The Quest for Salvation in an Ancient and a Modern Play,* London, 1941.

Forbes, P. B. R., "Law and Politics in the *Oresteia*," *Classical Review*, LXII (1948), 99ff.

Kuhns, Richard, *The House, The City, and The Judge: The Growth of Moral Awareness in The Oresteia*, Indianapolis, 1962.

Murray, Gilbert, Aeschylus, *The Creator of Tragedy*, Oxford, 1940.

Owen, E. T., *The Harmony of Aeschylus*, Toronto, 1952.

Sheppard, J. T., *Aeschylus and Sophocles: their Work and Influence*, 2nd ed., New York, 1946.

Smyth, H. W., *Aeschylean Tragedy*, Berkeley, Calif., 1924.

Solmsen, Friedrich, *Hesiod and Aeschylus* (*Cornell Studies in Classical Philology*, Vol. XXX), Ithaca, 1949.

———, "Strata of Greek Religion in Aeschylus," *Harvard Theological Review*, XL (1940), 211–26.

Thomson, George, *Aeschylus and Athens: A Study of the Social Origins of Drama*, London, 1941.

Treston, Hubert J., *Poine, A Study in Ancient Greek Blood Vengeance*, London, 1923.

Winnington-Ingram, R. P., "Clytemnestra and the Vote of Athena," *Journal of Hellenic Studies*, LXVIII (1948), 130–47.

———, "The Role of Apollo in the *Oresteia*," *Classical Review*, XLVII (1933), 97–104.

Mask of old man. Terracotta miniature, 4th century B.C. *American School of Classical Studies at Athens*

THE ORESTEIA

by Aeschylus

Translated by Sir John Tersidder Sheppard

AGAMEMNON

Characters

WATCHMAN

CHORUS *of Argive Elders*

CLYTAEMNESTRA, *wife of Agamemnon*

HERALD

AGAMEMNON

CASSANDRA, *a princess of Troy*

AEGISTHUS, *cousin to Agamemnon*

Soldiers attending Agamemnon; guards attending Aegisthus; slaves

Before the royal palace at Argos; night

WATCHMAN   Deliverance, O ye Gods! The same prayer still
This year of nights, high on the Atreidae's* roof
Couched like a watch-dog, till I know by heart
The stars in full nocturnal session met
With those particular shining potentates   5
That bring men sign of storm and summer-weather,
Waxing and waning—well I know the times—
And still I keep my watch for one bright sign,
One flash of fire from Troy, the beacon-voice
Of capture—Why? Because a woman's will,   10
Strong as a man's, constrains me, sanguine still.
    Pacing my beat, this dew-dank roof my bed,
Unvisited by dreams—no dreams for me,
But fear instead of sleep for company,
Fear of a sleep indeed that knows no waking—   15
Well, when I think to sing or hum a tune
My dose of cheerful song, sleep's antidote,
Turns to a sorrowful wailing for this house,
Which is not what it was, a home well governed.
    Come! It is time! Glad messenger of light,   20

---

² Sons of Atreus, whose family was under a double curse: once for the murder of Myrtilos by Pelops, the
father of Atreus; and once because Atreus, on learning that his wife had been seduced by his brother
Thyestes, had arranged to have two of Thyestes' sons killed and served to him as food. Aegisthus was
Thyestes' third son.

Shine out with good Deliverance on the night! (*He sees the Beacon*)
All hail, bright beacon, shining on the night
Like dayspring after darkness. Many a dance
Shall Argos celebrate for this glad event.
  Ho there within!   25
A clear call that for Agamemnon's wife
To rise with instant pious Hallelujah
And greet this light which tells us Troy is won.
Troy won! My master's luck indeed has won!
Three sixes,* says the beacon, and I'll make   30
Good use of that. I'll be the first to dance.
Soon may our King, the ruler of this house
Be home; soon may I clasp his hand in loyal friendship.
  As for the rest, I'm silent. A great ox
On the tongue. This House, if it could find a voice   35
Would tell a plain tale. As for me, I talk
To those who know. For others—I forget. (*Exit*)
        (CLYTAEMNESTRA'S *voice cries "Hallelujah" within the palace*)
                 (*Enter* CHORUS *of Elders*)

CHORUS   The tenth year this   40
Since Priam's great antagonist at law
King Menelaus*—yea, and Agamemnon—
Launched against Troy the thousand galleys of the Argive expedition,
With passionate hearts and a clamorous cry of the War-God,
Like vultures, which in grief for their high-nested children wheel and   45
                                        circle
With outspread wings, like a ship's beating oar-blades.
  They have lost
The labour for their young which kept them faithful to the nest,
They are heard in the height,   50
Apollo perhaps, or Pan, or Zeus
Heareth the lamentable cry of the birds, his guests, who dwell in his
                                dominion,
And with punishment at last
Sendeth upon the sinners an avenging Fury. (*The doors of the Palace open.*   55
  CLYTAEMNESTRA *is seen making an offering of oil and spices at the altar*)
Even so that greater Zeus, the Lord of Hospitality,
Sent against Paris the two sons of Atreus,
Purposing, on the day when the knee should be planted in the dust and
  the spear shivered in the first shock of the battle,   60
The battle, fought for a woman, every man's woman,
To lay on Greek as well as Trojan
Many a weary wrestling.
So the case stands as now it stands and Fate is moving to fulfilment.

---

30 In a popular dice game using three dice, a throw of three sixes was the highest score.

42 Menelaus was king of Sparta. Paris, the son of Priam, king of Troy, abducted Helen, wife of Menelaus, thus precipitating the Trojan War.

No kindling of the flame of sacrifice, 65
No pouring of an unburnt offering,
Can appease that stubborn Wrath. (CLYTAEMNESTRA *still stands silent at*
the altar, pouring the oil, burning the spices)
  We are old. Our flesh is weak.
We could not play our part in that great expedition. 70
Left behind, we linger,
And on staves we guide our steps. We are as weak as children.
For just as the young marrow, when it ruleth in the breast,
Hath no more strength than hath the old—the God of Battle is not
                                                        there— 75
What of extreme old age?
The leafage turns to stalk, and down the three-foot ways,
No better than a child, he wanders,
A dream abroad by day. (*At length they see and they address the Queen*)
  Daughter of Tyndareus, Queen Clytaemnestra, 80
What is your errand? What has befallen? What have you heard?
What message so convincing that you order sacrifice throughout the city?
All the altars of the gods who guard our state,
Gods of heaven and gods infernal,
Gods of the house-door, gods of the assembly, 85
Kindle to a blaze. Lo here! Lo there!
Towering to heaven, the flame rises,
Drugged by soft innocent persuasion of pure unguent from the royal store.
Tell us of these things what you can,
At least so much as pious custom will allow you, 90
And be the healer of this thought that weighs on me with evil presage,
Though from the sacrifices Hope reveals a face of promise
And bids the restless, heart-devouring Care begone.
  (CLYTAEMNESTRA *makes no answer, but passes, in religious silence, as if*
to visit other shrines; as they wait for her return the ELDERS *sing*) 95
The tale is for me to tell of the triumph and doom revealed
To the men in their warrior-prime when they took the field,
For the spirit of life yet moveth within me, a breath of fire
Divine, and the strength of song is the heart's desire:
So I can tell how the princes, the brothers in arms, who led 100
The youth of Greece with avenging arm and spear against Troy were sped
By the king of the birds—to the kings of the fleet two eagles in full sight
Of the palace, near, on the spear-hand side, one black, the other with
                                            tail-plumes white,
Devouring the brood of a hare, the young in the mother's womb, 105
Ere the last course home was run overtaken by doom.
  Sing woe for the death of delight, yet blessing come!

The prophet* looked on the kings with their differing nature, and read

---

[108] Calchas, the soothsayer of the Greeks, read these signs when the Greek task-force was delayed by winds
in Aulis.

The omen. The feasters devouring the hare, he said,
Were the warrior-kings. And he told them "Your army shall make a prey   110
Of Troy in the fulness of time, and before that day
Her cattle shall perish, the wealth of the fortress-town be spent,
Ravaged by destiny's violence. Only I fear for this armament,
Troy's curb, the frown of the wrath of heaven, the darkness, the bolt of
                                                              fire,   115
For the pure maid Artemis hath seen the wing'd hounds of her Sire
Fall on the victim and tear the timorous mother-beast.*
She is full of pity and full of wrath. She loathes the eagles' feast."
   Sing woe for the death of delight, yet blessing come!

      "Beauteous One" he prayed, "whose care   120
      Whelps of ravening lions share
      With every tender suckling child
      Born to the creatures of the wild,
      Now, if ever, hear our prayer!
      All the good these signs portend   125
      Accomplish, all the evil mend!
   Yea, and I call the Healer, the Lord of the Paean-cry,*
   Prevent her! Let her not send on us lingering contrary
   Winds that will bind the fleet, in her zeal for another life,
A sacrifice other than this, strange, lawless, unhallowed by feast, a   130
                                                 begetter of strife
In a house where the lord shall be honoured no more. Wrath never
                                                 forgets.
Dangerous, crafty, recoiling for ever, she lingers and waits,
A child to avenge." So Calchas from the portent on the road seen plain   135
For the king's household chanted loud much blessing with much bane!
      Whereto in just accord we also cry
   Sing woe for the death of delight, yet blessing crown the victory!

      Zeus, Whosoe'er He be,
      That be His name for me   140
   If He so please. I weigh the world and find
   Save Zeus no other Helper, if the mind
Oppress'd so strangely is to lift the burden and be free.
      Huge, insolent, uncouth
      Was One who ruled*—In sooth   145
   He hath no mention now. His day is done.
   And His successor? Thrice outwrestled, gone.
Give Zeus the glory. Hail Him Victor, and thou hast the truth.

---

117 Twin sister of Apollo and daughter of Zeus, Artemis was the goddess of the hunt and the protector of
    wild animals and virgins.
127 Apollo, the god of music, poetry, prophecy, and medicine.
145 This passage alludes to the successive dynasties of Uranus, Cronos, and Zeus and to the triumph of
    Zeus over his predecessors.

'Twas He who bade men tread
   The road of sober thought.   150
  'Twas He whose ordinance decreed
    Mankind must suffer to be taught
In sleep, when old wounds bleed and smart,
Discretion in man's own despite
From grief remembered in the night   155
    Steals on the stricken heart,
Stern grace, perforce by Spirits given,
By Spirits seated at the helm of Heaven.

  The elder prince,* the lord
   Of that Greek armament,   160
  Challenging no prophet's word—
    For as winds blew, that way he leant—
When in their sore distress they lay,
Longing for release in vain,
Idle ships and hungry men,   165
    Windbound in Aulis' bay
Opposite Calchis, camped beside
The baffled, backward-running tide,

  And winds from Strymon blew,
Keeping them idle, to starve in the perilous roadstead, and men's minds 170
                                       grew
Strange, and the timbers warped and the ropes rotted, and time stood still,
  While the flower of Argos withered, and then the cry
  Of the prophet was heard in the midst, alleging Artemis' will,
    And expounding a remedy   175
Strange, and worse than the storm for the princes, and when they heard,
They smote on the ground with their staves and wept at the word.

  The elder prince made known
His mind, for he said "It is hard to refuse. It is hard to destroy my own
Child, the delight of the home. How can a father stand at the altar and 180
                                    stain
  His hands with the blood of the virginal sacrifice?
  Every way there is wrong. Can I turn traitor, and fail my men?
    I should lose my allies—
They are right to demand a victim, right in their lust for the blood 185
Of the maiden to stay the storm! May the end be good!"
  As the wind veers, he wavered wickedly,
  Then took the yoke of sheer Necessity
And shrank from nothing vile. Sin breeds a spirit of ruthlessness,
  Distraction, by suggestion of things foul,   190
  Making hearts callous. So was the King's soul

---

[159] Agamemnon.

Steeled by the butchery of his child to bless
The voyage and in a woman's war achieve success.

Her prayers, her cry "Father!", her maidenhood
With judges bent on war for nothing stood.   195
Her father prayed, then gave the young men sign to lift her high

Above the altar, kid-like, the soul faint,
The body swathed, and a gag's harsh restraint
Clamped on those lovely lips, for fear a cry
Might fasten on the royal house calamity—   200
Therefore they gagg'd the child. The raiment slipp'd
From her body to the ground—a mantle dipp'd
In saffron. Her eyes lifted, and the dart
That sped to every sacrificer's heart
Begged pity. Like a picture, and yet fain   205
To speak, she seemed, as often, when men raised
The Paean in her father's hall, to bless
The house and wish her father happiness
At the third drink-offering, clear-voiced, lovingly the pure maid graced
The festal strain.   210

I did not see what followed, and I say
No word. The prophet Calchas had his way.
The law abides. The scales of Justice turn.
The hearts of men must suffer ere men learn.
The future, when it comes, shall be made known: 215
Be of good cheer till then: there's nothing won
By grief untimely. With the dawning day
The truth dawns. Be it good! As thus we pray
So prays the Regent, the Protector of this realm, who stands alone,
Nearest the throne.   220

(CLYTAEMNESTRA *has re-entered in time to hear the last words of the Ode;*
the LEADER *of the chorus addresses her*)

LEADER   Queen Clytaemnestra, I am here to show
Due deference to your state. When the King's throne
Is vacant of the male, authority   225
Rests with the consort and she must be honoured.
    Whether good news, or none, or hope of good
Inspire your sacrifice, I shall be glad
To learn, yet ready to respect your silence.

CLYTAEMNESTRA   Just as the proverb has it, with good news   230
May the Dawn issue from her mother, Night.
The message you shall hear is fraught with joy
Greater than hope. The Greeks have taken Troy.

CHORUS   Is it possible?

CLYTAEMNESTRA   It is true. The Greeks hold Troy.   235

CHORUS   I weep for joy of it.

CLYTAEMNESTRA   So the eye betrays
The good heart.

CHORUS   Have you proof?

CLYTAEMNESTRA   Yes, I have proof,
Unless some god deceive.

CHORUS   A happy dream?

CLYTAEMNESTRA   I am not one to prate of dreams.

CHORUS   A breath
Of rumour?

CLYTAEMNESTRA   Nor am I a witless girl
Whom thus you chide.

CHORUS   But when?

CLYTAEMNESTRA   Troy fell, I say,
On this same Night, the mother of to-day.

CHORUS   What messenger could make such swift despatch?

CLYTAEMNESTRA   The god of Fire himself!
Hephaistos launched from Ida a bright flame,
And beacon still sped beacon in relays
Of messenger-fire towards us. Ida first
To Hermes' hill on Lemnos, then the Mount
Of Zeus in Athos welcomed the great brand
Which rose to clear the sea's back, like a strong
And joyful courier. Like another sun,
It shot the golden glory of the flame
To the watch-tower of Makistos. Nothing loath
Makistos proved, no laggard, sleep-subdued
To shirk his office: past Euripos' flood
His ensign streamed, reporting to the watch
That holds Messapion, whence their countersign,
Fired from a heap of old grey heather, flashed
The message on and on. Still strenuous,
The travelling torch, still unabated, bright
As moonlight, swept Asopos' plain, and reached
The ridge of Mount Cithaeron, there to rouse
A fresh relay of missionary fire.
Nor was the far-flung message scorned. The watch
Kindled above their bidding, and the light
Swept over Lake Gorgopis to the cliffs
Of Aigiplanktos, where the cry was still
For swift observance of the rite of fire,
And swiftly came the answer. A great beard
Of flame flared higher than the promontory
That looks on the Saronic gulf, then swooped
To the Spider's Crag near Argos, and came home
On Agamemnon's palace-roof, this light
Whose first progenitor flashed from Ida's height.

240

245

250

255

260

265

270

275

280

So raced my flaming messengers. Each from each,
Successive, took his torch and reached his goal,
The last triumphant as the first. My proof   285
And evidence is my husband's word from Troy.
CHORUS   I will praise the gods hereafter, yet am fain
To hear and marvel at your tale again.
If it would please you, speak.
CLYTAEMNESTRA   This day the Greeks   290
Possess the town of Troy. I think her streets
Are loud with clamorous ill-accordant cries.
Your oil and vinegar, poured in the same flask,
Make you a sorry mixture, enemies
Not friends; and so, as their conditions are,   295
The voices of the vanquished ill accord
With the glad shouts of the victors. Hear them wail
For husbands, brothers, children dead. Or see
Yon greybeard with the body of his son,
Weeping, and yet not even free to weep.   300
    What of the victors? A night's foraging
Sets them down hungry to the morning meal
Of what the city offers—discipline
Forgotten—every man, as Luck provides,
Snatching at fortune. In the captured homes   305
Of Troy they lodge, delivered from the frosts
And dews of the cold sky. What happiness,
To sleep the whole night through, secure at last,
No guard kept! If they hold in reverence
The shrines of the conquered land, the city's gods,   310
Then may the spoilers not themselves be spoiled.
Only I pray no lust possess them now
Covetously to plunder what they should not.
They need safe passage home. If they return
Without offence to heaven, the wrathful dead   315
May spare them—if no stroke of accident
Befall. Such is my thought, a woman's thought.
    Rich is the promise. May the good cause win
Past doubt, and the ripe fruit be gathered in.
CHORUS   Lady, your language of good will has all   320
A man's discretion. Now I have heard your proof,
So cogent, I would fain address the gods
With praise for mercy worth all pains edured.
                    (*Exit* CLYTAEMNESTRA *into the palace*)
    King Zeus,   325
And Thou, O friendly Night,
In whose house the stars are jewels,
Who hast thrown about the towers of Troy the strong-meshed net

Which neither greatness can o'erleap nor youth escape,
Doom's universal drag-net of captivity and ruin:

Zeus, Lord of Hospitality,
Who hast aimed Thy bow so long at Alexander*
That neither should the bolt fall spent before the mark
Nor shoot beyond the stars and so be wasted,
Thine be the homage, as the work was Thine.

"The bolt of Zeus hath struck them." Any man
Can say it. And man from this event,
His will's accomplishment,
Can trace the plan.
"The high gods hold aloof"
One said, "too proud to care if mortals tread
Fair sanctities underfoot." 'Twas impiously said.
Here stands the proof—
Havoc, that pays the price of recklessness,
Wealth, puffed to pride in scorn of righteousness,
Palaces, crammed with plenty to excess,
Beyond the best—Ah, what is best? To be
Well-satisfied, possess
The mind in prudence and a harmless, safe sufficiency.
    No fortress-wall can save
    The rich, when what they have
    Turns to a surfeit, and they spurn from sight
    The altar of the Right.

Temptation is the offspring of designing
Ate.* She storms the sort. No remedy
Can cure that malady
Or mask the shining
Mischief. Temptation shows
The man's true nature, as the touch of the stone
And rubbing test the bronze: the fatal flaw's made known,
The black spot glows
Malignant, obdurate: the metal's base.
Lured like a child to covet and give chase
To a bird on the wing, he smirches all his race
With the taint of his own iniquity.
Heaven heeds not when he prays.
Who walketh in such ways, the man of sin, shall surely die.
    So Paris, though a guest
    At Menelaus' feast,

332 Another name for Paris.
355 The goddess personifying sinful impulse.

Disgraced the name of friendship, on the day   370
    He stole a wife away.

She fled, bequeathing to her townsmen tumult of an armament
Preparing, noise of shield and spear, and sailors fitting ships for sea,
And for dowry took to Troy destruction, when she went
Tripping through the gates into the city, sinning wantonly.   375
Moaning voices told the secret of the palace, mournfully—
"Woeful home and princes! Woeful marriage-bed, where even now
Prints of dear embracement show!" Deserted scornfully,
Unreproachful, silent—not one word of prayer, but silence—how
He sits alone, and pining for his bride beyond the sea,   380
Haunts the palace-courts, a shadow of authority.
    Her statued form is fair,
    But vexes now. The stare
    Of eyes where Aphrodite's beauty shone
    Seems vacant—the light gone.*   385

He dreams, and in his dreams he thinks he sees her. Fancies show
Shapes that flatter, joy, illusion—vanity of vanities.
All in vain he seems to see happiness near—and lo!
In that moment she has gone: she slips from his embrace, and flies,
Winged, along the paths of sleep. Such are the miseries   390
Of the King's own hearth and household—these, and worse than these.
What of other homes in Hellas? Have they no distress?
What of that great host of fighting-men who sailed from Greece?
Broken-hearted cries there were, loud lamentation everywhere,
And cause enough they had for grieving, grief enough to bear.   395
    The men they sent they knew.
    To every house a few
    Handfuls of dust, instead of men, return
    Stored in a tiny urn.

In the field the War-God plies a money-changer's trade. He weighs   400
Lives—his balance is the spear—and for men's bodies pays
And packs in decent jars and sends
From Troy full weight of precious dust, refined by fire, for friends
To welcome and to weep and give them praise.
"He was a clever fighter," "In the carnage he faced death   405
Well," "For a stranger's wife he died," they mutter under breath,
And hate is mingled with their grief. Resentment grows
Against the Atreidae in whose cause the quarrel first arose.
    Some in their beauty found
    A place in Trojan ground.   410

385 The passage alludes to the contest for the golden apple, in which Paris, then a shepherd on Mount Ida,
was asked to award the apple to the fairest among Aphrodite, Hera, and Athena. On the promise that
she would give him the most beautiful of women as wife, he chose Aphrodite.

Under the fortress-wall the victors have
Possession of a grave.

No light matter this, a people's talk, when grief breeds anger thus.
Like a public curse it works. It is most dangerous.
For something veiled in night my mind   415
Listens. The gods have eyes. They are not blind.
Who thrives by sin, his luck is hazardous.
The tide turns. The dark Furies* claim their prey. He dwindles, wanes,
Fades out, a shadow among shadows, where no help remains.
Dangerous too it is when flattering tongues are loud.   420
The eyes of Zeus flash lightning to consume the proud.
　　Be my prosperity
　　Unenvied. Not for me
　　Titles of conquest. These I no more crave
　　Than to be thrall and slave. (*Exit*)   425

───────────

The same place, some weeks later
(*Enter* CHORUS *of Elders*)

AN ELDER   Sped by the beacon's happy news swift rumour goes
　　Throughout the city—truth? or some divine deceit? who knows?
ANOTHER ELDER   Who is so crazed and childish, to take fire   430
　　From flaming signals, then let hope expire
　　Because talk changes?
ANOTHER　　　　　　　　　That's a woman's way—
　　Say "Yes" before you hear the proof, be gay
　　Before your luck comes true.   435
ANOTHER　　　　　　　　　　They take desire
　　For fact. Their fancy runs away like fire.
　　Their news admits no doubt till the flame flickers out.
LEADER   Soon we shall know for certain, was the tale
　　With all these torches, beacons and relays   440
　　Of messenger-flame the truth, or like some dream
　　To flatter fools and cheat them with delight?
　　I can see yonder, coming from the coast,
　　A herald, crowned with olive-boughs. The dust,
　　Mud's thirsty friend and sister, tells her tale,   445
　　This messenger has a voice. He'll make no blaze
　　Of smoky timber on the hills, but speak,
　　And by his speech confirm our joy, or else—
　　No! I'll have nothing else but good to crown
　　The signs of good already seen and known!   450
ANOTHER ELDER   If any man has other thoughts than this
　　For Argos—be the fruit of folly his.

───────────

418 The three horrendous female spirits who punished the doers of unavenged crimes. Also called the
　Eumenides.

(Enter a HERALD, *a veteran of the war)*

HERALD My fatherland, my Argos! Ten years gone,
And home this happy day! How many a hope   455
Turned traitor. One held good. I never thought
To die at home, and lay my body down,
Happy, to rest in this dear Argive country.
I give you greeting, Sun and Soil, and Zeus,
Supreme Lord of the Land, and you, great god   460
Of Delphi* too—but aim your darts no more
At us—you proved yourself our enemy
Enough beside Scamander!* Lord Apollo,
Be Healer now and Saviour. All of you,
Assembled gods, I greet, with my own patron,   465
Hermes, dear Herald, whom all heralds worship,
And Heroes, you who cheered us to the wars,
So welcome home what war has left of us.
  Hail to you, palace of our princes, halls
Of friendly entertainment, solemn seats   470
Of Judgment, deities that face the sun!
Bright-eyed to-day, if ever, greet your King
Who comes to end your darkness, brings back day
To you and all his people, Agamemnon,
With well-deserved good welcome. For indeed   475
He has deserved well. He hath made of Troy
A heap. The mattock of the Justicer
Zeus wielded in his hand hath turned the soil,
Broken the clods, and rooted out the seed
And left the land a waste.—So tamed he Troy,   480
So yoked her—he, the King, the elder son
Of Atreus, and he comes to you, this man
Of happy destiny, no man alive
Worth so much honour. Paris cannot boast,
Nor Troy, who shared the crime, and shares the payment,   485
That what they did was worse than what they suffer.
What was the charge? Rape? Theft? Well, he has lost
His plunder, razed his city to the ground,
Ruined his home. The sins of Priam's house
Are paid for, and the price is twice the purchase.   490

CHORUS You come from the army, Herald? We wish you well.
HERALD All's well. Come death, as the gods will. I surrender.
CHORUS You have been sore tried, heartsick for home?
HERALD So now I weep for joy.
CHORUS   If you were homesick   495
  It was a pleasing malady.
HERALD   Pleasing? How?
  Help me to get your drift.

---

461 Apollo.   463 A river which flowed across the plain of Troy.

CHORUS   Because your love
And longing were returned.   500
HERALD   You pined for us
As we for home?
CHORUS   Yes, in a maze of tears
Often.
HERALD   So gloomy? Come, why take the war   505
So hard as that?
CHORUS   For some time past I've known—
Least said, best mended.
HERALD   In the princes' absence
Have there been some you stood in fear of?   510
CHORUS   Death,
In your own phrase, were welcome.
HERALD   Nay, I said,
Because all's well. It's a good end. There's much
For satisfaction, plenty to regret   515
In the whole long story. If the blessed gods
Live on for ever and a day exempt
From trouble, no one else does. Shall I tell you
The sort of life we led, the narrow berths,
Bad bedding, that they gave us? The long days   520
With nothing new but hardships to complain of?
And then ashore, worse wretchedness—to lie
Close under enemy fortress-walls, with dew
From the dank drizzling sky and the drenched fields,
A chronic mildew, every strand and stitch   525
Of our clothing verminous—then freezing cold,
When Ida was all snow: it killed the birds:
Or sweltering heat at noon, when not a breath
Of wind stirred, not a ripple, and the sea
Sank in his bed and slept. Why think of it?   530
Why grieve? The griefs are finished, and the dead
Past even caring to rise up again.
Why count the roll of loss? Break living hearts
Because life's hard? Farewell, cross luck, say I!
For us, for every soldier left alive,   535
Loss is outweighed by gain, and the glad boast
Of this day's work shall crown the triumph, borne
On wings of glory over land and sea:
"The Argives hung these trophies from the spoil
Of Troy, subdued at last, to grace the shrines   540
Of all the gods of Hellas." 'Tis a tale
Should make your praise our Argos, and the man
Who led her, with all honour to the grace
Of Zeus, who wrought the deed. My tale is done.
CHORUS   I am convinced. I yield. Age cannot quench   545

Youth in a spirit teachable. Your great news,
Enriching me, should touch the royal house
Chiefly, and Clytaemnestra most of all.

(*Enter* CLYTAEMNESTRA)

CLYTAEMNESTRA   I raised my Hallelujah long ago   550
When the first fiery messenger proclaimed
Troy's capture and our enemy's overthrow.
Then there were some who chid me. "What? Believe
The beacons? Think Troy taken? Very like
A woman's credulous fancy!" Oh, 'twas plain,   555
I was a fool. And yet the woman's word
Prevailed. I lit my sacrifices. All
Thronging our shrines, lulling the hungry flames
Of the altar-fires asleep with fragrant spices,
Cried Hallelujah most religiously.   560
So now, what need for you to tell me more?
My lord will tell me all. I must make haste
To greet him as I honour him. No day
Dawns brighter for a woman than the day
She flings her gates wide open for her lord,   565
Saved by some god from war. Bid the King come
His people's well-beloved, right welcome home,
And find at home his wife, the faithful ward
No truce for her with miscreants—not one jot
Changed from the wife he left, no seal of love   570
Broken through all this length of weary years.
I know no touch of joy, no breath of shame
With any other man, more than I know
The way to temper swordblades. (*Exit*)

HERALD   So she protests. Take every word for truth,   575
What of the modesty that becomes her station?

CHORUS   She has said her say. You hear and apprehend.
Specious it sounds, to ears of understanding.
But tell me, Herald, what of our loved prince
Menelaus, shall we greet him soon, safe home?   580

HERALD   I could not keep a friend beguiled for long
With falsehood painted fair.

CHORUS   Then let your news
Be true as well as good. That partnership
Must hold, or else the breach is soon discovered.   585

HERALD   Then you shall have the truth. The prince is missing,
He and his ship lost.

CHORUS   Did you see him sail
From Troy alone? Or did a storm that swept
The whole fleet part him from you?   590

HERALD   There you shoot
Straight to the mark. In one short phrase you sum

A tale of trouble.

CHORUS   What was thought of it
By the other sailors? Do you talk of him   595
As living or as dead?

HERALD   No one can give you,
Save the all-nurturing Sun, the truth of that.

CHORUS   Tell us your story, how the visitation
Broke from the angry heavens, and how it left you.   600

HERALD   To speak of inauspicious news profanes
This day of praise. Grief's office may not blend
With worship of the gods. It were unseemly.
The surly-visaged messenger who proclaims
Defeat and death, the body of the state   605
At one blow crippled, droves of citizens
Whipped out of doors, made excommunicate
By that fell curse the war-god loves, the lash,
The double scourge of havoc twinned with slaughter—
Bears such a load of mischief in his pack   610
As justified a Paean of the Furies.
But when your messenger comes with news from home
Of saving mercies to a city crowned
With glad prosperity—how adulterate
The good with evil? How rehearse the tale   615
Of a storm manifestly sent by wrathful gods?
   Two ancient enemies, fire and the sea,
Conspired like friends, and to confirm their pact
Joined for destruction of the Argive fleet.
At night the sea grew troubled and the waves   620
Ran high, and a wind blew from Thrace that dashed
The ships together, and they rammed, then drove
Pell-mell, through rain-swept surges, like a flock
Ill-shepherded by the hurricane, and so vanished.
But when the sun brought back the day, we saw   625
The wide Aegean like a field aflower
With wreckage and with bodies of our men,
Though we ourselves were safe. No human hand,
Some spirit touched the helm, kept the hull sound,
By trickery or through intercession. Luck   630
The Saviour was our passenger, and we rode
Securely, neither swamped at anchorage
Nor drifting helpless to the rock-bound coast.
Then, in the white light of the dawn, escaped
From death at sea, still barely crediting   635
Good Luck, we mused and pondered on the strange
Fate of the o'erwearied, sorely buffeted fleet.
   So now, if any of them live, they speak—
It must be so—they speak of us as dead,

And we suppose the same of them. We'll hope   ₆₄₀
The best still! Menelaus certainly
You must presume in evil plight, and yet,
If any beam of the sun still reaches him,
Hale and alive, by the design of Zeus
Who would not see the race quite blotted out   ₆₄₅
As yet, some hope remains, He may return.
    You have my story now. You know the truth.

CHORUS Who named her? In good sooth
      Well named was she
    With premonition of the truth.   ₆₅₀
      Some spirit we cannot see
      Made the name fit the life
        The destiny.
    Helen! The prize of war, the bride of strife!
      Husband, fleet, citizens shall read   ₆₅₅
        Her title—Hell indeed!
From the veiled luxury of the bower she fled,
      By earth-born Zephyr sped,
By troops of huntsmen, hard on the invisible trail of oars
      Hotly pursued,   ₆₆₀
Fighting-men, who beached their ships on Simoeis'* leafy shores
      In murderous feud.

    Who sealed the marriage-bond
      As pledge of doom
    For Troy? Wrath, mindful of the fond   ₆₆₅
      Host cheated, and the home
      In scorn of Zeus betrayed.
      It needs must come,
    Requital. Soon or late such debts are paid,
      As Troy pays for the bridal-song   ₆₇₀
      Chanted so loud and long
    When the gay rout of groomsmen hailed the bride,
      And "Hymen, Hymen!"* cried.
The music changes. "Woeful Paris! Woeful bridal-bed!"
      The new refrain   ₆₇₅
Grows too familiar. Priam's ancient city mourns her dead
      Untimely slain.

    A herdsman took a lion-cub to rear
Straight from the mother's breast, in life's fair prelude mild,
      Sharing the children's play,   ₆₈₀
      Their darling, even to the old a dear
      Delight, the homestead's harmless foster-child.

---

[661] A small river near Troy; a tributary of the Scamander.
[673] The Greek god of marriage, Hymen is invoked in song at weddings.

How often in the herdsman's arms it lay
Like a babe, bright-eyed, fawned on his hand and coaxed for food.

But soon the creature's nature was made clear.   685
True to its parentage it grew, and with a wild
   Red frenzy, to repay
   Kind nurture, made a feast of no good cheer,
   A massacre of the flocks, a home defiled,
   A household helpless while it tore the prey,   690
Revealed a fiend by heaven's will reared, Ruin's High Priest of Blood.

So Helen! For the moment Helen brought
   To Troy the halcyon thought
     Of deep content,
    Wealth's modest ornament,   695
   Love's flower, without a thorn
Save Love himself, kind eyes that flashed no scorn
    Only Love's dart
   To strike, not wound the heart.

She changed. How Love turned bitter! How the spell   700
   Was broken in the end!
Friendship with her was fatal. Zeus, who wrought
   For sin against a friend
Havoc in Priam's house, launched her from Hell,
   A Bride of Tears, a Fiend.   705

(*Enter* CLYTAEMNESTRA, *who makes preparations for the
reception of* AGAMEMNON *while the* ELDERS *chant the
remainder of the Ode*)

There is an ancient proverb which, men say,
   Can teach us wisdom's way—   710
    That wealth grown great
   Comes not to full estate,
   Nor dies, without a child.
Wealth breeds, they say, disaster. Has Luck smiled?
   The change must come.   715
   The house is marked for doom.

Not so! I think my own thought. Wickedness
   Breeds woe. The first foul deed
Litters a pack of children to obey
   The prompting of the breed.   720
As for the righteous, fruits of happiness
   Grow from the happy seed.

In sinners the old Insolence breeds new
Sooner or later, at the appointed time,

A Spirit invincible, 725
Dark, irresistible,
Exacting crime for crime, a reckless mood,
Till Ruin triumphs and Distraction reigns and sons imbrue
The father's house in blood—to prove it true,
The brood is like the parents of the brood. 730

Justice may shine in smoky cottages.
To men of honest mind she gives all grace.
From gorgeous palaces
And gilded fineries
She turns away her face. She will not lend 735
Countenance to the power of wealth, stamped with the world's false
praise.
With Righteousness for friend she goes her ways,
And guideth all things to the appointed end.
(*Enter* AGAMEMNON *in a chariot, followed by another in which* CASSANDRA 740
sits; she remains motionless and silent throughout the following scene)
Offspring of Atreus, Conqueror of Troy, my King,
How can I pay due homage, how express
My reverence, neither scanting your good pleasure,
Nor overshooting the just meed of praise? 745
Many there are who care not overmuch for justice,
Thinking rather of the outward show.
Every man is ready with his tears for a misfortune,
Though no pang of sorrow touch the heart.
And in joy false friends, as if rejoicing, 750
Force their faces to a smile, yet feel no joy.
A good judge of the flock will watch the eyes. Is friendship watered?
Is the good will they seem to show a flattering feint? The eyes will tell
him.
So I confess, 755
When first you raised your expedition
For Helen's sake,
My thoughts of you were jangled, and my picture out of drawing.
It seemed to me bad steering, to redeem a willing wanton at that price—
The lives of men. 760
But now in all sincerity and truth of friendship
I say "The end crowns all. The toil is blest when all's well done."
Presently your own questioning will tell you
Which of your citizens has proved a righteous steward
And who have not done well. 765
AGAMEMNON   To Argos first just praise, and to the gods
Of Argos who have furthered my return
And seconded my work of Justice wrought
On Priam's town. Heaven heard the cause—not words,
But the just cause, and by consent the gods 770

Cast votes into the urn of blood for death
And doom of Troy. Hope seemed to spy a hand
Moving towards acquittal, but no vote
Followed. The urn stood empty. Still the smoke
Proclaims Troy captured. Still Doom's hurricane   775
Lives, and the smouldering ashes in fat gusts
Of opulence puff away the life of Troy.

    For this we owe the gods our memorable
Thanks. The full price of arrogant rape is paid—
Troy for one woman's sake a heap of ruin.   780
Just at the setting of the Pleiades.*
Hatched from the horse in form of fighting men,
Our Argive beast, our lion, overleapt
The ramparts, and supped full of royal blood.

    From which long prelude to the gods I pass   785
To your thought. I remember and approve.

    You have my advocacy. Men are rare
Who find it in their nature to admire
A friend's good luck and feel no jealousy.
Envy's a poison to the heart. It makes   790
The sick man's malady twice as hard to bear:
He knows his own distress and shoulders it,
But sighs to find his neighbour prosperous.
I speak with knowledge. Close companionship
Is truth's best glass. In some who most pretend   795
Devotion is the phantom of a shade.
Just one, who sailed reluctantly, Odysseus,
Once in the traces, pulled right loyally;
Whether he lives, or while I speak of him,
Lies dead. For the rest, the business of the state   800
And what concerns the gods, we shall confer
Hereafter in the general congregation
Which I shall hold. We shall deliberate
How to ensure continuance of the good,
And use our best endeavour, where the need   805
Of remedy appears, by cautery
Or the knife well applied, to check the mischief.
Now home! Now to the palace, greeting first
The gods who sent us forth and have vouchsafed
Return. My victory, well approved our friend   810
At Troy, continue steadfast to the end.

CLYTAEMNESTRA   Good citizens, my reverend Argive Elders,
    I shall not blush to publish openly
My love for this my husband. Modesty
Fades out in time. The story I shall tell you   815
Of my own life—no lesson learnt by rote

781 Seven girls whom Zeus placed among the stars; hence a group of stars.

From others, but my own—shall be the truth
Of all those years when this man lay at Troy.

   First, for a woman it is no good thing
To sit at home alone without a husband, 820
Hearing malignant rumours, messengers
Hot on each other's heels, and every man
With news to cry more cruel than the last.
Why, had my lord been hit as many times
As flooding rumour gave him out for wounded, 825
He had been more full of holes than any net.
If dead, as often as report alleged,
He might have been some triple-bodied monster,
Once dead for every body, with a cloak
Of earth for each above him. We'll not speak 830
Of what's below. These same malignant rumours
So moved me, many a time I have essayed
To die by my own hands, freed from the noose
Against my will and purpose, forced to live
By others. 835
         This, my lord, is why your son,
Our child, our pledge of equal faith, Orestes,
Is not here present. Make no wonder of it.
He is with a friend, well tended. Your ally
Strophios the Phocian urged it, for he said 840
There were two risks, your jeopardy at Troy,
and fear at home, lest the seditious mob
Might hatch some plot against us. This is common.
When great men fall, the mob will trample on them.
Therefore I sent him. There's no guile in that. 845

   As for myself, the fountains of my tears
Have run themselves quite dry, not one drop left.
And my late-watching eyes have suffered hurt
With weeping for my candle, lit for you,
My lord, yet unregarded. If I slept, 850
I dreamt of you, and woke at sudden stir
Of the thin-piping gnat from sights of woe
Too many for the time that slept with me.
   All that is past, all now endured, and now
I greet my husband gladly, the strong stay 855
And saviour of our vessel, the high roof's
Main pillar, watchdog of the homestead, land
Sighted by hopeless mariners, a sole child
Born to a father past all hope.
               How fair 860
The morning after storm, like a fresh well
Of water to thirsty traveller!
How sweet it is to be free, constraint all past!

These are my titles for him. May the praise
Evoke no envy. We have had our share   865
Of troubles in the past. Now, my loved lord,
Leave the car. Nay, the foot that trampled Troy
Is not for common earth. Slaves, you are slow!
You know your office. Spread the broideries.
Straight let his road be carpeted with crimson,   870
That Justice lead him to a home scarce hoped for.
 The rest our vigilance, undefeated still
  By sleep, shall order justly, if God will.
AGAMEMNON Daughter of Leda,* guardian of my home,
Your long-drawn speech at least is suitable   875
To my long absence. But the proper meed
Of praise should come from others. For the rest,
Leave flatteries alone. I'll not be pampered
In womanish ways. Base oriental clamour
And grovelling—I'll have none of it. I forbid you   880
By strewing robes to make my path invidious.
The gods should have such honours. For a man
To step on broidered beauties—there's some fear
Lurking in that for me. Pay the respect
Due to a man, your husband, not a god.   885
Fame needs no broideries, no foot-wipers.
She cries her own worth. Modesty of mind
Is God's best gift, and happiness a title
 To keep for lives that end well. What you hear
  I shall confirm by action, conscience-clear.   890
CLYTAEMNESTRA Nay tell me this. Tell me of your true mind . . . .
AGAMEMNON My mind is fixed and not to be corrupted.
CLYTAEMNESTRA In time of peril might you not have vowed
Just such an act of worship to the gods?
AGAMEMNON I might, had competent authority   895
 Prescribed it.
CLYTAEMNESTRA What of Priam, had success
 Been his?
AGAMEMNON He would have trod the broideries.
CLYTAEMNESTRA No reason then to shrink from human censure.   900
AGAMEMNON Our citizens? A free people's voice has power.
CLYTAEMNESTRA A man unenvied is not enviable.
AGAMEMNON Heat in contention ill becomes a woman.
CLYTAEMNESTRA Submission well becomes the warrior
 Entitled "happy."   905
AGAMEMNON   Do you care so much
 For such a victory?
CLYTAEMNESTRA   Yield. If your own will
 Dictates surrender, you are master still.

874 Clytaemnestra is the daughter of Leda and Tyndareus; Helen is the daughter of Leda and Zeus.

AGAMEMNON   Well, since it is your pleasure—I must have   910

    The shoes unloosed that served me on the road. (*A slave removes them*)
    And as I tread the empurpled path, I pray
    No stroke of ill befall me from the eyes
    Of jealous gods afar. It much concerns
    My conscience thus to waste our household store   915
    Trampling these silver-purchased stuffs. No more
    Of that. Here is a maiden I would have you
    Welcome with favour. Masters who are kind
    Find favour with the gods. She comes with me
    As the army's gift, the choice flower of the spoil.   920
      So, as your captive, you will have it so,
      Home by this path of purple I will go.

      (AGAMEMNON *descends from the chariot and moves toward the Palace,*
                   while CLYTAEMNESTRA *speaks*)

CLYTAEMNESTRA   There is the sea, and who shall drain it dry?   925
    Breeding fresh purple, every drop worth silver,
    Oozing abundantly for dipping robes.
    Praised be the gods, my lord, our house is full
    Of such rich furniture. Penury's here a stranger.
    And many a costly robe I would have vowed   930
    For trampling underfoot, had oracles
    Enjoined that price for purchase of your life.
    The root lives, and the tree puts forth fresh leaves,
    To shield the house against the dog-star's fever,*
    And the hearth feels your presence, like the breath   935
    Of warmth in winter, whispering "I am here."
    Nay, coolness in the house in summertime,
    When Zeus from the virginal grape matureth wine—
    The master takes possession of his home!
      Zeus, Zeus, Accomplisher, fulfil my prayer.   940
      What Thou intendest to accomplish be Thy care.

                (*She follows* AGAMEMNON)

CHORUS   What wind of Fear is this
    That so persistently
    Haunts my prophetic soul?
    What music, piping prophecies,   945
      A tune of dole?
    Unwelcome minstrelsy!
      And no good cheer
    Mounts the heart's throne to help me spew away   950
  Misgiving, like a riddling dream, dismissed at break of day.
        How long ago it is
  Since the ships left their moorings and the cables chafed the sand

---

[934] The Dog Star is Sirius; the hottest part of the year in Greece was associated with the rising of this star;
    hence, the heat of the day.

And the fleet put to sea,
Bound for the Trojan land. 955

We have them here. These eyes
Bear witness. They are home.
Yet the self-taught refrain
Still pipes the dolorous prophecies,
    A jangled strain, 960
Some Fury's dirge of doom!
    And still no cheer
No friendly hope bids the foul Fiend depart.
Truth works in all this turmoil! From the welter of the Heart
    Waves of true presage rise, 965
Surge to Fulfilment, on the reef of Reason break and beat!
    God grant it may not come!
    May the Fear prove a cheat!

    Though narrow walls divide
Rude Health from Fever, Wealth unsatisfied 970
Craves more, and keeps no bounds. Prosperity
Takes ship in Fortune's galley, crammed with treasure,
    Full sail on a calm sea,
Then strikes the reef. From derrick of Due Measure
    Caution may fling 975
Wealth's surplus overboard—such jettison
May stave off ruin, keep the house from foundering—
    And still, by benison
    Of Zeus on furrowed field,
The barns may be replenished, plague of famine banished, 980
    By one year's yield . . .

    But the red blood, once shed,
Is lost, past cure. No voice can wake the dead,
No spells of healing. He* whose master-skill
Had virtue to recover souls departed, 985
    Was crushed beneath the Will
Of Zeus, for fear Fate's ordinance be thwarted,
    Whereby each part,
By check and countercheck, subserves the Whole . . .
Were it not so, ere tongue could speak, the heart 990
    Had voiced the Truth . . . My soul
    Is darkened . . . gropes in vain
For hope to cure the fever, or unravel ever
    The twisted skein.

---

984 Orpheus, the music of whose lyre had the power to charm beasts, trees, and even rocks. Through his
musical skill, he almost succeeded in leading his wife Eurydice back from the dead.

CLYTAEMNESTRA   You also, you, Cassandra—get you in!
  Since Zeus vouchsafes you in all clemency
  A share in our drink-offerings and a place
  At the altar of Possession, with a throng
  Of slaves, be modest. Leave the car. We are told, 1000
  Even Alcmena's son took the slave's bread
  With patience.* If the turn of chance impose
  The yoke, at least it is a boon to serve
  Masters of old-established wealth—your new
  Rich reapers of a harvest unexpected 1005
  Are harsh to slaves. They keep no rule. With us
  You have exactly what is customary.

CHORUS (*To* CASSANDRA)   To you she spoke, and she awaits your answer
  To plain instructions. You are in Fate's toils.
  Will you not hear and yield? Perhaps you cannot? 1010

CLYTAEMNESTRA   Unless her only speech is that uncouth,
  Outlandish, unintelligible noise
  The swallows make, she hears and understands me.

CHORUS (*To* CASSANDRA)   Go with her. Leave this chariot-throne. Her
                                             counsel 1015
  Is the best possible now. Yield and comply.

CLYTAEMNESTRA   I have not leisure now to squander time
  Abroad. The victims at the central hearth
  Stand ready for the slaughter that shall grace
  The consummation of joy unhoped-for. 1020
  You—if you mean to do my bidding, come!
  Or, since such dullness cannot cope with language
  Do you lay hands on her in true foreign fashion.

CHORUS   Madam, her need is someone to interpret,
  I think. She seems like a wild creature trapped. 1025

CLYTAEMNESTRA   She is mad, swayed by a vicious mood—to leave
  A city just made captive and refuse
  To handsel bit and bridle till she foam
  Her fury off in blood. But I'll not waste
  More words to be insulted. (*Exit*) 1030

THE LEADER OF THE CHORUS   I shall not
  Grow angry, for I pity her. (*Then, to* CASSANDRA)
  Come, leave the car, and yielding to the stress
  Of present need, take the new yoke upon you.

CASSANDRA   Otototototoi!* O Earth, Earth! 1035
      Apollo! Apollo!

1002 The great Heracles was made a slave to Omphale, Queen of Lydia. He often complained about the
  food.
1035 A wail of woe.

CHORUS   What have such cries to do with Loxias?*
He claims no mourner for his ministry.
CASSANDRA   O bridal, bridal of Paris, fatal to the home!
Scamander, my father's river . . . long ago   1040
I was a nursling on your banks, but now,
        Ah me! soon, very soon
Beside Cocytus' waters, by the streams
Of Acheron,* I am like to dream my dreams.
Otototototoi! O Earth, Earth!   1045
Apollo! Apollo!
CHORUS   Apollo's name again, with lamentable
Cries, that profane his presence and his godhead!
CASSANDRA   Apollo! Apollo!
Lord of the Ways, Apollo, my Destroyer!   1050
Utterly, a second time, thou hast destroyed me.
CHORUS   Some prophecy this will be of her own troubles.
She is a slave now, yet the spirit still moves her.
CASSANDRA   Apollo! Apollo!
Lord of the Ways, Apollo, my Destroyer! Ah!   1055
What way is this you have led me? What is this House?
CHORUS   Can you not grasp it even now? I'll tell you.
You are at the Atreidae's house. You'll find it true.
CASSANDRA   It is loathsome—the gods loathe it—a place intimate with sin,
Privy to butcheries, where kinsmen kill   1060
Kinsmen—a shambles—splashes on the floor!
CHORUS   She has the hound's keen scent for blood. Her trail
Leads presently to discovery of murder.
CASSANDRA   There's evidence here to prove it. Look! My witnesses
Are children—why do they wail so bitterly?   1065
For murder—for a roast of flesh a father tasted.
CHORUS   We have long been acquainted with your fame
For prophecy, but we need no prophets here.
CASSANDRA   Fie, Fie! What have we here?
What strange device? What horror?   1070
Someone is plotting in this house a thing
Intolerable to love, incurable.
There's no help near.
CHORUS   I cannot read that prophecy. The other
I knew at once: the whole town rings with it.   1075
CASSANDRA   Woman! Wretch! Is it this
You have in hand—your husband—
After the bath—How can I tell the rest?

1037 Applied to Apollo, particularly as a source of prophecy. Cassandra had been loved by Apollo, and he
    had given her the gift of prophecy. When she offended him, he ordained that she should retain the gift
    but never be believed.
1044 Rivers in Hades.

It comes apace, hand stretching after hand,
The end comes soon. 1080
CHORUS   I am in a mist. Dark riddles first, and now
veiled oracles that elude my understanding.
CASSANDRA   Ah me! Fie on it, Fie! What is this I see?
A net of Hell? Yes, but the wife's the net,
Shares the bed, shares the killing! 1085
Sing Hallelujah over the House, you ravening revel-rout,
To crown the damnable sacrifice.
CHORUS   What! Do you call a fiend from Hell to cry
Her triumph in the House? Is this your comfort?
My blood drains to the heart, 1090
The red drops jaundiced yellow—such a change
As comes to mortally wounded men—a sick faint glow,
Timed with the sunset, proves
The end is near.
CASSANDRA   Beware! Stand on your guard—on guard, I say! 1095
Keep clear of the Cow! See! She has caught the Bull
In a robe—with a black-horned
Instrument strikes, and he falls in the water. The tale is told,
The caldron's murderous treachery.
CHORUS   I fear there's mischief in it, though I claim 1100
No mastery in the art of reading oracles.
Have oracles ever brought
Light to the world, good news of happiness?
No, they are always evil, always a web of words
Innumerable, to teach 1105
Nothing but fear.
CASSANDRA   Ah! Woe is me!
Ah me for my own sad fortune. I pour my own
Grief in the general cup.
Why did you bring me here? What destiny 1110
Waits me? To die with you—only to die.
CHORUS   You are brainsick, by some spirit possessed,
In tuneless melody
Lamenting your own fortune, like the brown sad nightingale,*
Forever piping low 1115
"Poor Itylos, poor Itylos"
Her whole life through.
CASSANDRA   Ah, woe is me!
What is the nightingale's portion? A clear sweet song,
Wings and a feathery form 1120
The gods gave—save for tears a happy life.
And mine? The cloven flesh, the two-edged knife.

[1114] The passage alludes to the story of Philomela, who was ravished by her sister's husband, Tereus, and who, together with her sister Procne, killed Tereus' son Itylos. Having accomplished this revenge, she was changed into a nightingale to sing the death of Itylos ("Poor Itylos") forever.

CHORUS   Whence comes this ecstasy of sorrow,
          Unearthly, meaningless,
          Fears woven into music, passionate, discordant, shrill?   1125
          What makes your spirit brood
          So terribly, incessantly,
          On one sad road?
CASSANDRA   O bridal, bridal of Paris, fatal to the home!
          Scamander, my father's river . . . long ago   1130
          I was a nursling on your banks, but now,
              Ah me! soon, very soon
          Beside Cocytus' waters, by the streams
          Of Acheron, I am like to dream my dreams.
CHORUS   What have you said? That was a presage all too plain. A babe   1135
          Could understand you now. Your pitiful plight,
          Your songs of sorrow, fasten on the mind
          Like fangs, and the flesh feels the wound, My heart
              Breaks, as I listen . . .
CASSANDRA   O wasted labour, and sorrow wasted. What is Troy?   1140
          A ruin, utterly desolate . . . Wasted too
          The pastured kine—my father's sacrifice
              For the ramparts was no cure.
          What came to Troy, came . . . So the toils are set
          For me now—passionate still, I run into the net.   1145
CHORUS   You harp, as ever, on the same unvaried prophecy.
          Some Spirit of Evil, crushing you beneath
          A weight of malice, tunes your minstrelsy
          To the same burden, Death. I am in a maze . . .
              What will the end be?   1150
CASSANDRA   No longer shall my oracle peep and peer
          From veils, like a young bride, but fresh and strong
          Shall seek the sunrise, like the rushing wind
          That washes to the coasts of orient light
          Huge waves of worse disaster. You shall hear   1155
          No riddles. You shall be my witnesses.
          Come with me, as I hunt the trail of wrong
          Committed long ago. There haunts this House
          A choir that sings together, all one tune,
          Yet out of tune it sounds, and in the words   1160
          There's no good meaning. Drunk they are—yes, drunk
          With blood, to make them bold, a revel-rout
          That stays beyond its welcome—will not budge.
          These are the sister Furies, and the strain
          They chant when they infest the chambers, tells   1165
          Of the first fatal sin*—then presently
          They sicken at a marriage-bed, defiled
          And loathing the defiler. 'Twas the man's

1166 The "first fatal sin" probably alludes to the murder of Myrtilos at the hands of Pelops.

Own brother! Have I missed the mark of truth
Or hit? Am I some fortune-telling cheat, 1170
Knocking at doors with lies, or do I know
The story of this House, the sins committed long ago?
I'll have your oath for that. Swear.
CHORUS   Could an oath,
Plighted however honourably, help 1175
Or cure? And yet I marvel you, a stranger
Bred overseas, relate these histories
As an eye-witness might.
CASSANDRA   That is the power
The seer Apollo gave me. 1180
CHORUS   Was he swayed
By love, despite his godhead?
CASSANDRA   I have been
Ashamed to speak of it.
CHORUS   The fortunate 1185
Are ever proud.
CASSANDRA   Ah, but he strove with me
In passionate ardour.
CHORUS   So in course of nature
The union came? 1190
CASSANDRA   I promised Loxias,
Then failed him.
CHORUS   Had he laid on you the gift
Of mantic skill already?
CASSANDRA   Yes already 1195
I told Troy all the future.
CHORUS   Were you left
Unscathed then, by his anger?
CASSANDRA   Not one word
With any soul in Troy after my sin 1200
Found credence.
CHORUS   We believe your oracles true.
CASSANDRA   Oh, Oh, the pain! Oh me! It comes again,
The torment, in a whirl of dizziness
Preluding visions of the truth. See! See! 1205
Who are these—haunting the House—young creatures, like
Shapes seen in dreams? Children they seem—dead children,
Killed by their own kinsmen, their hands full
Of flesh—it is their own flesh—you can see,
What they are holding is a pitiful load, 1210
The heart and entrails which their father tasted.
    For this I tell you vengeance is afoot,
Planned by a lion, recreant to the breed,
Who wallows in the royal bed, keeps house
Forsooth for the Master—I must bear the yoke 1215

Of slavery—for my Master! Little dreams
The fleet's high admiral, Troy's conqueror,
What evil work the lecherous she-hound's tongue,
With long-drawn flattering speeches and the smile
Of cunning, cringing Ate, means to compass.   1220
So bold she is, so shameless. She will kill
Her husband, the wife kill the man! What beast
Is this? What loathsome creature shall I call her?
An amphisbaena?* No—not that—she lures
A sailor to destruction—she shall be   1225
A Scylla,* housed in rock, a bacchanal
Of hell, a frantic mother, breathing war
To the death against her dearest. How she cried
Her Hallelujah! Utterly perverse
She is, and sticks at nothing! Like a shout   1230
Of triumph in the field! And the pretence
Was joy to have her husband home from war.
Whether you think this true or not, all's one.
What shall be, shall be—soon—and you shall say
In pity "This was a true prophetess."   1235

CHORUS Thyestes' banquet of his children's flesh
  I understand, and shudder. It is true,
  No guess-work, and I am appalled to hear you
  Speak of it. After that I lose the track.

CASSANDRA I say, you shall see Agamemnon murdered.   1240

CHORUS Hush! Good words, woman!

CASSANDRA   There's no Healing God
  Concerned—this is no case for good words.

CHORUS   No,
  Not if it has to be. But Heaven prevent it.   1245

CASSANDRA You pray—they plan the business of the killing.

CHORUS What man in Argos plans a deed so fearful?

CASSANDRA What man? In sorry sooth you have lost the track.

CHORUS If there be such an one, I do not see
  How he could compass it.   1250

CASSANDRA   And yet I know
  Your language all too well.

CHORUS   The oracles
  Of Delphi are in Greek, but they are riddles.

CASSANDRA Oh, the fire! How it burns. It surges on me!   1255
  Ototoi! Lycian Apollo, Woe is me! Woe's me!
  Here's a two-footed lioness takes the wolf
  To bed when the brave lion's gone. She means
  To kill me miserably. That's a brew
  Of poison she concocts. She swears she'll put   1260

1224 A mythical serpent with a head at each end of its body.
1226 A female monster who inhabits a cave opposite Charybdis, a whirlpool, and lures sailors to destruction.

My wages in spite's potion, and the man
For whom she whets the knife, shall foot the bill
In blood because he brought me. Why do I keep
This gear, the magic wand, the mantic Wreaths
At the throat? They mock me now. I'll have you dead   1265
　　　　　(*She breaks the wand and tears off the garlands*)
Before my own time comes. So! Lie you there!
Get you to Hell—I'll follow. (*She slips off the mantic robe*)
　　　　　　　　　Here's a wealth
Of costly stuffs. Enrich some other wretch   1270
With ruin. Lo! Apollo comes to strip
The prophet's mantle off—the livery
In which fools mocked me, while He watched them—friends
And foes combined for that! What were the names
They had for me? Wretch, starveling, mountebank,   1275
The beggar, the madwoman. I endured
All that, and He who laid the ministry
Of truth upon me, brings me here to die,
Far from my father's altar—Here's a block with gore
Hot from the sacrificial victim slain before!   1280
　Yet the gods will not leave us in our death
Neglected. There will come to vindicate
Our cause a young avenger, a new shoot
Of the stock, the sire's revenge, the mother's death.
A wandering exiled outlaw, he shall come   1285
To crown the fabric, fix the coping-stone*
Of sin. There is an oath in Heaven, the Doom
Stands fast. His father's body draws him home.
　Why do I wait and moan? Why pity them?
I go. I will go bravely, meet death well.   1290
Are these the gates of Death? Thus I salute them
With prayer. Be the blow mortal. May the blood
Flow freely. I would have no agony
At the end. I would just close my eyes and die.
CHORUS　Lady of many sorrows, and withal   1295
　Much wisdom, tell me—though you have discoursed
　At length already—if indeed you know
　Your fate, how is it that you pass to death
　So bravely, like the victim which the gods
　Speed willing to the altar?   1300
CASSANDRA　　　　　　No delay
　Could save me, friends.
CHORUS　　　　　　And yet the last hour still
　Seems best.
CASSANDRA　My time has come. I have not much   1305
　To gain by flight.

1286 The top stone in a wall or building; hence the culmination.

CHORUS   A brave heart gives you strength
     To endure bravely.
CASSANDRA   That is not the praise
     Men give the fortunate.   1310
CHORUS   Yet there is comfort
     Even in death with honour.
CASSANDRA   Oh my father,
     You and your noble children! (*She moves towards the Palace, then recoils*)
CHORUS   What turns you back? What is it frightens you?   1315
CASSANDRA   Foul! Foul!
CHORUS   What makes you cry "Foul! Foul!"? Your own sick fancy?
CASSANDRA   There's blood—blood in the air. The House smells of it.
CHORUS   No, no. That is the stench of the sacrifice
     Slain at the hearth.   1320
CASSANDRA   The fumes of the charnel-house.
CHORUS   Only the fumes of the rich Tyrian incense!
CASSANDRA   I will go in and there bewail my own
     And Agamemnon's fate. Enough of life.
     Ah me, friends, friends,   1325
     I do not thrill and startle like a bird
     At any bush that trembles. When I am dead
     Say that of me, and when the woman dies
     For me, a woman, and another man
     For this ill-mated man, say this of me,   1330
     "She told the truth." I ask it as at point to die.
CHORUS   Brave soul, I pity your sad fate of prophecy.
CASSANDRA   Yet once more I would speak—no, it shall be
     My own dirge. To this last light of the sun
     That I shall ever see, be this my prayer   1335
     That when my champions come my enemies
     May pay together the like price for this
     Their easy conquest—a slavewoman's murder.
          Alas for mortal lives—their happiness
     A shadow-picture: their unhappiness   1340
     A sketch, by a wet sponge at a touch dashed out.
     And this I pity more than that, far more. (*Exit*)

CHORUS   Mankind are all alike in this—Prosperity
     Is never satisfied:
     No man ever says to her "Go hence, come here no more!",   1345
     Shutting her out, driving her away from famous palaces.
     Here is a man to whom the blessed gods vouchsafed
          The conquest over Troy,
     And safe return, still glorious.
     If he should pay the price for sins of others, blood shed long ago,   1350
     By his own death crowning the account,

What mortal man can boast
A harmless destiny for birthright?
AGAMEMNON (*Within*) Ah me. I am wounded mortally! Here in the House!
CHORUS Silence! Who shouted? Wounded mortally?   1355
AGAMEMNON Ah me, again—I am wounded—a second blow.
CHORUS That was the King groaning. Indeed I fear
The worst has happened. Come, we must consult—
Find some safe way—
AN ELDER   Here is my judgment. Call   1360
The city to the rescue. Sound an alarm!
ANOTHER ELDER No, best break in at once, I say, and catch them.
Red-handed—
ANOTHER   I agree—to this extent—
I vote for action. There's no time to waste.   1365
ANOTHER It is evident! A plot to overthrow
All government, and enslave us. This first stroke
Proves it.
ANOTHER   And here we talk! Delays and dreams
Are not for them! They act!   1370
ANOTHER   I cannot tell
What should be done. Your man of action, he's
The best adviser.
ANOTHER   True—I see no way
To raise the dead with talk.   1375
ANOTHER   But surely, here's
Foul murder in the house. Can we submit
Even to save our lives?
ANOTHER   Intolerable!
Die rather! Slavery is far worse than death.   1380
ANOTHER Come, come. Are we diviners? Can we take
Groans as a proof of death?
ANOTHER   No, no, indeed.
Conjecture is not knowledge. We should have
The facts before we grow so passionate.   1385
LEADER That sums the many voices. We must have
Assurance, how it stands with Agamemnon.
                    (*As they move towards the Palace, the doors open,
                    disclosing* CLYTAEMNESTRA *with the bodies of*
                    AGAMEMNON *and* CASSANDRA)   1390
CLYTAEMNESTRA I have said much before to serve the time
Which now I shall not blush to contradict.
How, if you show plain hatred for a foe
Esteemed your friend, how shall you fence the toils
Of ruin high, too high for overleaping?   1395
The encounter, long premeditated, sprang
From an old feud. My moment came at last,

And I stand where I struck, my work well done.
I left no loophole for escape, no way
Of warding off the blow—I'll not deny it.   1400
I wrapped the rich robe round him, caught my fish
Fast in the blind inextricable net,
Then struck two blows, and with a groan for each
He slacked his limbs there. On the fallen body
I struck a third blow, grave of prayer to Zeus   1405
The Saviour, who keeps dead men safe below.
So down he fell, gasping his life away,
And the sharp jet of blood which suddenly
Gushed and besprinkled me with a dark shower
Was welcome as the god's own gift of rain   1410
To cornland at the birth-time of the bid.
Such are the facts, yet reverend Argive Elders.
Rejoice, if so you will. I glory in them.
If we could pour it, what drink-offering
Were fit for this dead man, just, more than just?   1415
      (*She shows the blood on her hands and garments*)
This—for the bowl of curses and of wrong
He filled high in his home, now drinks it and is gone.
CHORUS   This was your lord and man. Have you no shame
    To brag and boast? I cannot understand.   1420
CLYTAEMNESTRA   You play on me as a light-minded woman.
    There's no fear in my heart. You know the truth—
    Whether you blame or not, no matter now—
    And thus I speak it. This is Agamemnon,
    My husband. He is dead, by this right hand's   1425
    Most righteous workmanship. The case stands so.
CHORUS   What venomous herb of the land,
    What drug of the restless sea,
    Woman, infected thee
    With frenzy when thy hand was raised to slay,   1430
    To cut and cast away? So shalt thou be
    A loathed abomination, cursed, cut off and cast away.
CLYTAEMNESTRA   You sentence me to banishment, and cry
    "Abominable." You curse me, cut me off
    From the people. What of him? With no more thought   1435
    Than for a beast, though fleecy multitudes
    Grazed in his pasturelands, he sacrificed
    My dearest pang of travail, his own child,
    To charm the winds of Thrace. Was there a word
    Of protest then from you? This was the man   1440
    To banish for pollution! Now you hear
    What I have done, you judge it harshly. Listen!
    I'll counter threat with threat. Look to yourselves!

Conquer me, if you can, by force. I'll own
Your government then. If God decides the issue   1445
Otherwise, I shall teach you greybeards prudence.
CHORUS   Arrogant was the sin,
And hers is shamelessness
To match the wickedness.
The tainted mind within   1450
Shows on the brow—the blood-fleck on the brow.—What wretchedness
Awaits thee in thy shame when blow shall answer blow.
CLYTAEMNESTRA   What I have sworn has sanction. You shall hear.
By Justice, in my child's revenge made perfect.
By Hate, Hell's Fury, by the fiend Distraction,   1455
To whom I slew this sacrifice, my Hope
Treads not the house of Fear while on my hearth
The fire burns, kindled by a faithful friend,
Aegisthus, the strong shield of my defence.
   Here lies the man who shamed his wife, the toy   1460
And comfort of the Chryseids* under Troy,
And here the slave, the prophetess, his mate,
His fortune-telling concubine. They shared
The galley-bench, good partners. Now they get
Just what they merit. This for him—for her   1465
One last shrill swan-song—then this extra-bride,
This quaint new garnish for my marriage-bed,
His lover—crowns my triumph. She is dead.
CHORUS   Kind gods, only to sleep, and never wake!
No agony of the flesh, nor wasting bed   1470
Of sickness—Woe is me! My friend is dead,
Who shouldered for a woman's sake the toil and strife
And by a woman's hand has paid the last toil, life.
Ah fatal, fatal Helen. Many gave
Their lives at Troy to pay thy folly's price.   1475
And this, the last, most perfect sacrifice,
Most memorable, of blood that none can lave,
Crowns thee, the fatal wife,
The non-pareil of strife.
CLYTAEMNESTRA   You should by no means pray   1480
For death, nor turn away
Your wrath, to rail on Helen. Leave the thought
That by one woman all those Greeks were slain,
And all this tangled mystery of pain
Only by Helen wrought.   1485
CHORUS   O Spirit of Death and Doom, haunting the home,

1461 An allusion to the episode that provoked the quarrel between Agamemnon and Achilles, the subject
   of *The Iliad*. Agamemnon had taken Chryseis, the daughter of a Trojan priest to Apollo, as a prize of war,
   but then was forced to give her up. When he did, he forced Achilles to give over his prize, a young
   woman named Briseis, to him.

For ruin of those twain,
The sons of Tantalus, though didst make strong
Two women of like temper, equal ministers of wrong.
It breaks the heart. See how the Fiend, elate,
Perched like a raven on the body croaks the triumph-song of hate.   1490

CLYTAEMNESTRA   Ah! Now you guide aright
Your sentence, and indict
The Spirit of the House. Thrice-fed with gore
He fosters in the heart of us the mood
Insatiate, yea, ere the feast of blood   1495
Is finished, craving more.

CHORUS   Yea, terrible indeed
That spirit of Wrath and Hate,
Insatiate,
Fraught with Distraction, even as thou hast said.   1500
Yet were these things decreed
By Zeus, nor could befall
Save to fulfil
Heaven's purpose and the Will   1505
Of Zeus, the author and the cause of all.

My King, my King, how shall I weep for thee?
With loving heart what shall I say of thee?
Caught in the spider's web, ah me,
Breathing away the life,   1510
Betrayed by treachery,
And by the blow of the keen two-edged knife
On bed of shame laid low.

CLYTAEMNESTRA   You speak as if my hand
Had slain him. Leave the thought.   1515
I am not Agamemnon's wife who stand
Before you, but a Spirit wrought
In woman's flesh—the ancient stern Avenger of the feast
Which Atreus gave his guest,
Heaping upon the children slain by him   1520
This other sacrifice, fresh, full-grown, grim.

CHORUS   Your innocence of blood
No voice will testify,
Nor yet deny
The foul Fiend may have steeled the murderous mood   1525
And helped you. 'Tis a flood
Of slaughter, till in full the price be paid
For sacrifice of children, flesh for flesh and blood for blood.

My King, my King, how shall I weep for thee?
With loving heart, what shall I say of thee?   1530
Caught in the spider's web, ah me,

Breathing away the life,
Betrayed by treachery,
And by the blow of the keen two-edged knife
On bed of shame laid low.   1535

CLYTAEMNESTRA   What of the King's own deed?
Was that no treachery?
What of the fair shoot sprung from his own seed,
Iphigeneia? Was not she
My own lamented fruit of travail? As he wrought   1540
On her, he suffered. He has naught
To boast in Hades. By the sword he drew
He perished, slaughtered even as he slew.

CHORUS   I have lost the clue, alas! I am helpless, blind.
The House shakes. The first shower of blood abates.   1545
Yet apprehension waits
The deluge that shall dash the roof in pieces. Even now
Justice on a new whetstone whets the sword for a fresh blow.
O Earth, Earth, would you had covered me
Ere I had seen my King   1550
In bath of silver huddled. He must be
Buried! Who shall bury him and sing
His dirge with lamentation true, and grace
The hero with just praise?

CLYTAEMNESTRA   That is not your concern. We slew! We laid him low!   1555
And we shall make his grave,
Nor shall he have
Lamenting from his household, customary rites of woe.
Only his child shall meet him,
Iphigeneia, at the straits of tears in Hell,   1560
And, as a daughter should, shall greet him
With a kiss, lovingly and well.

CHORUS   Taunt parries taunt. The truth is hard to find.
The spoiler is despoiled, the slayer slain.
So shall the law remain,   1565
While Zeus abideth on the Throne, the sinner pays.
How banish the foul Spirit? Doom if fastened on the race.

CLYTAEMNESTRA   You preach true doctrine now. For my own part
I find it in my heart
With the dark Spirit of the House to swear   1570
A solemn treaty. Be it mine to bear
This load, however hard, if he consent
To leave us, go his ways
And plague some other race
With kindred murder. Little wealth I need,   1575
Once I have freed
These halls from that mad lust for blood, I stand content.

(*Enter* AEGISTHUS.)

AEGISTHUS Bright day of Justice! Happy retribution!
I'll now acknowledge that in heaven the gods   1580
Look down with vengeful eyes on mortal sin,
Since I have seen this man, to my heart's joy,
In the net woven by the Furies pay
For Atreus' cunning work. Atreus was King
Of Argos, this man's father. You shall have   1585
A plain tale. When his brother, prince Thyestes,
My sire, challenged his title, claimed the throne,
He turned him out of doors. He banished him.
Then, when he came again, a suppliant
At the hearth, vouchsafed him this much clemency—   1590
Not to be killed forthwith, not to pollute
His father's house with bloodshed. Zealously
He made him welcome, with more zeal indeed
Than loving-kindness, making much pretence
Of sacrificial cheer, he served his guest   1595
With a rich feast of his own children's flesh.
He kept the fringes of the hands and feet
Apart: the rest he gave him in a mess
Confused, and straightway, ignorant, he took
And tasted—'Twas a banquet, as you see,   1600
Unwholesome to the race. At last he knew
The abominable fact, and groaning reeled
Backwards, and vomiting the foul flesh, kicked
The table, as he fell, and while it crashed,
Cursed all the line of Pelops with a cry   1605
"Thus perish the whole House of Pleisthenes!"*
So comes it that you see this man here dead,
And I, the just contriver of this plot,
I, that unhappy father's youngest child,
His third, last hope, a babe in swaddling clothes,   1610
Cast out with him to banishment and reared
In exile—Justice brought me home—I reached
My man, though far away. The subtlety
Was mine, and now I see my enemy
Fast in the toils of Justice, I can die   1615
Content.

CHORUS   Aegisthus, you insult distress.
I like it not. You say this wretchedness,
This murder, was your doing. Wilfully,
You say, you killed him. On your own head be   1620
The Justice you yourself invoke, the voice
Of cursing from the city, and the death
By stoning.

1606 According to some mythographers, Pleisthenes was the son of Atreus and the father of Agamemnon and Menelaus.

AEGISTHUS   Is it so? You, you who sit
   On the bottom bench, prate! We of the upper tier   1625
   Control the ship. The order for to-day
   Is "Prudence." Must we send you back to school,
   Greybeards, to learn that lesson? You will find
   The schooling hard. Chains and the pangs of hunger
   Can physic old men's folly. Have you eyes   1630
   And cannot see? Kick not against the pricks
   For fear you stumble.

CHORUS   Woman! So you kept
   A soldier's house, you shamed a soldier's bed,
   And when the fighting-men came home, contrived   1635
   The murder of their captain!

AEGISTHUS   Words, mere words!
   Your tears shall pay for them. Your eloquent speeches
   Have none of Orpheus' charm. His music led
   All nature captive with delight. Your crude   1640
   And childish whelpings prove you must be tamed
   By prison, taught to recognize your master.

CHORUS   You to be master here! To tyrannise
   In Argos! You, who plotted the King's death,
   But did not dare to kill him with your own   1645
   Right hand.

AEGISTHUS   To trick him was the woman's work
   Clearly. I was a suspect, his old foe.
   However, with the help of his estate
   I shall attempt to rule you. When I find   1650
   A malcontent among you, I shall make
   The yoke press harder on him. He shall prove
   No pampered corn-fed trace-horse. Hunger, lodged
   In solitude with darkness, shall reduce
   His high heart.   1655

CHORUS   Coward! What prevented you
   From killing him yourself? Why must the woman
   Defile her country and her country's gods?
   Because you dared not! If Orestes lives,
   Prosper him, Fortune! Speed him home again   1660
   To conquer and avenge and kill these twain!

AEGISTHUS   Since in word and deed you threaten, you shall have your lesson.
                                          Ho!
   Up, my spearmen! Here is work, my friends, for you to do!
                    (*Enter a Bodyguard of Soldiers*)   1665

CAPTAIN OF THE GUARD   Fighting order! Ready! Forward! Company, draw
                                          swords!

CHORUS   I too
   Stand ready for you. By the sword I'll not refuse to fight and fall.

AEGISTHUS Fight and fall, you say. We greet the omen! Fight and die you   1670
                              shall.
CLYTAEMNESTRA No, my dearest husband, by no means! We'll have no
                                more
   Wrong-doing. We've a full crop now of trouble for the reaping,
   Surely cause enough for grief. Indeed we'll have no bloodshed.   1675
   Go you, reverend Elders, home. Submit to what is fated.
   Now believe, before you suffer. What we did, we had to do.
   If this hard affliction prove enough, we shall submit,
   Content, though we are crushed beneath the feet of this dark Spirit.
   These are a woman's thoughts, if any of you deign to listen.   1680
AEGISTHUS Who are they to let their tongues run riot? Here's a crop indeed
   Of idle insolent threats to reap! They tempt their fate too far.
CHORUS Shall I cringe before a scoundrel? That is not the Argive way.
AEGISTHUS You shall pay for this hereafter, settle this account some day.
CHORUS Never if by God's good guidance our own Prince Orestes come!   1685
AEGISTHUS Starveling exiles, well I know the story, feed on thoughts of
                                home!
CHORUS Take your pleasure now. Wax fat, polluting Justice, while you may.
AEGISTHUS Fools you are, and for their folly, when the time comes, fools
                              must pay.   1690
CHORUS Struts the cock beside his mate! Brag and swagger! Challenge Fate!
CLYTAEMNESTRA Do not heed their idle yelpings. We together, you and I,
   Masters of this House, will order all things well.
                    (*Exeunt* CLYTAEMNESTRA *and* AEGISTHUS *to the Palace*)

THE CHOEPHOROE

Characters

ORESTES, *son of Agamemnon*
PYLADES, *his friend*
CHORUS *of Trojan slavewomen*
ELECTRA, *daughter of Agamemnon*
A servant of Clytaemnestra
CLYTAEMNESTRA, *widow of Agamemnon*
Nurse of Orestes
AEGISTHUS, *Clytaemnestra's lover*
A servant of Aegisthus

Before the palace at Argos; night; in the foreground Agamemnon's grave

(*Enter* ORESTES *and* PYLADES)

ORESTES Nether Hermes, hear me. Thou who keepest watch
On every father's cause, hear me and save.*
At last returned from exile, here I stand,
Before this mounded sepulchre and call
My father's spirit to hear. (*A woman's cry is heard within the palace;* ORESTES   5
      proceeds with a ritual of offering and supplication)
This lock of hair I give to Inachus,*
As grateful for my nurture. This to thee,
Father, for token of my grief. Alas!
I was not with thee at thy death, nor wept   10
With hands outstretched to bid thy corpse farewell.
(ELECTRA, *attended by a train of Trojan slavewomen, issues from the palace*)
ORESTES Ah, what is this I see? A company
Of women—mourners, so their sable robes
Proclaim them. What event should I surmise
For cause? Some fresh disaster to our House?   15
Or shall I guess aright to say they bear
Drink-offerings for the dead, gifts to appease
My father? Surely that. I seem to see
Electra. In such bitter grief she moves—
Surely, my sister! Zeus be gracious to me,   20
Succour me. Let me avenge my father's murder.
   Stand we aloof, Pylades. I must know
For certain who they are and what their errand.

---

2 Hermes is invoked as the watcher of the souls in Hades and as the helper of suppliants.

7 The hero-founder of Argos, identified with the river that bore his name. It was the custom for youths to
  keep one lock of hair as consecrated and upon reaching maturity to cut it off and offer it to the river-god
  of their country in thanks for their nurture.

(ORESTES *and* PYLADES *withdraw, and the procession of women*
approaches the gravemound)

CHORUS I am sent from the Palace, beating my breast, to bring
    Libations for the dead.
    Behold my cheek, stained crimsom by the nail's fresh furrowing,
    My soul with a life's long lamentation fed.
    I have rent the robe on my bosom. It shrieks as I tear
    The folds. I have beaten my breast for a thing hath befallen of no good
                        cheer.

It was heard in the heart of the Palace, a piercing cry,
    Panic, with lifted hair,
    Waking the sleeper at dead of night in wrathful prophecy,
    Haunting the woman's chamber, a dream of fear,
    By the readers of dreams in the name of the gods interpreted thus—
    That the nether powers are angry, the slayers loathed by the wrathful
                        dead.

    Such are the woes this godless Woman who sends me here
Seeks to avert and appease, but the rite must fail—
Alas! Earth Mother, I speak my thought in fear—
Blood hath been shed, and for blood what rites avail,
What ransom can atone? The House is down, overthrown,
Wrapt in a cloud of hate by the Master's doom,
Shrouded in sunless gloom.

    What of the ancient Majesty, once in the people's ear,
And in their hearts, pre-eminent? Reverence, proved, in stress
Of war invincible, now yields place to fear.

    Justice hath eyes! The scales turn. Sinners pay,
Some in this light of day,
Some between day and dark in the twilight realms,
Some total darkness whelms.

    Hath blood been shed and drunk by nurturing Earth
It melteth not away, but sticketh fast,
Congealed, malignant, while the infected soul
Sickens to ruin in a waste of Self-Delusion.

    Even so, hath any man deflower'd the shrine
Of pure virginity, he can find no cure:
Even so, though streams from many fountains mingle,
Many waters cannot cleanse a hand by blood polluted.

    But I, because the gods, encompassing
My city with constraint, have brought me here
For this—'tis proper in the slave—must brook
Authority's prescription, right or wrong,
Assent despite my thought, and still control
My loathing, though beneath my cloak I weep
Despite my thought, compliant, hiding tears
Under my cloak, and, though I weep, control

My loathing of such infamies
As freeze the blood and harrow up the soul.
> (*They have now reached the gravemound;* ELECTRA *speaks*)

ELECTRA   Women who tend the service of the house,
 Since you are here to bear me company   75
 In this my intercession, well advise me.
 What shall I say, how pray, to please my father
 When at his grave I pour these offerings?
 Shall I say, "From a loving wife these gifts
 To a dead husband?" From my mother? No,   80
 I am not so bold, nor have I words to grace
 The pouring of these oils. Or should I use
 The customary form and fashion, "Bless
 The friends who send these garlands with a gift
 Of blessing, good in recompense for good?"   85
 Or silently, and with no rites of honour
 Even as my father died, pour out the drink
 For Earth to take, then fling the vessel back
 Behind me, with averted eyes, like one
 Who throws away offscourings?* Join with me   90
 Your counsel, even as in the house we share
 A common enmity. Friends, speak your hearts free thought,
 Nor let the fear of one you dread restrain you.
 Fate governs all, and what must come the free
 Must bear no less than those whose destiny   95
 Is bondage. Speak, if you have better counsel.

CHORUS   You bid me, and I speak. In reverence
 Before your father's grave, as at an altar—

ELECTRA   In reverence for my father's grave, say on.

CHORUS   As you pour, invoke a blessing on true friends. 100

ELECTRA   Who are my friends? What friends can I call true?

CHORUS   First yourself—then, whoever hates Aegisthus.

ELECTRA   That is a prayer for you and me.

CHORUS   You take
 My meaning. Think!   105

ELECTRA   Who else? What other friend
 Am I to count of the company?

CHORUS   There is one,
 Though far away. Do not forget Orestes.

ELECTRA   Good counsel. I am schooled.   110

CHORUS   Do not forget
 The murder, and upon the guilty, pray—

ELECTRA   For what? Instruct my ignorance.

CHORUS   Thus—pray
 That there may come spirit or mortal man—   115

---

90 The passage alludes to the Athenian custom of cleansing a house, morally or physically. The cleanser
 threw the filth ("offscourings") away without turning to look.

ELECTRA To judge? Or, do you mean, to punish them?
CHORUS Speak in plain terms—then kill them, as they slew.
ELECTRA Is that a righteous thing to ask of heaven?
CHORUS Surely, to repay your enemy with evil.
ELECTRA Nether Hermes, Herald of the realm below   120
    As of this world above, help me! Proclaim
    This message! Bid the powers below attend,
    The guardian spirits of my father's House,
    Yea, Earth herself, who giveth all things life,
    Nurtureth, and to the quickening womb again   125
    Receiveth all. Bid them attend my prayer,
    While thus, in solemn converse with the dead,
    I pour the lustral water, name his name,
    Cry, "Father, pity me, and in thy house
    Make dear Orestes, like a flame of fire   130
    Shine on our darkness. Both thy children now
    Are outcasts, bartered by their mother's lust
    For a new lord, Aegisthus, who with her
    Compassed thy death—I, even as a slave,
    Orestes, exiled, portionless, while they   135
    Wax wanton in the wealth thy labour gathered.
    Hear me, O father, and in happy time
    I pray thee, send Orestes home again.
    And for myself, may my own spirit prove
    More modest than my mother's, and my acts   140
    More innocent by far. This for ourselves,
    And for thine adversaries, even as they slew,
    So may they justly perish. Thus I call
    The Avenger, and with evil interweave
    The good prayer. Father, send us from thy grave   145
    All blessing! Earth, Heaven, and triumphant Justice save!"
                (*She pours the drink-offerings at the tomb*)
    This is my prayer! For this I make libation!
    (*To the* CHORUS) It is your part to crown the ceremony
    With keening and the Paean for the dead.   150
CHORUS Bitterly wail at the grave,
    Bitterly weep for the lord   ·
    Cruelly, cruelly slain.
    So the libation is poured,
    So hath the grave where the body was lain   155
    Potency, evil to banish and that which is good to save.
    Hear us, O Master, Hearken, King revered.
    Rouse thy dim spirit to hear.
    (*With growing excitement*) Otototototoi!
    O for a champion to appear,   160
    A champion mighty with the spear
    Or with the back-drawn Scythian bow that shoots afar,

Or bludgeon, dealing havoc in the close grim press of war.
For the deliverance of the home
Soon may he come.   ₁₆₅

ELECTRA   The earth hath drunk, my sire received, the gift.
But now I have strange fresh news for you to share.

CHORUS   What news? My heart leaps up with dread.

ELECTRA   A lock of hair at the grave.

CHORUS   Whose! Can it be   ₁₇₀
A man's? A maid's?

ELECTRA   That is not difficult
For anyone to guess.

CHORUS   I am your elder,
But let me learn from you.   ₁₇₅

ELECTRA   Could there be one,
Save I, who might have made that offering?

CHORUS   Not one, since those who should have mourned for him,
Hate him.

ELECTRA   And yet this lock of hair is like—   ₁₈₀
So very like—

CHORUS   Whose? I have still to learn,
And I am eager—

ELECTRA   Mine! It is like mine!

CHORUS   Is it—oh, could it be, a secret gift   ₁₈₅
Brought by Orestes.

ELECTRA   Very like, most like
It seems!

CHORUS   And yet how could he dare to come.

ELECTRA   Perhaps from exile he has sent this gift   ₁₉₀
Of love and sorrow.

CHORUS   Then still I must weep,
If he should never more set foot in Argos.

ELECTRA   I too am in deep waters, and my soul
Is moved as if a sword had pierced the heart,   ₁₉₅
And from the surging flood of that Heart's tears
Some drops I needs must weep—these thirsty eyes
Indeed are fain to weep. Have they not seen
This lock of hair. Whose? Whose, can I believe,
Of all who dwell in Argos? Surely not   ₂₀₀
That godless mother, who has forfeited
Her motherhood by murder?
                              'Twas not she—
And yet, what proof have I, to make me sure
This gift of beauty came from him I love   ₂₀₅
Best in the world, Orestes—though the hope
Beguiles me still! Ah me! If it could speak
And like a messenger, turn this misery
Of doubtful hope and fears to certainty

Am I to spurn it as a loathsome thing   210
Shorn from some enemy's head, or welcome it
And cry "Behold my brother who hath graced
His father's tomb with beauty and with honour?"
   The gods who hear us know in what distress
We pray, like baffled mariners, adrift   215
In stormy seas—and yet, if destiny
Intend our safety, even the smallest seed
Of hope may spring into a mighty tree.
   Look! Look! Here is fresh evidence, the print
Of feet—his and some fellow-traveller's—   220
There are two different outlines here—and see!
These heels are like my own and, measuring
The whole, these imprints pair with mine! Alas!
I am in sore travail, and my wits distracted.
                (ORESTES *and* PYLADES *return;* ORESTES *comes forward*)   225
ORESTES   Pray that the gods hereafter may approve
   Your prayers as now, with a like glad fulfilment.
ELECTRA   How has heaven helped me now?
ORESTES   You stand in sight
   Of him you so long prayed for.   230
ELECTRA   Do you know
   For whom I prayed?
ORESTES   I know. It is Orestes,
   For whom you so much care.
ELECTRA   What makes you think   235
   My prayers are answered?
ORESTES   I am here. No friend
   Shall you find dearer.
ELECTRA   Stranger, is it a plot
   Contrived against me?   240
ORESTES   Then it is a plot
   Contrived against myself.
ELECTRA   It pleases you
   To mock my misery.
ORESTES   If I make a jest   245
   Of yours, I mock my own.
ELECTRA   You ask me, sir,
   To welcome you, as if you were Orestes.
ORESTES   You see, but do not know me. I am he.
   Yet, when you saw this votive tress of hair,   250
   And while you scanned the footprints, you were all
   On wings! You fancied it was I you saw!
   Come, put the shorn lock to the tonsure—Look!
   It fits. It *is* your brother's, very like
   Your own. And look you, here—This was your work.   255
   This broidery you wove. That is your trick

Of threading, and these beasts are your design.
Be calm, I beg you. Let not joy distract you.
Those who should love us most, I know, most hate us.

ELECTRA Dear presence, four loves in one love conjoined,   260
I needs must call you father; what regard
I owe my mother falls to you, for she
Is utterly harsh and hateful; and my love
For her, the sister whom they killed, is yours,
With all my loving pride in you, my brother!   265

CHORUS O darling of thy father's house, and hope
Which we have watered with our tears, for seed
Of our deliverance, strong in faith and deed,
Thou shalt retrieve thy father's heritage
If Justice fight with thee, and Victory,   270
And Zeus, the third, and greatest of the three.

ORESTES Zeus, Zeus, look down and see what here is done.
See the great eagle's offspring, of their sire
Bereft, their father in the tangled skein
Of a fell viper perished—and the young   275
Pinched, starving, fatherless, not yet mature
To hunt and fetch their father's quarry home.
Even so thou mayst behold us, robbed alike
Of home and sire? Electra here and I
Are orphans both, yet children both of him   280
Who with abundant sacrifice and praise
Worshipped thee? Wilt thou then destroy his brood?
Who shall be found henceforth to render thee
Rich festal honours? Kill the eagle's young,
Thou canst no more to mortals here on earth   285
Send trusty signs—even so, if once this stem
Withers, no branch of royal stock remains
For service on thy day of sacrifice.
Raise and restore the plant now laid so low.
Let the stock live, and strength from weakness grow.   290

CHORUS Hush, children. Saviours of your father's house,
Dear children, silence! What if you were heard,
What if for sake of talking, all were told
To the tyrants—May I live to see their flesh
In flaming pitch-pine's resinous ooze devoured.   295

ORESTES Apollo's potent oracle cannot fail,
Which bade me tread this perilous road, in strains
Of high-uplifted prophecy, many times
Rehearsing to the fevered soul such threats
As freeze the blood, should I neglect pursuit   300
Of those who slew my father. Life for life
He bade me take. Yes, I myself must kill them,
Even as they slew, steeled, so Apollo said,

By wrath for my lost heritage—else the debt
Is mine, and loathsome evils fall on me.   305
He published it to the world. Resentful powers
Of Earth will breed malignant plagues.* He spoke
Of leprous ulcers, mounting the clean flesh
And eating up its goodness, hungry mouths
Beneath a mildew of white, tufted hair.   310
He spoke of Furies too, whose visitation
Becomes effectual through a father's murder.
When kindred blood cries for revenge, he said,
Strange instruments of darkness by the powers
Of Hell are wielded, frenzies, sudden fears   315
That start in the night at nothing to distract
And trouble, till the body by the scourge
Of excommunication scarr'd, expelled
The city, roams at large. Where others mix
The wine and pour drink-offerings, or approach   320
Heaven's altars, still his father's wrath unseen
Prevents him. None may lodge with him, none welcome.
Disfranchised, friendless, scorned, a living death
Conserves him till he withers and so dies.
    Must I not trust such oracles as these?   325
Though I believed not, I must do this thing,
So many promptings of my heart's desire
All to one purpose join—the god's command,
My sorrow for my father, and the pinch
Of disinherited hunger challenge me   330
To save the world's most famous citizens,
Whose valour conquered Troy, from slavery
To this vile brace of women—Is not he
Indeed a woman? Else—he soon shall see.
CHORUS   Yet potent Fates, by Grace of Zeus   335
             Vouchsafe this matter end
             There where the ways of Justice wend,
             That stern executor of dues.
             "For cruel word by cruel deed,
             The penalty," she cries,   340
             "But for the deed of blood the doer pays the price:
             The price of blood is death."
             So age-old Wisdom saith. (*All take their places at the Mound for the*
                 ritual by which they seek to rouse the Spirit of the murdered King,
                 constraining him to steel ORESTES *for his task*)   345
ORESTES   Father, stricken father, how shall word or deed of mine
             Waft a message where afar thou sleepest in the grave?
             Light is foil to darkness, and the name our dirges have
             Is comfort, for they praise the famous King of Atreus' line.

[307] That is, if Orestes does not avenge his father's murder.

CHORUS   Child, the spirit of the dead is not subdued   350
   By the fire's ravening jaws;* he yet makes manifest his mood.
   For the slain the mourners mourn,
   And the slayer is made known.
   True and righteous lamentation for a prince, a father, like a hunter goes
                                          abroad   355
   Yea, will hunt the world for blood.
ELECTRA   Therefore, hear us, Father. We, thy children, at the tomb,
   Suppliants and fugitives, weep and sing thy dirge together in responsive
                                          strain.
   Is not grief made perfect here? Doth any good remain?   360
   Over all triumphant rides inexorable Doom.
CHORUS   Yet, if a god so will, the day may come
   To chant in sweeter strain and tones less drear
   Instead of dirges for the dead a hymn of praise and triumph and good
                                          cheer   365
   To welcome a friend home.
ORESTES   O Father, hadst thou died at Troy in war
   By Lycian* spearman slain,
   Thy children honoured in the sight of men,
   Thy fair fame for their legacy, and thou, in mounded sepulchre afar,   370
   At rest, it were indeed a grief less hard to bear.
CHORUS   So thou, a hero to all heroes dear,
   Majestic still, their comrade and their peer,
   Even as thou wert a monarch in this land
   Once of the living, still with sceptred hand   375
   As Minister to that realm's dread Potentates,
   Wouldst cast the lots that govern human fates.
ELECTRA   I would not have it so,
   I would not Father thou among the rest
   Hast died beneath the walls of Troy in war,   380
   And lain beside Scamander. It were best
   That those who murdered thee had been laid low
   By their own kinsman, so that we might hear a message from afar
   That they themselves were dead, nor grieve as now we do.
CHORUS   Ah, daughter, that were bliss more precious than fine gold,   385
   And yet to pray for but a boon, though dreams are free,
   Is vanity.
   Only of realms beyond the north-wind's rage such tales are told.
            (*With growing excitement and gestures as of scourging*)
   Beneath a double scourge our spirit groans.   390
   Twice the lash falls, twice moans—
   Our champion lies, long dead, and Victory
   Is theirs, the blood-polluted! Can there be
   For you, his children, a worse infamy?

---

351 The funeral pyre.
368 The Lycians were the Trojans' chief allies.

ORESTES   That was a shaft well sped,   395
      Straight to the heart from the bow!
      Zeus, Zeus, on mortal hands befoul'd with blood
      Send Ruin and Distraction from below,
      Swift to avenge the dead,
      An Offspring like the parents of the brood.   400
CHORUS   Soon, soon, glad Hallelujahs crown the cry
      Over a man stricken to death, a woman doomed to die!
      My spirit is moved within me—why should I hide it? Passionate,
      Crying for vengeance, it beats on my heart in a storm of hate!
ELECTRA   Ah me! When shall the hand   405
      Of Zeus in plenitude of might
      Fall on the guilty heads to smite and slay?
      O God, vouchsafe the land
      A sign. Let evil-doers have
      Their just reward. That, only that I crave.   410
      Hear me, O Earth, and ye majestic spirits of the darkness and the grave.
CHORUS   It is the law. Once shed,
      Blood will have blood, and Havoc cries aloud
      Till from the bodies of the dead who sleep
      A Fury springs, to heap   415
      Ruin on Ruin's head.
ORESTES   Fie on it, Earth! Ye sovereignties of darkness, die, for shame!
      Ye, potent curses of the dead,
      Look on us here, sole remnant of the seed and of the name
      Of Atreus, homeless, lost. O Zeus, where shall we turn for aid?   420
CHORUS   And yet, my faint heart trembles, and to hear
      Such pitiful clamour shrouds the darkling soul in fear,
      Till courage, armed for combat bids my passion banish pain,
      And I rejoice again.
ELECTRA   What words, what pleading can avail? No plea   425
      More potent than that mother's cruelty!
      In vain she flatters now: the heritage
      Of hate abides: our mother gave it me,
      A spirit of loathing, nothing can assuage,
      Wolfish like hers, true to its parentage.   430
CHORUS   As mourner from the East, in Arian, Cissian mode,*
      We tear the flesh, we beat the breast. Yea, even unto blood.
      Beneath the rain of blows my head
      Is bowed and bruised and buffeted.
ELECTRA   O cruel mother! Fiend!   435
      To bury him unmourned,
      A King unwept by folk or friend,
      A husband scorned.
ORESTES   My father scorned, you say?

---

431 Again the Trojan chorus mourns in Asiatic style, with breast-beating and robe-tearing. The Arians and
      Cissians seem to have been famous for their extravagant lamentations.

Buried in shame? Alas! She needs must pay.   440
The gods and the right hand
Shall take the price. I stand
Ready to strike, and then
To perish, having slain.
CHORUS   Yea, and his body mutilated. Know,   445
She who thus buried him contrived it so.
To make your life a thing
Intolerable by his death, she dealt the King
That foul, dishonouring, last blow.*
ELECTRA (To ORESTES)   Even so our father fared, while I, his child,   450
Disowned, esteemed a thing of nought, was kept,
Like a malicious dog that might run wild,
Close prisoner in my chamber, where I wept
Secretly. Tears, not laughter, were my part
In childhood. Hear, and write it in your heart.   455
CHORUS   Yes, let it pierce the heart. These things are so.
And yet remember this. We yearn to know
Much that is still uncertain. What you do
Calls for your best,
Your stern resolve unmoved, your heart at rest.   460
ORESTES   Father, I call thee. Hear thy children's cry.
ELECTRA   I join my voice. Alas! All tears am I.
CHORUS   With one accord, all as one company,
We call thee.
ORESTES, ELECTRA AND CHORUS   Come, dread spirit, to the light!   465
Help us. Against thine enemies we fight.
ORESTES   Cause shall meet cause, and might encounter might.
ELECTRA   Ye gods, attend. Judge the just cause aright.
CHORUS   I hear them pray, and in my own despite
I tremble.   470
ORESTES, ELECTRA AND CHORUS   Fate hath waited long. This day
Reveals the issue, even as we pray.
CHORUS   Ah, grim inheritance, inborn, inbred,
Bloodshed begetting bloodshed, blow on blow,
To spoil life's music still, and breed fresh woe,   475
Endless, unbearable, uncomforted.
Alas, no cure can come
From others for a house polluted so.

Only the children of the home can cleanse the home,
And they themselves, alas!   480
Through blood must pass.
Therefore in solemn strain we chant our song of woe—
"Hear us, ye blessed powers who reign below!

---

449 This passage refers to the practice of cutting off a murdered man's hands and feet and tying them around
    his waist so that he could not seek vengeance.

Be gracious to these children. Hear them pray,
And give them strength to triumph in the fray." 485

ORESTES Grant me, dear Father, so unkingly slain,
This boon, as master of thy house, to reign.

ELECTRA I ask the like boon, Father. I would be
A wife, no more Aegisthus' slave, but free.

ORESTES Then shall the customary feasts our laws ordain 490
Be paid thee; else, in high solemnity
Of rich burnt-offering, none shall honour thee.*

ELECTRA I too from my own portion, on my day
Of marriage will bring gifts; and I will pay
First honour always to thy grave and thee. 495

ORESTES Earth, send my sire to watch and succour me.

ELECTRA Persephone,* crown the end with victory.

ORESTES Think of the bath wherein they slew thee, father.

ELECTRA Their fell device, the net they spread for thee.

ORESTES Those unforged fetters that entrapped thee, father. 500

ELECTRA That cloak, devised to shroud thee, shamefully.

ORESTES Have not these taunts the power to wake thee, father?

ELECTRA Art thou not rearing up that well-loved head?

ORESTES Send Justice here, herself to fight with me,
Or, to retrieve defeat by victory 505
Give me that self-same grip they took on thee.

ELECTRA With one last cry this one best boon we crave,
Thy nestlings, son and daughter, at thy grave
Crouching together, Pity us, and save.

ORESTES Rescue from death this remnant of the seed 510
Of Pelops. So, in death, thou art not dead.

ELECTRA Children are voices, when a man is dead
That hold him close to life, like floats that keep
The submerged net from foundering in the deep.

ORESTES For thine own sake thy children at thy grave 515
Make moan, that, hearing, thou thyself mayst save.

(After some moments of solemn silence, the LEADER *of the Chorus speaks)*

LEADER Enough! For the lament so long denied
You have made full amends, and well performed
Your office. Now to work! Your spirit is ripe 520
For action. Put your fortune to the touch.

ORESTES I shall. But first—it is not from the purpose—
Why did she send these offerings? What induced her
To seek so late a cure for things past cure?
Can she have thought such gifts as these would prove 525
Her good will to the dead? For such a sin
Such paltry penance? No, I cannot think it.

---

[492] The continuing dishonor to Agamemnon consists in part in the facts that his children have not come
into their inheritance and have not been in a position to celebrate his yearly funeral banquet.
[497] Queen of Hades.

What saith the word? For blood of one man slain,
Pour out the whole world's store—the labour's vain.
Tell me, if you can tell. What was her purpose?   530
CHORUS   I know, child. I was there. From dreams and fears,
Haunting the night, that godless woman woke
Distraught, and therefore sent drink-offerings.
ORESTES   What was the dream? Did you hear? Can you tell me truly?
CHORUS   She fancied she had given birth, she said,   535
To a snake—
ORESTES   And then? How did the vision end?
CHORUS   In swaddling-clothes she nursed it, like a babe.
ORESTES   What food did the strange new-born creature need?
CHORUS   She suckled it. She gave it her own breast.   540
ORESTES   Fie, fie, so foul a thing! And was the breast
Unwounded?
CHORUS   With the milk, she dreamt, it drew
A clot of blood.
ORESTES (*Aside*)   'Tis true. The dream runs true.   545
CHORUS   She woke, screaming in panic. Many a torch,
Blinded before in darkness, flared again,
Kindled for the Queen's comfort. Then she sent
These offerings to the dead, in hope to lance
And cure the mischief.   550
ORESTES   Now to this Earth I pray
That holds my father's body, be the dream
Fulfilled for me. Thus I interpret it,
And thus it fits. From that same womb as I
A serpent came, and in my swathing-bands   555
Was nursed. It mouthed the breast that suckled me
And with the sweet milk mixed a clot of blood,
Whereat she cried in panic. She has nursed
A brood unnatural and by violence
She needs must be destroyed. That snake am I,   560
And, as the dream saith, surely she shall die.
CHORUS   You shall interpret for us. May the event
Confirm your truth. Teach us, your friends, our part,
What some should do, what others leave undone.
ORESTES   That is simple. You, Electra, go within,   565
And keep our purpose secret, all of you.
So as they killed that noble gentleman
Cunningly, they themselves, in the same trap
By cunning caught, shall die, as Loxias,
The Lord Apollo, proved a prophet true,   570
Foretold they should. I shall present myself
At the palace-gates, dressed as a foreigner,
In traveller's guise, with Pylades, as friend,

Ye, guest-friend to the household. Both of us
An imitation of the Phocian* tongue   575
Will talk as people from Parnassus talk;
And if, because this household is obsessed
By evil, no kind doorkeeper appears,
To greet us, I shall wait till passers-by
Ask, "Does Aegisthus know? Is he at home?   580
Why should his doors be barred to suppliants?"
But once I cross the threshold, if I find
Him on my father's throne, or if perchance
He comes to meet me face to face, and speaks—
Dropping his eyes—you may be sure he will—   585
Ere he can say "Who is the stranger," I
With one swift sweep of the sword shall strike him dead.
So shall the Fiend unstinted sup her fill
Of vengeance, a third draught of unmixed blood.
  Electra, keep good watch within the house   590
That the event may jump with our design,
And you (*to the* CHORUS) keep guard upon your tongues, to speak
Or to be silent as the time requires,
While you, my friend, (*to* PYLADES) watch o'er me in the fight
And see to it, I wield my sword aright.   595
        (ELECTRA *enters the Palace;* ORESTES *and* PYLADES *withdraw*)
CHORUS   Earth teems with creatures grim and shapes of woe:
    In the embraces of the sea
    Lurk deadly monsters: from Heaven's canopy
    Rain fiery torches, harbingers of death   600
    On all who fly aloft or walk below,
    Consider too the fury of the storm-wind's breath.

    What of Man's own proud spirit? Is not he,
    Past telling, fierce and bold?
    Nay, what of Woman? Passions uncontrolled   605
    Drive her to ruin: lawless lust and blind
    Distraction triumph, and their mastery
    Breaks every bond of peace in beasts and human kind.

    Ye who are not light-minded, learn of one—
    A wretch who slew her son,   610
    Thestius' daughter.* Very well she knew
    When on the flames the ruddy brand she threw,
    It was his talisman

---

575 Phocis was an ancient territory in central Greece.

612 This was Althaea, who was told that her child, Maleagrus, would live only so long as a firebrand then
   burning was not consumed and who extinguished the firebrand to prevent his death. When he was
   grown, however, she took her brothers' part against him and re-lit the firebrand to cause his death.

Of life since life began,
From the babe's cry at parting from the womb   615
To that grim day of doom.

And yet not less abominable she
Who to his enemy
Betrayed old Nisus.* With a chain of gold
Minos the Cretan bribed her, and she sold   620
Her nearest. While he lay
Asleep, she cut away
Her father's thread of life, and he was led
By Hermes to the dead.

FIRST VOICE   Such tales of ancient woe   625
　　We tell—
SECOND VOICE   Who speaketh so,
　　Strays from the purpose. What of that abhorr'd
　　Adulterous union and the subtle woman's plan to slay her lord?
　　What think you of her cunning? Have you praise   630
　　For that, as traitors have? A woman's grace
　　For me is modesty,
　　A heart at peace, home-keeping, passion-free.
FIRST VOICE   Of many mischiefs done
　　By woman's passion, none   635
　　Can match the sin of Lemnos.* Even today
　　It is a proverb, and if aught abominable chance, men say
　　" 'Tis like the Lemnian horror." That whole race
　　Was blotted out by heaven—and who would praise
　　A thing by heaven abhorr'd?   640
　　What is there from the purpose in my word?
FULL CHORUS   The man of sin, the man who doth the deed,
　　And wantonly defies
　　The majesty of law by Zeus decreed,
　　May trample Justice down.   645
　　Yet is he overthrown,
　　Her sharp sword pierceth to the heart, and so he dies.

Firm-planted still the stem of Justice stands,
And on that anvil Fate
Forgeth fresh weapons for avenging hands.   650
Even so a child hath come
To cleanse this blood-stained home.
A deep-designing Fury leads him to the gate. (*During the singing of the
last stanza* ORESTES *and* PYLADES, *disguised as Phocian merchants have*

---

[619] Scylla (not to be confused with her of Scylla and Charybdis fame) betrayed her father, Nisus, by revealing to his enemy and her lover, Minos, that Nisus' life was protected by a charmed lock of hair. She cut the lock.

[636] The Lemnian women rose up and put their husbands to death.

ORESTES   Boy, boy! You hear me knocking at the door.
Who is within, Boy? Boy! who is within?
So, I have called three times. Let someone answer,
If great Aegisthus welcomes guests at all.

(*Enter a* SERVANT)   660

SERVANT   Oh yes, I heard you. Who is this fellow? Where
Do you come from?

ORESTES   Tell the rulers of the house,
I bring them news, and it is news indeed.
And make good haste. Night's dusky chariot   665
Rolls on space. High time for travellers
To anchor in a place where guests are welcomed.
Fetch someone in authority—perhaps
Your Mistress—that would serve—or, better still,
The Master were more seemly. Man to man   670
Can speak plain truth more boldly, and make clear
The meaning with no veil of modesty.

(*Enter* CLYTAEMNESTRA)

CLYTAEMNESTRA   Friends, tell me what you wish. Here you will find
Such welcome as befits our house, warm baths,   675
Beds to refresh the weary, and true eyes
To wait on you and watch you. If you bring
Matter for action or important counsel,
That is for men, to whom we will impart it.

ORESTES   I am a stranger here, a Daulian,*   680
From Phocis. I was on my way with goods
To trade in Argos, when, on setting out,
I met a man I knew not, nor he me,
Who asked my way, and told me his. The name
Was Strophios, the Phocian—so I learnt   685
In course of talk. "Friend, anyhow," he said
"You are bound for Argos. Bear it well in mind
To tell Orestes' parents he is dead.
Do not forget. And bring us their instructions,
Whether his friends decide to fetch him home   690
Or have him here interred, our foreign guest,
For ever. As it is, a brazen urn
Contains his ashes, well and truly wept for."
That was the message. Whether I am speaking
To the rulers of his household, to his kinsmen,   695
I do not know. His father should be told.

ELECTRA   Woe is me! Cruelly, ruthlessly undone!
O Curse unconquerable, how keen thou art
To spy what we have stored away for safety
Far off, and shoot and hit the mark and kill,   700

---

[680] Daulis was a city in Phocis.

Bereaving me of all the friends I love.
And now Orestes—he was wise, and thought
To stand aloof, clear of the mire of ruin—
Now that one hope which might have cured us all
And stopped this dance of death, this carnival   705
Of evil—mark it "absent," it has failed us.

ORESTES   I could have wished, with hosts so fortunate,
To make acquaintance first on score of news
More happy, and so earn my entertainment.
For what could be more happy than a guest   710
Whose host is glad? And yet it were a sin,
I thought, since you have welcomed me, and I
Am pledged to tell you, to neglect that office.

CLYTAEMNESTRA   Nay, you shall not be robbed of the reward
You merit, nor the less be held our friend.   715
Some other messenger would have brought the news.
(*To* ELECTRA)   It is high time for guests, after the day's
Long journey, to be suitably entreated.
Take him to the men's guest-chambers, with these
His followers and fellow-travellers,   720
And see they have such comfort as befits
Our house. Be warned. You are responsible.
As for ourselves, we shall impart this news
To the master of the house, and, since we have
No lack of friends, take counsel on the event.   725

(*Exeunt to the Palace all except the* CHORUS)

LEADER OF THE CHORUS   Beloved handmaidens of the house, when shall we
                                                                raise
The song of triumph in Orestes' praise?

CHORUS   O sacred Earth, O sacred Mound   730
That coverest the body of the King,
The Lord of Ships, now hear! now help!
Now is the time
When cunning Suasion should come down into the lists
And fight for us,   735
When nether Hermes, he that walketh in the night, should stand at watch
Over the deadly clash of swords. (*A woman's cry is heard from the Palace*)
The stranger-guest, it seems, is working mischief.

(*Enter Orestes'* NURSE)

See, yonder comes Orestes' nurse, in tears.   740
Where are you going, Kilissa, from the palace
With grief in close attendance—though you pay
No wage to such a follower?

NURSE   The Mistress
Gives orders, I am to fetch Aegisthus home   745
To meet the strangers, and, as man from man,
To hear their news exactly—oh, she wears

Before us servants a pretence of gloom
In the eyes, to hide her laughter at a thing
Well done indeed for her—but for this house   750
Most miserably ill done is the tale
Of which the strangers tell the news so plain.
Aegisthus will be glad of it. His heart
Will warm to hear the news, but, woe is me!
I have supped my fill of horrors long ago   755
In this grim house of Atreus—yes, a brew
Of strangely mingled grief that made the heart
Ache many a time; but never a grief like this.
Indeed I have borne my troubles patiently—
But this—my dead Orestes—my heart's child,   760
I took from his mother's womb to nurse, and all
The shrill calls in the night, when he cried for me,
And all that weary waste of work—all wasted
It was—and yet I bore it. A young babe,
Still senseless, must be nursed, indeed it must,   765
Like a dumb animal. You must humour it.
It cannot tell you anything, a child
In swaddling-clothes. It cannot say if hunger
Or thirst it is, or wanting to make water
That peeves it. The young body will have its way.   770
All that I had to guess, and I suppose
I guessed wrong often, by the swaddling-clothes
I had to wash, combining in one office
Laundress and nurse, for both these handicrafts
Were mine, when his father handed to my care   775
Orestes—Now he's dead, they say, and I
Am on my way to the man who ruined all
Our host, with news he will rejoice to hear.

CHORUS   How did she say he was to come?

NURSE   Explain.   780
I do not understand. What do you mean
By "How"?

CHORUS   I mean, with bodyguard or alone?

NURSE   She says he is to bring a guard of spearmen.

CHORUS   Then give the accursed master no such message.   785
Tell him to come alone, and hear the news
At once, with joyous heart and not one jot
Of fear.

NURSE   Can you be glad of news like this?

CHORUS   What if Zeus means to send a change of fortune?   790

NURSE   How can he now? Orestes, the one hope
Of the home, is dead.

CHORUS   Not yet! A poor diviner
Could tell as much as that.

NURSE   What do you mean?
    Do you know something more than we were told?
CHORUS   Go your way with the message that you bear.
    What the gods purpose to accomplish is their care.
NURSE   I will be ruled by you and go my way.
    The kind gods grant a good end, as we pray. (*Exit*)   800
CHORUS   Sire of the gods, O Zeus, we pray to thee
    That these, who yearn to see
    The spirit of their father's house again
    Restored and sane,
    May prosper in the fight.   805
    Our prayer is righteous. God, defend the right.

    Ah me!
    For him who stands within the gates, ah me! For him of Zeus, we pray.
    Advance him, high above his foes, that he
    Gladly two-fold, three-fold, the price may pay.   810

    Look on this colt whose sire was dear to thee,
    Yoked to a destiny
    Of anguish. Only measure and control
    Can reach the goal.
    Guide him, that in the race   815
    Stride after stride may keep an ordered pace.

    Ah me!
    For him who stands within the gates, ah me! for him, O Zeus, we pray.
    Advance him high above his foes, that he
    Gladly two-fold, three-fold, the price may pay.   820

    Gods of the home, who share
    In your dim treasure-house our hopes, our prayer,
    Grant that for evil done
    Long since, a fresh requital may atone,
    And murderous hate, grown old, no longer breed   825
    Fresh murder, blood for blood, from that same seed.

    And thou, whose cavern shrine*
    Became a stately temple, grant that we
    May weave in victory
    A garland for a mortal hero's home, that it may shine   830
    Forth from the veil of gloom on eyes of friendship, fair and free.

    Also let Maia's son,*
    Great Hermes, help and guide him. There is none

---

827 Apollo in the shrine at Delphi.
832 Hermes is invoked again, both as the patron of the dead and the god of craft.

More fitting. He hath sight,
Swift to discern and publish to the light   835
All secrets, if he please, or hide away
His thought in riddles, dark both night and day.

And thou, whose cavern-shrine
Became a stately temple, grant that we
May weave in victory   840
A garland for a mortal hero's home, that it may shine
Forth from the veil of gloom on eyes of friendship, fair and free.

Then, when the day shall come
That wafts deliverance on a fair breeze home,
My woman's voice shall cry   845
In that old wizard-strain,
"The vessel speeds. Thereby
My friends are saved!"

Be of good cheer. Strike home,
And do what must be done.   850
Yea, when you hear her cry,
"My child," make no reply save this alone,
"I am my father's son."

Take courage. Perseus' mood*
Possess your heart and help you, that the blood   855
You needs must shed may prove
To friends below a joy,
And to the gods above
A blameless sacrifice, the root of evil to destroy.

Be of good cheer. Strike home,   860
And do what must be done.
Yea, when you hear her cry,
"My child," make no reply save this alone,
"I am my father's son."
Be of good cheer. Strike home.   865

(*Enter* AEGISTHUS, *unattended*)

AEGISTHUS   I come in answer to a summons. News,
Brought, we are told, by foreign travellers,
By no means welcome news, imports the death
Of Prince Orestes. That were a fresh load   870
Laid on our stricken house, an opening
Of old sores, not yet healed, still festering.
What should I think? Is the news living truth,

---

[854] Like Perseus, who could defeat the gorgon Medusa only by turning his eyes away so that he would not
be turned to stone, Orestes must avoid his mother's glance.

Or talk, bred by a woman's fear, vain fancy
That flames to heaven, then leaps to swift destruction? 875
What evidence have you, reason can approve?

CHORUS   We have but heard the story. Go within.
Question the strange guests. Never was report
So sure as a man's own first-hand enquiry.

AEGISTHUS   I must see the messenger and question strictly 880
Was he at hand, or present at the death,
Or is his knowledge based on some vague rumour.
My wits have open eyes. He cannot trick me. (*Exit to the Palace*)

CHORUS   Zeus, Zeus, what shall I say, and where begin
My charge, my supplication? 885
How shall the loyal heart find words for the zeal within?
Now is the time when the bloodstained edge of the murderous
sword-blade
Either shall ruin the house of our lord Agamemnon,
Or a fire shall be kindled, a light of freedom and honest rule shall prevail 890
And the son shall inherit the great wealth of his father,
That is the stake. And the hour has come when glorious Orestes
Wrestles with twain for the prize. Be the victory his.

AEGISTHUS (*Within*)   Eh, Eh, Ototoi!
CHORUS   Aha! What was that cry? 895
How is it in the house? What has been done?
Let us withdraw while the event moves on
To fulfilment. We must seem innocent of the evil
Here compassed. How the issue lies with the word. (*The* CHORUS *withdraw*)
(*Enter from the Palace a Servant of* AEGISTHUS) 900

SERVANT   Woe is me! Woe is me! They are killing my master.
Woe is me again makes up the third last cry.
Aegisthus is no longer. Open, Open!
Make haste. Unbar the women's gates. Draw back
The bolts. A strong man's arm is needed here— 905
No, not to rescue him. He's dead. All's over.
Ho there with!
I waste my breath. I call them to no purpose.
They are deaf, or sleeping. Where is Clytaemnestra?
What is she doing? Now her own neck too 910
Seems near the block—ripe for the stroke of Justice.
(*Enter* CLYTAEMNESTRA)

CLYTAEMNESTRA   Why do you make this clamour? What has happened?
SERVANT   I'll tell you. The dead are murdering the living.
CLYTAEMNESTRA   Ai me! I understand. I read the riddle. 915
We are to die by cunning, as we slew.
Quick! Fetch the axe that slays men. Give it me.
We'll know now, are we conquerors or conquered?
To such a pass on this grim road I have come.
(*Enter* ORESTES, *and* PYLADES) 920

ORESTES   It is for you I am looking. *He* has enough.

CLYTAEMNESTRA   Ai me! You are dead, my love, my strong Aegisthus.

ORESTES   You love the man? Then both of you shall have
One grave. You shall not play him false in death.

CLYTAEMNESTRA   Forbear, my son. Respect and pity, child,   925
This breast, at which so often, while you slept,
You sucked with toothless gums that good sweet milk.

ORESTES   For pity and shame, Pylades, shall I spare
My mother?

PYLADES   What of Apollo's oracle?   930
What of your own pledged word? Make enemies
Of all mankind rather than of the gods.

ORESTES   I judge your counsel best. You school me well.
Follow. I mean to kill you at his side
Whom living you esteemed more than my father.   935
Sleep with him still in death, because you love
This man, and him you should have loved, you loathe.

CLYTAEMNESTRA   I nursed you. I would fain grow old with you.

ORESTES   What, live with me? Could you? You killed my father.

CLYTAEMNESTRA   My son, the cause in part was Destiny.   940

ORESTES   And Destiny has brought this doom on you.

CLYTAEMNESTRA   Have you no fear, child, of a mother's Curse?

ORESTES   A mother's? Yours? You cast me out to ruin.

CLYTAEMNESTRA   Never. I sent you to a friendly home.

ORESTES   My sire was royal, and shamefully you sold me.   945

CLYTAEMNESTRA   How sold you? Say, what price had I for you?

ORESTES   A price that shames me, even to taunt you with it.

CLYTAEMNESTRA   How sold? What price had I for you?

ORESTES   A price
Too shameful even to taunt you plainly with it.   950

CLYTAEMNESTRA   Your father wronged me. Speak of his follies too.

ORESTES   You take your ease at home. Blame not the toiler.

CLYTAEMNESTRA   We suffer, left without a mate, my son.

ORESTES   You take your ease, I say. The man's work feeds you.

CLYTAEMNESTRA   It seems, you mean to kill your mother, child.   955

ORESTES   Not so. Your death is your own work, not mine.

CLYTAEMNESTRA   Look you. Beware the hounds of a mother's wrath.

ORESTES   If I shirk now, shall I escape my father's?

CLYTAEMNESTRA   All's vain. I chant my own dirge to a tomb.

ORESTES   What dooms you is the death you dealt my father.   960

CLYTAEMNESTRA   Ai me! This was the snake I bore and suckled.

ORESTES   Indeed your dream-born fear was true. You killed
Him whom we should not. Suffer what you should not.

(Exeunt to the Palace all except the CHORUS)

LEADER OF THE CHORUS   Both suffer, and I pity both, yet praise   965
The deed whereby Orestes' anguish crowns
The long dark tragedy of death, to save,

Even at this last, the light of the home unquenched.
CHORUS   As to the sons of Priam Justice came—
Heavy the retribution—   970
So hath the lion of vengeance, the spirit of War, in double measure
                                                                   swooped
On Agamemnon's House.
Sped by the oracle, led by the gods, our fugitive reached his goal.

Sing Hallelujah for the Master's House,   975
So long by that grim bloodstained pair
Most lamentably abused.
But now from squandering of treasure and from sorrow free at last.

One who fighteth in secret, Hermes, came—
Crafty the retribution—   980
Touching the fighter's hand a Spirit strove—Justice we name her
And she is just in truth.
Hath she not laid them low by the breath of her Wrath? The Child of
                                                                   Zeus.

Sing Hallelujah for the Master's House,   985
So long by that grim bloodstained pair
Most lamentably abused,
But now from squandering of treasure and from sorrow free at last.

The word of Loxias proclaimed,
God of Parnassus, Lord of Earth's deep cavern-shrine,   990
Fails not but moves against the wrong deep-rooted in the home.
A Power Divine there is, whose mastery
Serves not the cause of evil. To heaven's will
All mortal flesh should now.

The light hath shone! The chain that held the house   995
In thraldom breaks! Our bonds are burst asunder.
Lift up your heads, ye gates.
Ye have lain in the dust too long.

Soon, soon, shall Time, made perfect, move
Within the House when that which hath defiled the hearth is urged   1000
By cleansing remedies, and Mischief out of doors.
Then shall the eyes of those that weep behold
The fair aspect of Fortune, and the vile
Usurpers be laid low.

The light hath shone! The chain that held the house   1005
In thraldom breaks. Our bonds are burst asunder.
Lift up your heads, ye gates.

Ye have lain in the dust too long. (*The central doors of the Palace open and disclose* ORESTES *standing over the bodies of* CLYTAEMNESTRA *and* AEGISTHUS) 1010

ORESTES Look on these twain who held our land in thrall,
Who killed my father and despoiled his house.
And, as I read their present state, still friends,
Sworn friends, they have kept faith with one another.
They swore to kill my father and to die 1015
Together. All they promised stands fulfilled.

Look also, ye who judge this tragedy,
On the device, the toils in which my father
Was caught, bound hand and foot, fettered and foiled.
Spread it out. Stand around it. Show this net 1020
That took a man's life. Let the Father see it—
Not mine—I mean the Sun-God, who beholds
All that we do on earth; and, having seen
My mother's foul work, now in my hour of trial
Bear witness I did right in compassing 1025
Her death—I do not count Aegisthus' end,
The customary wage of the seducer,
But hers—she plotted this abomination
Against the man whose children she had borne
Beneath her girdle, once a load of love, 1030
Now manifestly hateful—what of her?
What think you of a lamprey that could rot
A man's flesh with a touch, a viper, steeped
In such malignity, so accursed in nature,
She had no need to sting? I'll speak fair terms— 1035
What shall I call this thing? A hunter's trap
For a beast, a coffin-cloth, a shroud to wrap
A corpse well, feet and all?—No, no, a net,
A snare, a woman's robe to catch the feet.
Here's a fine instrument for a cheat, who lives 1040
By tricking travellers and cozening
Their silver from them. Such a lure as this
Catches and kills them to his heart's content.
Ye gods, let no such mate keep house with me,
No wife like that! Rather destroy me, childless. 1045

CHORUS O sorrow, sorrow! Fearful were thy deeds,
And a terrible death
Has come in this flowering time of sorrow.

ORESTES Was the deed hers, or no? Here's evidence.
The robe shows where she dipped Aegisthus' sword. 1050
These many stains of blood, not time alone,
Have dimmed the colours of the broidery.
Now I can praise and mourn him. Now I stand

In presence of the web that slew my father,
Grieved for the deeds, the sorrows, all our race, ₁₀₅₅
The victory mine, unenviable, unclean.
CHORUS   There lives no mortal man his whole life long
Unhurt, unscathed.
Alas! Grief come today or tomorrow.
ORESTES   But for your knowledge—since I cannot tell ₁₀₆₀
How this will end—my mind is like a team
The driver cannot master, and I swerve
A little from the course—I have fear,
Ready to sing at the heart, and the heart waits,
Ready to dance to the tune. While I am sane, ₁₀₆₅
I solemnly declare to all who love me,
I killed my mother justly. She had killed
My father. She was loathed by heaven, unclean.
What magic steeled me to it? There I cite
The Pythian prophet, Loxias, whose word ₁₀₇₀
Pronounced me guiltless if I did this thing;
If I failed, the price—no I'll not speak of it;
It is fearful, past the furthest range of thought.
So now you see me ready. With this bough,
Enwreathed for supplication, I shall seek ₁₀₇₅
Earth's central shrine,* Apollo's sanctuary
And altar-flame, the light men call immortal,
An exile, for this act of kindred blood,
Bidden to seek no other hearth than His.
Therefore I call on all my countrymen ₁₀₈₀
To witness how these things have come to pass,
While I, fugitive outcast, have to bear
In life and death, no other fame than this.
CHORUS   Nay, you have done right well. Pronounce no word
Ill-omened, nor speak evil of yourself, ₁₀₈₅
Since you have freed all Argos by the stroke
Which lightly lopped the heads from both these serpents.
ORESTES (*On hearing the word "serpents"*)   Ah, Ah!
Bondwomen, see—there—they are Gorgon-like—*
Their robes are murky. They are coiled about ₁₀₉₀
With swarming snakes. I may not tarry longer.
CHORUS   What fancies vex you? Fear not, dearest son
That ever father had. You are the victor.
ORESTES   These are no fancies that afflict my soul,
But manifestly the hounds of my mother's Wrath. ₁₀₉₅
CHORUS   That is because you bear the stain of blood
Still on your hands; therefore the mind's distraught.

[1076] Apollo's shrine at Delphi contained the navel-stone, or *omphalus,* the center of the earth, at which
consecrated widows tended a perpetual flame.
[1089] He sees the Furies, or Eumenides.

ORESTES   O Lord Apollo, they are crowding on me.
　　Their eyes drop loathsome blood.
CHORUS　　　　　　　　　　　　There is one cure, 　　1100
　　One purge. The touch of Loxias shall free
　　Thy spirit.
ORESTES　　　You do not see them, but I see.
　　They drive me hence. I may not tarry longer. (*Exit*)
LEADER OF THE CHORUS   Fortune attend thee, and with gracious eye 　　1105
　　The god watch over thee and prosper thee.
CHORUS   So for a third time hath the hurricane
　　Broken upon the royal house and run its course;
　　First in the misery of children slain
　　And devoured at a feast; 　　1110
　　Then in the fall of a King,
　　When the Captain who led the Greeks to war
　　In the bath was slain;
　　And now, for the third time, there has come
　　A Saviour—or should I call his name 　　1115
　　Destruction? What shall the end be?
　　When will the Fury of Doom find its fulfilment?
　　When will it cease to rage and fall asleep?

Reconstruction drawing by A. von Gerkan (1921) of the Hellenistic form of the theater at Priene. *Hirmer Fotoarchiv, Munich*

THE EUMENIDES

Characters
The Pythian Priestess
APOLLO
HERMES
ORESTES
The ghost of CLYTAEMNESTRA
CHORUS *of Furies, or Eumenides*
ATHENA
Twelve Athenian jurymen; herald; citizens

Delphi, before the temple of Apollo; early morning

THE PYTHIAN PRIESTESS   First among gods I call in reverent prayer
To Earth,* the first diviner. After her
To Themis, her successor and her child,
So runs the story, who in turn resigned
The seat prophetic, with no mischief done   5
To any, of her own free will, to one
Who also was Earth's child, the Titaness
Phoebe.* She gave this place, a birthday gift,
To Phoebus, and he bears her borrowed name.
From Delos, with its lake and ridge of rock,   10
He sailed, and landing on the harboured coast
Of Pallas, journeyed onward to his seat
Parnassian here, with all solemnity
Escorted by Hephaestus' sons, who tamed
The wilderness and made a road for him.   15
So he came, and the people of this land,
With their Prince, Delphos, welcomed him with honour,
And Zeus, who fired his soul with mantic skill,
Fourth in the line enthroned him, Loxias,
Priest and Interpreter of Zeus, His Father.   20
   These gods I make my prelude, and I name
With the like worship Pallas, our near neighbour,*
Also the Nymphs of the Corycian cave,
Where birds frequent, and spirits haunt a place
By Bromios* (I forget it not) possessed   25
Since, as a god, he led the Bacchic rout

---

² Gaia, wife to Uranus.
⁸ Phoebe was the mother of Leto, or Latona, and so the grandmother of Apollo.
²² A shrine or statue to Pallas Pronaia stands close to the temple of Apollo.
²⁵ Another name for Dionysus.

That hunted Pentheus* like a hare to death.
I call too on the springs of Pleistos,* and the strong
Poseidon, and to crown my prayer I call
On Zeus Himself, Accomplisher, who crowneth all.   30
  So to my office. And if heretofore
The gods have blessed my coming, be this day
Most blest. Let any here who are of Greece,
Draw lots and enter, as is customary,*
For as the god dictates, I prophesy.   35
    (*The* PRIESTESS *enters the shrine; her cry is heard within; she returns*)

PRIESTESS Things terrible to see, dreadful to tell,
Drive me from Phoebus' shrine. I have no strength
Even to walk. Nor can I run. My legs
Fail, and I grope my way with my hands. An old   40
And frightened woman is as weak as a child.
On my way to the laurelled sanctuary I saw
A suppliant at the navel-stone, a man
Polluted, for his hands dropped blood. He held
A drawn sword and a high-grown olive-branch,   45
Modestly wreathed with dazzling-white fine wool.
Of so much I am sure, and can speak plainly.
But, throned in front of the man, there crouched, asleep,
A wondrous company of women—no,
Not women—Gorgons call them—yet not like   50
The Gorgon shapes I saw once in a picture
Snatching at Phineus' feast:* these have no wings.
They are black and utterly loathsome. A foul breath
They heave in unapproachable gusts: their eyes
Distil a noisome rheum, and their attire,   55
Outrageous even for the homes of men,
Sorts ill with holy images of the gods.
I never saw one of this tribe before,
Nor heard of any country that could breed
Such beasts unharmed and not repent its travail.   60
What is to come of it must be the care
Of Loxias. He is the Master here.
He is the Healer. Other homes than this
He purifies, and reads all mysteries. (*The doors of the temple open and disclose*
        APOLLO, HERMES, ORESTES, *and the sleeping* FURIES)   65
APOLLO (*To* ORESTES) I shall not fail thee. I shall be thy guide
And guardian to the end, though far removed,
A present help, ungentle to thy foes.

---

[27] See *The Bacchae.*

[28] A river flowing through the valley of Delphi; mythically, the father of the Corycian nymphs.

[34] After they had made their offerings, the pilgrims cast lots, and the doors were opened to the winner.

[52] The "shapes" alluded to are the harpies, birds with women's faces, or women with birds' wings; they tormented Phineus for his cruelty to his children.

So now thou seest these raveners for blood
Subdued, o'ercome by sleep, these hateful virgins,   70
These ancient hoary children, with whom none,
Not god nor man nor beast, hath intercourse.
For evil they were born, and in the murk
Of evil dwell, in Tartarus,* abhorr'd
Of mortal men and gods Olympian.   75
   Fly from them. Grow not faint. They will pursue
O'er the wide continent, wher'er the feet
Of wandering men have trodden, beyond seas
And wave-encircled cities. Keep thy soul
From brooding on thy burden. Faint not. Go   80
To the city of Pallas.* There take session, clasp
Her ancient image in thin arms, and pray,
There, having judges for the cause, and speech
That weaveth spells, we shall discover means
To give thee full deliverance from these troubles,   85
Since at my suasion thou didst slay thy mother.
ORESTES   Apollo, Lord, thou knowest what is just,
And since thou knowest, be not negligent.
Thy strength, sufficient for the need, is sure.
APOLLO   Remember. Let not fear dismay thy soul.   90
Hermes, my very brother—for we twain
Are seed of one great Father—guard him well,
True to thy name and office, shepherding
My suppliant. Even to outlaws from the world
Zeus hath regard, if sped by gracious escort.   95

      (APOLLO *vanishes;* ORESTES *and* HERMES *leave the shrine;*
         Enter the Ghost of CLYTAEMNESTRA)

CLYTAEMNESTRA   Sleep would you? Fie! What use are you asleep?
I am nothing to you, though among the dead
My shame lives, and incessant voices cry   100
"Murder"—I tell you, I am shamefully
Abused, a homeless outcast, utterly
Neglected—I, who suffered such great wrong
From my dearest—He who killed me killed his mother—
Can find no spirit indignant. See my wounds!   105
Let the heart see. The sleeping mind hath eyes
To read the fate none can discern by day.
How often have you supped my offerings,
Wineless liberations, sober soothing draughts,
Grim feasts, burnt on the brazier in dead night   110
When none save you are worshipped. Under foot
You trample all, I see, and, like a dawn,
Your quarry's gone. Fled from your net, escaped

---

[74] An underground prison below Hades, where rebels against Zeus' will were confined.
[81] Athens.

By one light leap, He mocks and mouths at you.
Hear and attend, ye goddesses of Hell!   115
Hear and attend! I plead for my own soul!
I am your dream. I, Clytaemnestra call you.
> (*Muttering from the* CHORUS *of Furies*)
You whine and mutter, but the man has fled.
His friends are not like mine. He's lost and gone. (*More muttering*)   120
You sleep too well! You pity not my wrong!
Orestes—he who slew his mother—gone! (*Cries of "Oh. Oh!"*)
"Oh, Oh!" you cry, and sleep. Awake! To work!
Indeed what work have you, save to do harm? (*More cries*)
Two strong conspirators, sleep and weariness   125
Have robbed the deadly dragon of its venom. (*Loud and shrill ejaculations*)

CHORUS   Fie! Up and at him! Up, up, up and at him! Mark there.

CLYTAEMNESTRA   You dream the chase is up, and you give tongue
Like a keen hound that never flags or falters,
And yet what do you do? Shall weariness   130
Master you? Or shall sleep so soften you
That you forget your injuries. Nay, feel
Even in your inmost entrails the reproach
Of taunts that sting a righteous soul to action.
Breathe on him, waft against him, hot with blood,   135
Fumes of the belly, blasts that burn and shrivel.
Hunt him afresh! Pursue and wither him. (CLYTAEMNESTRA *vanishes, but
> her voice is still heard in the distance twice during the first stanza of the
> Ode which follows. The* CHORUS *of Furies, one after the other, wake*)

CHORUS   Awake, awake thy sister, as I thee.   140
Art still asleep? Spurn sleep. Awake and see
In this grim prelude what of truth there be.

1ST FURY   Fie on it, sisters, Fie! They have done us wrong.

CLYTAEMNESTRA'S VOICE   Wrong they have done me, grievous, wanton
                                       wrong.   145

2D FURY   Alas, Intolerable anguish, bitter wrong.
Fie, fie. Alas the day!

CLYTAEMNESTRA'S VOICE   Your quarry's gone—slipped from the toils and
                                       gone.

3D FURY   Sleep mastered me. I slept and lost the prey.   150
> (*For a moment* APOLLO *reappears*)

CHORUS   Aha! Thou son of Zeus, Thou art a thief,
A god, whose youth rides down divinities
Most venerable, thou hast taken to thy care,
Nay stolen him away,   155
A child unnatural, and a son who slew
His mother. Who shall say thou hast done well? (*Exit* APOLLO)

In a dream I have heard a voice that taunted me,
And struck me, like the goad of a charioteer,

Gripped at the centre to strike. 160
Under the ribs at the heart
It smote. It is icy cold and sore,
Like flesh lashed by the scourger.

That is the way of these younger gods. They grasp
At power over all, beyond the measure of right. 165
See, there is blood. It is blood
Of murder. From head to foot
The navel-stone is red with the clotted gore,
And the black stain of pollution.

A Prophet, he, of his own choice and motion, 170
Hath fouled the sacred hearth of his own home,
And, caring for things mortal, hath o'erthrown
The Age-old Fates, and even Heaven's own laws undone.

I hate him, and the man shall not go free.
There's no deliverance for him. Though he flee 175
To Hell, there's no atonement. On his head
Still hangs the Curse, and a fell Spirit waits to avenge the dead.

(APOLLO *reappears*)

APOLLO   Out of my shrine, I charge you. Hence! Away!
Avoid this holy ground. Go instantly, 180
For here you feel a serpent's sting, a bright
Shaft from my silver bow, to make you belch
In anguish clots of foul black gore and froth
Of the red blood you sucked from living men.
Here is no home for you. Seek out some place 185
Where throats are slit, eyes gouged, heads taken off,
Boys mutilated to destroy the seed,
Others dismembered shrieking, or impaled
And stoned to death. You hear me? Festivals
Like these delight you. That is why the gods 190
Hate you. Your very shape and manners fit
Your disposition. It were better far
A den of lions lapping blood should house you,
Than that a holy shrine, so opulent,
Should be so tainted. Go. You are a flock 195
Unshepherded. No god in heaven loves you.

CHIEF FURY   Hear us in turn, Apollo. Not in part,
But wholly thou thyself art answerable.
Thine was the deed, and thine the guilt for all.

APOLLO   How so? Speak on to make all plain. 200

CHIEF FURY   Thy word
Enjoined the matricide.

APOLLO   My word enjoined

Due vengeance for his father.

CHIEF FURY   That same word   205
Promised acceptance of fresh blood.

APOLLO   I bade
The slayer come to me for absolution.

CHORUS   Yes, and we drove him here; then you insult us.

APOLLO   Because my house is not for such as you.   210

CHIEF FURY   All that we do is our appointed office.

APOLLO   What office? Say. What boasted privilege?

CHIEF FURY   A son who kills his mother we drive out
Homeless.

APOLLO   What of the wife who kills her husband?   215

CHIEF FURY   They are not of one blood. She has slain no kinsman.

APOLLO   You make of slight account, nay, hold as nought
The covenanted faith of Zeus and Hera,
The Queen of all true marriage; and you slight
The source of all best joys and nearest ties,   220
The Cyprian goddess.* Man and wife once joined,
The troth-plight, pledged by Fate and fenced by Justice,
Standeth, a bond more binding than all oaths:
If, then, with eyes of mercy, not of wrath,
On some of these you look, who slew their consorts,   225
I say, unjustly you pursue Orestes.
Against him you run passionate, I know:
Others, I see, you judge more equably.
But Pallas, with pure eyes, shall judge the cause.

CHIEF FURY   I will not let him go. I will not leave him.   230

APOLLO   Pursue him then. Add to your toil fresh toil.

CHIEF FURY   Seek not to lessen my prerogatives
By talking.

APOLLO   Such prerogatives as yours
I would not have, if offered.   235

CHIEF FURY   You are great
Already at the throne of Zeus, while I
Shall never leave this trail. A mother's blood
Calls me. I needs must hunt him to the end.

APOLLO   While I shall help and save. To men and gods   240
Alike, the wrath of supplication scorned
Were fearful, should I fail him willingly.

                  (*He drives the Furies from the temple*)

          The scene changes to Athens
    (*Enter* ORESTES, *who takes sanctuary at a shrine of* ATHENA)   245

ORESTES   Goddess Athena, welcome me with favour.
I come by the command of Loxias.

221 Aphrodite.

An outcast and as thy suppliant, yet I crave
No absolution, since the stain of blood
Grows faint at length through many wanderings   250
And visitations of the homes of men
By land and sea alike. Obedience
To the prophetic word of Loxias
Hath brought me, goddess, to thy shrine and image,
Here to abide and to await thy judgment.   255

(Enter the CHORUS *of Furies)*

CHIEF FURY   Aha! Here are his traces manifest.
Follow the dumb informer's evidence,
For, as the hound pursues the wounded fawn,
We trail him by the droppings of the blood,   260
Till, worn and weary with long days of toil,
My heart pants. Every quarter of the earth
My flock has ranged, and now across the sea,
In wingless flight, fast as his ship could sail,
I followed in pursuit and follow still   265
The trail. Here, crouching somewhere, he must be.
The scent of mortal blood rejoiceth me.

1ST FURY   Scan every nook. Search everywhere! See! See!
For fear this matricide escape scot free.

2D FURY   Aye, there he sits, with holy ground   270
For refuge. Flings his arms around
The image of the deathless goddess, prays
For judgment and for grace.

3D FURY   That may not be. A mother's blood once shed
Is not recovered.   275

4TH FURY   Ah me!
The blood, once shed upon the earth, is lost, lost utterly.

5TH FURY   Yet art thou doomed to render me again
A draught that is not good, though I am fain
To quaff it—from the living limbs the thick red blood—and so   280
Living I'll wither thee, then drag thee down in pain
To pay the full price for a mother slain.

6TH FURY   And thou shalt see below
Others, for sin
Against a god, or guest,   285
Or dearest, best of kin,
A parent, pay the recompense they owe.
For there, below,
Hades, the great corrector of mankind doth sit.
He watcheth all,   290
And whatsoever thing befall,
As in a book, on tablets of the heart he writeth it.

ORESTES   Distress hath taught me much, the healing rites
Of purification, speech, where speech is best,

And silence also. In this present matter 295
A wise instructor bids me speak. My guilt
Sleeps, and the blood-pits on my hand grow dim—
Yea, there is cleansing even for the stain
Of matricidal blood. When it was fresh
Upon me, Phoebus drove away pollution 300
At his own hearth with blood of slaughtered swine,
And I can tell of many who received
And dwelt with me, and had no harm from it.
So now with unpolluted lips, I call
Athena, this land's queen, to rescue me. 305
So, with no spear uplifted, she shall win
Myself, my country and my Argive people
To true, enduring friendship and alliance.
Whether in Libyan regions, by the ford
Of Trito, in the land that gave her birth, 310
She sits, perchance, enrobed, or stands upright,
Befriending those who love her, or surveys
Like some bold captain, the Phlegraean heights,*
Oh, may she come—She hears. A god can hear
Far off—to rescue and deliver me. 315

CHIEF FURY Neither Apollo nor Athena's power
Can save you. Every thought of happiness
Abandon. You must perish wretchedly.
A bloodless shadow, and a feast for fiends.*
  You do not even answer? You despise 320
My words, though bred and consecrate my victim?
Slain at no altar, living, you shall feed me.
Now hear the hymn that binds your soul my prey.

CHORUS Come, let us dance and sing. Join hands, and show
We are at one, determined to make known 325
The power of our grim music, and make plain
How we administer our solemn trust
For the affairs of men.
In what we do we think that we are just.
If any man can show 330
Clean hands, unscathed he goes and still shall go
Through life. But for the sinner, who hath shed
Blood, and is fain to hide the blood-stained hands, there can be no
Such mercy. We are near him and exact in full the price he owes the dead.

FULL CHORUS Mother Night, Oh hear me. Mother, who didst bear me, 335
Justicer of souls who walk in darkness or by day.
Leto's whelp would rob me of my rights and steal away
The hunted hare, marked by a mother's blood, my lawful prey.

---

313 Athena had helped Zeus in a war against the giants fought in the Phlegraean plains.

319 As I could not hope to improve George Thomson's version of this line, I have ventured, with his kind consent, to borrow it [translator's note].

Over the victim sing we the spell
That wastes and warps and withers, till the mind,   340
Helpless, distracted, blind,
Runs mad, and the heart breaks. It is the spell
That binds the Will, the Furies' tuneless chant of Hell.

Destiny that reigneth through the world ordaineth
This, my charge and portion, whosoever wilfully   345
Sheddeth kindred blood, we haunt and harry tirelessly,
Until he dies and soon after death he is not free.

Over the victim sing we the spell
That wastes and warps and withers, till the mind,
Helpless, distracted, blind,   350
Runs mad, and the heart breaks. It is the spell
That binds the Will, the Furies' tuneless chant of Hell.

Such the power at birth assigned us by the ordinance of fate.
Yet the gods we touch not; in the feasts we celebrate
No Olympian god hath part. From festal joy and raiment white*   355
We stand aloof. Far other things than these are our delight—

Wreck of the home, when, through the strife
Of kindred with kin, murder is rife.
As we swiftly pursue the doer of wrong
Blood hath been spilt; it is blood that we taste,   360
Yea, though he be strong, in the end he shall wither and waste.

Gladly we relieve the gods immortal from the trust we bear,
Gladly would exempt them past all question from this care.
Yet, because our hands are bloody, we are loathed, and Zeus denies
All converse. We are outcasts, vile and filthy in his eyes.   365

Wreck of the home, when, through the strife
Of kindred with kin, murder is rife.
Blood hath been spilt. It is blood that we taste
As we swiftly pursue the doer of wrong;
Yea, though he be strong, in the end he shall wither and waste.   370

What is the glory of man? Though the pride of it mount to the sky,
Night falls. In the murk of disgrace it shall dwindle and die
When the beat of our sinister dance is heard and the black-robed choir
                                                    is nigh.

Up to the light   375
Nimbly we leap,

355 The special color of feasts.

Then in a trice, heavily down,
Swoop to the deep,
Where the sinner is tripped and o'erthrown.

He falls, but he knows not he falls. His iniquity maketh him blind. 380
Over his House reigns darkness. The tale of his doom shall afflict
mankind.

Such is our charge, our care.
Brooding on mortal ill,
Swift in resource, majestic, we fulfil 385
Our ministry, unmoved by human prayer.
What all despise, we cherish, regions vast,
By gods unvisited, a rugged waste
Of foul corruption, noisome to the tread
Of all who see the light and of the sightless dead. 390

What mortal can there be
Who heareth not with dread
The ordinance of power, by Fate decreed
And by the gods' own gift confirmed to me?
This age-old privilege and power we bear, 395
Which all must reverence and all mortals fear.
Therefore we lack not honour, though our home
Be sunk beneath the earth in sun-forsaken gloom.
(*Enter* ATHENA; *the* CHORUS *of Furies, startled by her sudden intervention,
fall back from* ORESTES, *baffled and indignant*) 400
ATHENA I heard a suppliant's cry, though, far away
From Athens, on Scamander's banks I stood,
Taking possession of the part assigned
By the Achaean chieftains from the land
Of conquered Troy, to me, to have and hold 405
As mine for ever, and their chosen gift
To honour Theseus' people. Thence I sped,
Swift, wingless, on the swelling folds of this,
My lusty team, my chariot, my aegis
Hither to Athens, where the unwonted sight 410
Of this strange company of guests—although
I fear them not—astounds me, and I ask
Who are you? To you all I speak, to you,
The stranger, who sit suppliant at my image,
And you, who seem unlike aught else begotten, 415
For never were such goddesses beheld
By gods, nor are you shapes of human kind,
Though to speak ill of any without cause
Ill sorts with justice or with piety.
CHIEF FURY Daughter of Zeus, you shall hear all in brief. 420

We are Night's drear, age-old children, and are called
The Curses in our home beneath the earth.

ATHENA So, of your name and birth I stand informed.

CHIEF FURY My great prerogative you soon shall know
As plainly.   425

ATHENA   Tell me. I shall understand.

1ST FURY All who do murder we thrust out of doors—

ATHENA Where ends the slayer's flight?

2D FURY   Where every thought
Of happiness is lost.   430

ATHENA   And is this youth
Hounded by you on such a flight?

3D FURY   He is.
He made himself his mother's murderer.

ATHENA Was there some power compelled him? Was there one   435
Whose wrath he feared?

4TH FURY   By what compulsion spurred
Should a man kill his mother?

ATHENA   That is half
The case. We have not heard the counterpleas.   440

5TH FURY He would not swear his oath of innocence,
Nor accept ours, of guilty.

ATHENA   I perceive,
You wish to be called just, not to do justice.

CHIEF FURY How so? Explain. You have good wits. Instruct me.   445

ATHENA Seek not by oaths to make an unjust cause
Prevail.

CHIEF FURY Well, question him yourself, and judge
Fairly.

ATHENA You trust the cause to me?   450

CHIEF FURY   I do,
For I respect you and your parentage.

ATHENA Stranger, what answer have you? Tell me first
What are your country and your race. Relate
The tale of your own life. Then, after that,   455
Try to refute the charge. To every count
Give a plain answer, if, in confidence
Of a just cause, if, as a suppliant
Such as Ixion* was, so near my hearth
You sit and clasp my sacred image, speak.   460

ORESTES Athena, Queen, to these last words of thine
I answer first—thus, to relieve thy care.
I came not to your image as a man
With hands polluted, seeking absolution;
And can vouch for it with this proof. The Law   465

---

459 Ixion was the prototype of all suppliants for purification. Having killed Deioneus, he appealed to Zeus,
who had compassion for him and cleansed him of guilt.

Forbids a suppliant stained with blood to break
His silence till by purifying hands
In the blood of a new-born creature he is purged.
Long since at other shrines, on land alike
And water, I have been thus purified. 470
So, having set this doubt at rest, I now
Can tell you of my birth. I am an Argive.
My father—I am glad you ask of him—
Was high commander of the fleet, your helper
When you laid Troy in ruin, Agamemnon. 475
On his return he died. My black-souled mother
Caught him in those elaborate toils that proved
The blood-bath's shameful work, and murdered him.
I was in exile then. On my return—
I'll not deny the truth—I killed my mother. 480
Loxias too in part was answerable,
Since, if I spared the guilty, he foretold
What anguish should afflict my soul. Be thou
My judge. Was this done righteously or no?
Whate'er befalls me, I accept thy judgment. 485

ATHENA   Here is a cause too grave for mortal man
To deem himself its judge, and to pronounce
On savage blood-feuds ill befits my godhead.
Moreover, though you come to me a pure
And humbled suppliant, whom I respect, 490
As harmless, innocent of any wrong
To Athens, these your adversaries fate
Hath blessed with nothing gentle in their nature
And their indignant spirits, if they lose
Their cause, will drop such poison on my land 495
From their fierce bellies, that a pestilence
And blight will waste it. If I let them stay,
Or without conflict bid them go, for me
Each course is fraught with grievous injury.
Yet, since this task has fallen to our Athens, 500
I will appoint as justicers of blood,
By solemn oath constrained, an ordinance
That shall abide for ever. As for you,
Call witnesses and evidence to support
The plea of justice, while I go to choose 505
The first flower of my city, and return,
That well and truly they may try this cause. (*Exit*)

CHORUS   Should the mother-slayer's cause,
And the wicked plea prevail,
Ancient customary laws 510
Of right and wrong shall fade and fail.
Lightly, if this thing is done,

All mankind will turn to sin,
And parents everywhere make moan
For wrongs inflicted by their own
Children, their own kith and kin.

Even we, the Watchers dread
Of all men do, no more shall send
Wrath and Ruin on the head
Of Murder, but shall rather lend
Death free licence. Then shall he
Who, telling of his neighbour's fate,
Asks what comfort there can be,
Find, alas, no remedy
To cure the evil or abate.

Never more let mortal cry,
"Justice, to my plea give ear,
And ye, enthroned Furies, hear!"
In vain a father's misery,
In vain a mother's grief, may show
All the stricken heart's distress,
If once the house of Righteousness
Itself is stricken and laid low.

Times there are when Fear is good;
Nay, enthroned Fear should rule
As the warder of the soul.
By constraint to learn the mood
Of wisdom profits much. And how
Shall State or citizen, unfed
In heart and mind by wholesome dread,
To Justice reverently bow?

Pray from lawless tyranny
And lawless licence to be free.
Zeus, though manifold his ways,
Giveth Measure sovereignty,
And our word is true that saith,
Sin breeds only pride and death,
And the boasted happiness
All men follow, none may find
Save in health of heart and mind.

This forget not ever. Low
At the shrine of Justice bow,
Nor, by thought of gain beguiled,
Spurn that altar. Even though

Retribution seem to wait
For time to ripen, soon or late
The end comes. Therefore, let the child
Honour the parents, and the guest
Find welcome and in safety rest.

To him who follows willingly
The good, by no compulsion driven,
Blessing surely shall be given,
Nor shall he perish utterly.
Not so the fool, who soon shall find
His cargo of ill-gotten gain
Swamped and scattered by the wind.
Then down he'll haul his sails—in vain,
For a sudden squall will wreck
The vessel, and the mast-head break.

In vain he wrestles, in the pool
Of the swirling waters caught,
And calls on gods, who answer not—
Save that one voice answers "Fool":
'Tis his own life's Demon mocks
The wretch who wind and wave defied,
Now drifting, helpless, to the rocks,
Sans power, prosperity and pride,
Till, from the reef of Justice swept,
He died, unnoticed and unwept.

The scene is arranged as for a Court of Justice
(*Enter* ATHENA, *a* HERALD, *Citizens and Jurymen*)

ATHENA   Make proclamation. Bid the folk be still.
And, Herald, let the Tyrrhene trumpet, full
Of mortal breath, with high uplifted challenge
Pierce heaven, and call my people to attend.
For, while this court of justice is enrolled,
It will be good, in order that the case
Be well and truly tried, that all of you,
Whether you plead or judge, should hear in silence
My Ordinance which shall abide for ever.
(*Enter* APOLLO)

ATHENA   My Lord, Apollo, rule thine own domain.
How in this present cause art thou concerned?

APOLLO   I come both to bear witness—since this mortal
Is in due form the suppliant of my shrine
And has by me been purified of blood—
And to be tried myself. I was the cause

Why this man slew his mother. Open then
The Case, and of thy Wisdom pronounce judgment.

ATHENA (*To the Furies*) The court is open, and it is for you,   600
Because it is the prosecutor's right,
To speak and to instruct us of the facts.

CHIEF FURY We are many voices, but will plead our cause
In sum thus briefly. Point by point make answer.
Tell us first—is it true you killed your mother?   605

ORESTES It is true. I killed her. I will not deny it.

1ST FURY Three falls make up defeat. Here is the first.

ORESTES You make your boast too soon. I am not yet down.

2D FURY Next you must tell us in what way you killed her.

ORESTES I will tell you. With the sword-blade, at the throat.   610

3D FURY Who moved you to it? Whose was the design?

ORESTES The god's own oracle. He is my witness.

4TH FURY The god, you say, moved you to kill your mother?

ORESTES Nor have I blamed him yet for what has followed.

5TH FURY Wait. Once convicted, you will change your tune.   615

ORESTES I still have trust. My father from the grave
Will help.

6TH FURY   So, mother-slayer—put your trust
In a dead man.

ORESTES   She was by double guilt   620
Defouled.

7TH FURY   How so. Explain to these who judge you.

ORESTES She killed my father when she killed her husband.

8TH FURY She hath atoned by death. You are alive.

ORESTES While she still lived, why did you not pursue her?   625

9TH FURY She was not of one blood with him she slew.

ORESTES What bond of kindred have I then with her?

10TH FURY She nursed you in the womb. The blood you scorn,
Orestes, is the dearest bond of all.

ORESTES (*To* APOLLO) Do thou bear witness now, instructing me,   630
Apollo, if in truth I slew her justly.
The fact is not denied. I have confessed it,
But whether to thine heart it seemeth just
Or unjust, say, that I may tell my judges.

APOLLO To this high court of Athens I shall speak   635
Plain truth. I am a seer and cannot lie.
Nor have I ever on the mantic throne
Of man or woman or of any State City
Spoken, save as the sire of all the gods,
My Father Zeus, commands.   640

CHIEF FURY   You say that Zeus
Gave you this oracle, wherein you charged
Orestes, in requital for a father
Murdered, to set a mother's wrongs at nought?

APOLLO It was far worse that a great gentleman,   645
       Vested by Zeus with royalty, should die,
       And by a woman's hand, not by a shaft
       From some fierce Amazon's archery afar,
       But thus, as thou shalt hear, Pallas, and you
       The court, assigned by lot to try this cause.   650
       He came home from a war, where in the main
       His traffic prospered, and she welcomed him
       Home with kind words. Then, while he bathed, she stood
       As if to help, and, when the bath was done,
       Just as he rose, threw over him a cloak   655
       Of rich embroidery, from head to foot
       Entrangling him in endless coils of stuff,
       Trapped, helpless. It was thus she struck him down.
       Such was his end, who was a Man, a King
       Much venerated, a great Admiral,   660
       And such as she, as I have shown, to move
       Your hearts, as you, the judges, try this case.
1ST FURY You say that Zeus prefers the father's cause.
       Yet Zeus himself threw into chains his own
       Old father, Cronos. Can you reconcile   665
       These doctrines? Judges, take good note of that.
APOLLO O loathsome creatures, heaven-detested monsters,
       Chains may be loosened. There are many means
       To free the captive. 'Tis remediable.
       But for a man once dead, when earth has drunk   670
       His blood, there is no waking any more.
       My father has devised no healing spells
       For that, though all the world with effortless might,
       Now, high, now low, he mouldeth to his will.
2D FURY How can you plead then for this man's acquittal? 675
       He hath shed kindred blood, his mother's blood.
       How shall he dwell in Argos, how possess
       His father's house? What altars of the gods,
       What brotherhood of men can welcome him?
APOLLO That too I will expound. Give ear, and mark   680
       The truth. The mother of her so-called child
       Is not the parent but the nurse, who rears
       Safely unless fate prove unkind the seed
       Implanted by the father, his, not hers.
       Which doctrine I will prove by evidence   685
       Thus—There can be a father who begets
       Without a mother. Here in presence stands
       My proof, the daughter of Olympian Zeus,
       Nursed in no darkling womb, a plant more fair
       Than any goddess in the world could bear.*   690

690 Athena sprang, full-grown, from the head of Zeus.

And, as in all things, Pallas, I shall use
My wisdom to make Athens great and help
Your people, so this suppliant I have sent
To be your friend for ever, that with him
And his successors, goddess, you may build   695
A strong and everlasting covenant
Between your folk and his posterity.

ATHENA   Are the pleas finished? Shall I bid the court
Vote now according to their mind and conscience?

CHIEF FURY   We have shot all our shafts, and now await   700
Pronouncement of the judgment.

ATHENA (*To* APOLLO *and* ORESTES)   What of you?
Are you content if I so order it?

APOLLO   You have heard what you have heard. Now, as you vote,
Pay reverence, friends, to your oath and conscience.   705

ATHENA   People of Athens, hear my ordinance,
Judges in this first trial for shed blood.
Hereafter Aegeus'* people shall maintain
For ever this same court of Justicers
On this same Hill of Ares, once the field   710
Where Amazons encamped, when, for the hate
They bore to Theseus, they made war on him,
And built and fortified a city here
With towers to rival his, and sacrificed
To Ares, whence these rock-bound heights are called   715
The Hill of Ares, Areopagos,
Where Reverence and her sister Fear shall keep
My city day and night from all injustice,
So long as my own citizens refrain
From tampering with their laws.* Adulterate   720
A fair bright stream with mire, you will not find
Its water sweet and drinkable. So now
I counsel you, maintain and reverence
A State neither despotic nor ungoverned,
Nor wholly from your city cast out Fear.   725
Can any man who has no fear be just?
    If in such reverence ye are scrupulous,
Your borders shall be safe. Ye shall possess
A strong defence no other people hath,
No, not in Scythia or in Pelops' realm;   730
This incorruptible Council, swift to wrath,
Yet grave and full of ruth, I constitute
As watchful, wakeful guardian of my land.
    Thus for the future guidance of my folk
I have discoursed at length. The time has come   735

---

708 Aegeus was a legendary king of Athens; father of Theseus.
720 With this speech Athena institutes the Areopagus, the highest judicial court in Athens.

To rise, take up your votes, and every one,
As you have sworn, do justice. I have done.   (*As the chosen citizens cast
their votes in the Urns of Condemnation and Acquittal the following
exhortations are uttered by* APOLLO *and the Furies*)

CHORUS   Beware! The visitation of our wrath   740
Is fearful to the land. Despise us not!
APOLLO   Nay, rather fear my oracles and the word
Of Zeus, nor seek to rob them of their fruit.
CHORUS   Your charge forbids you in affairs of blood
To meddle; your own shrine you will pollute.   745
APOLLO   Was my own Father's wisdom, then, at fault
To cleanse Ixion, the first murderer?
CHORUS   You talk—but if I shall return
And grievously I shall afflict this land.
APOLLO   No, I shall win. You are the scorn of heaven,   750
The younger and the older gods despise you.
1ST FURY   This part you played for Pheres and beguiled
The Fates to make a mortal man immortal.*
APOLLO   Is it not good to help a worshipper,
Always, and most of all in time of need?   755
2D FURY   With wine Fate's ancient rule you overthrew;
With wine you tricked primaeval goddesses.
APOLLO   Soon you will lose your cause, and, though you spit
Your poison, it shall do your foes no harm.
CHIEF FURY   I am old. Your youth rides roughshod over age.   760
I wait to hear the verdict, doubtful still
Whether to wreak my vengeance on the city.
ATHENA   I must declare my judgment last. My vote
Is to be added to Orestes' score.
I have no mother, none. With all my heart,   765
Save that I will not marry, I approve
The male. Indeed I am wholly for the father.
Therefore I less regard the woman's fate
Who killed her lord, the ruler of the home.
If half the votes be his, Orestes wins.   770
Judges, to whom that office is assigned,
Turn out the ballots from the urns forthwith. (*The judges obey her*)
ORESTES   Bright god, Apollo, what will be the judgment?
CHORUS   Black Mother Night, dost thou behold these things?
ORESTES   My Fate comes—to be lost or worshipped still.   775
CHORUS   Our Fate comes—to be lost or worshipped still.
ATHENA   With scrupulous regard for equity,
Count, friends, and make division of the votes.
Where judgment fails, great mischief comes of it;
Often one single vote hath saved a house.   780

---

753 In the story of Admetos, son of Pheres, Apollo interceded with the Furies to enable Admetos to live if
his father, mother, or wife were willing to die for him. Alcestis, his wife, sacrificed herself.

(The votes are counted and ATHENA *announces the result)*

ATHENA   The man goes free, acquitted on the charge
 Of blood. The number of the votes is equal.
ORESTES   Goddess Athena, Saviour of my House,
 Thou hast restored me to my fatherland   785
 Which else were forfeit, and the Greeks will say,
 "This man, again an Argive, dwells again
 In his paternal heritage, by the grace
 Of Pallas and Apollo and the Lord
 And Saviour, Zeus, Accomplisher of all."   790
 In face of these, my mother's advocates,
 In pity for my father's death, He saved me.
  Now, as I go, to Athens and to all
 Thy people, solemnly I pledge my oath,
 That in the fullness of all time to come   795
 Shall stand. No Captain of an Argive host,
 Arrayed for battle, shall attack this land,
 Or we ourselves shall from the grave afflict
 Transgressors against this my covenant
 With such ill-omened, such disheartened passage   800
 That they shall soon regret their enterprise.
 But while the pledge is kept, while Argos pays
 The city of Pallas honour and in arms
 Stands true, my blessing still then shall rest on Argos.
 Hail, Pallas, with thy people. May ye prove   805
 In wrestling with all foes invincible,
 Saved and secure and crowned with victory. *(Exit)*

CHORUS   Fie on you, fie!
 You younger gods have ridden down
 The ancient law, and from my hand   810
 Torn my prerogative, yet I,
 The wretch, despised and overthrown,
 Cry out for Justice, and shall breathe
 In wrath upon this land
 Corruption, my heart's poison, drop by drop,   815
 In blighted birth and mildewed crop
 To fester, dealing death.

 What can I do? I make my moan.
 The children of the Night, forlorn,
 Disparaged, laughed to scorn,   820
 Claim Justice. For the evil done
 The city shall atone.
ATHENA   Yield to my Suasion. Grieve not angrily.
 You are not defeated. In this cause the votes

In truth were equal. Naught was done to slight you.   825
From Zeus himself flashed the bright testimony,
Brought by the god who gave the oracle,
That for this deed no harm befall Orestes.
Be you no more indignant. Spare this land
Such visitation of your wrath. Distil   830
No poison to destroy the fruitful seed
With canker and corrosion and decay.
For solemnly I promise you, for shrines
Of habitation in this righteous land,
Caverns where, on bright altar-hearths enthroned,   835
Ye shall be worshipped by my citizens.

CHORUS   Fie on you, fie!
You younger gods have ridden down
The ancient law, and from my hand
Torn my prerogative, yet I,   840
The wretch, despised and overthrown,
Cry out for Justice, and shall breathe
In wrath upon this land
Corruption, my heart's poison, drop by drop,
In blighted birth and mildewed crop   845
To fester, dealing death.

What can I do? I make my moan.
The children of the Night, forlorn,
Disparaged, laughed to scorn,
Claim Justice. For the evil done   850
The city shall atone.

ATHENA   Ye are not scorned. Let no excess of wrath
Move goddesses to afflict a land of mortals.
I put my trust in Zeus. Must you be told?
None but I know the keys that will unlock   855
His armoury, wherein the bolt of thunder
Lies, sealed. We shall not need it. Graciously
Yield to my Suasion. Leave your empty threats.
Curse not my country. Calm the swelling flood
Of black and bitter fury. Be content   860
To share my residence and be worshipped here.
And when, from year to year, from this wide land
First fruits are brought you, that our marriage-rites
Be blest and fruitful, you will praise and thank me.

CHORUS   That I should suffer thus! Is it not shameful, vile,   865
That I, the goddess of old wisdom, should be housed beneath the earth?
                                              Ah me!

I am full of fury. Earth, I cry to thee!
What is this agony? It racks me. Mother Night,

Look on my passion. The triumphant guile   870
Of these young gods hath robbed me of my right.
ATHENA   You are my elders. I will bear with you
And yet, though you are wiser far than I,
To me too Zeus hath given understanding.
And if you seek some other land and folk,   875
Your hearts will turn to Athens, I forewarn you.
The future on the stream of time shall bring
Honour to these my citizens, and to you,
Housed honourably near Erechtheus' shrine,*
Where men and women of this land shall bring   880
More gifts than all the world beside can offer.
Therefore I pray you, cast not on my land
Such provocations as will heat the blood,
And spoil the hearts of youth, infecting them
With Fury, as with wine.   885
Such stings, such irritants, as heat the blood
And spoil the heart of youth, infecting it
With fury, as with wine. Infuse not here
The spirit of fighting-cocks, embroiling these
My citizens in war against each other.   890
War let them wage abroad; if any man
Lust after glory, he shall have his fill
Of fighting, but not here, for I despise
The brawling of domestic fowl. The choice
I freely offer you, is this—to give   895
And to receive rich blessings, and to share
With me my honours in this god-loved land.
CHORUS   That I should suffer thus! Is it not shameful, vile,
That I, the goddess of old wisdom, should be housed beneath the earth?
                                                      Ah me!   900

I am full of fury. Earth, I cry to thee!
What is that agony? It racks me; Mother Night,
Look on my passion. The triumphant guile
Of these young gods hath robbed me of my right.
ATHENA   I shall not weary, but still speak you fair,   905
Lest you should say that I, a younger goddess,
With these my mortal citizens, refused
Such ancient, such revered divinities,
A welcome here, or slighted you at all.
Come, if you reverence the gentle spell   910
Of my Divine Persuasion, you will stay.
Or, if you will not, it will be unjust
To do my people or my city harm
By visitation of revenge or wrath,

879 A legendary hero and king of Athens.

Since you are offered freely, if you stay,   915
    All honour as a partner in my realm.

CHIEF FURY Athena, Queen, what is this home you offer?

ATHENA A home from sorrow free. Accept the gift.

1ST FURY If I accept, what honour shall I have?

ATHENA This, that no home shall thrive without thy blessing.   920

2D FURY Wilt thou indeed achieve such powers for me?

ATHENA Yes, we shall prosper those who honour thee.

3D FURY Will you give surety to fulfil that promise?

ATHENA Why promise if I purpose not fulfilment?

4TH FURY It seems the charm works, and my wrath abates.   925

ATHENA Live with us. You will find you have won friends.

5TH FURY What would you have us sing? What song for Athens?

ATHENA Sing of a victory that hath no taint
    Of evil. Sing that earth and sea and sky
    May waft over the land propitious winds   930
    And sunshine, that the fruits of earth may show
    Rich increase and the cattle of our fields
    Flourish and multiply, while human seed,
    Unharmed, unfailing, swells to happy offspring.
    Especially I bid you bless the seeds   935
    That grow to righteous fruit. A gardener
    Am I, and love the plant that breeds no mischief.
      Such is your part, while I, in every field
    Of honour fighting, shall not stoop to see
    My city scant of fame or victory.   940

CHORUS I consent. Yes, I will dwell
    With Pallas. Nor will I despise
    The city, gracious in the eyes
    Of Zeus, the sacred citadel
    Of Ares, the bright crown of Greece,   945
    Guarding the altars of her deities.
    Therefore now, with all good will,
    We pray that ever, day and night,
    Soil and Sun alike may fill
    Her ways with plenty and delight.   950

ATHENA In that which now I do, my kindness is
    Towards my citizens. I give a home
    To these divinities, so great, so hard to please,
    Only that good may come.
    Of all that touches Man, it is their lot   955
    To make disposal, yet the mortal whom
    In wrathful mood they visit, knoweth not
    Whence come the strokes of doom,
    Nor how the evil by his fathers wrought
    Waits to arraign him at the throne   960
    Of Justice. Recking naught

Of danger, loud he boasts, while silently
The doom creeps on, then suddenly
All's lost. To dust he dwindles, and is gone.

CHORUS Winds of evil, shun this place!   965
Such the promise of my grace.
Never breeze of pestilence
Pass her borders. Mildews, hence!
Never fierce sirocco's breath*
Scorch her tender buds to death.   970
On her orchards, ne'er alight
Wasting canker, bane or blight.
Pan* protect her flocks, and bless
At the season of increase
With double births. Such fruitfulness   975
Fill the land that all may sing
My praise for the good gifts I bring.

ATHENA Elders who guard my city, you have heard
The blessings which their word
Confirms for you and Athens; and you know   980
What powers to them belong,
Alike by gods above and gods below
Honoured; and how they sway
This living world of men—for it is they
Who make of one man's life a happy song,   985
But of another life a tear-dimmed mystery of wrong.

CHORUS Hence, untimely Death. Befall
No son of Athens in his prime.
And you, O sacred Powers that bind
Marriage fast, confirm it so,   990
That every lovely daughter find
A home and husband—Grant it too,
Dear Sisters of our Mother's womb,
Heavenly Fates, who make your home
In every house at every time,   995
Righteous and revered by all.

ATHENA My heart is glad indeed that they invoke
With such good will such blessings on my folk.
Divine Persuasion too I reverence and thank, for she
Kept watch upon my lips, instructing me   1000
How I should win the hearts that spurned so fiercely every plea.
But Zeus, the Lord of Wisdom's Word, hath triumphed, and his victory
Is this, that in a rivalry
Of blessing only, we contend
Henceforth, as friend with friend.   1005

CHORUS Never may Faction flood the State
From unexhausted founts of hate

969 A hot, oppressive wind from the Lybian deserts.

With civil blood that cries for blood.
Rather let a gentler mood
Prevail, and every heart be bent 1010
To love and hate with one consent
Together. Thus and thus alone
Can mortal happiness be won,
And ill convert to good.

ATHENA (*To the Citizens*) Are they not wise? Are they not quick to learn 1015
The way to bless? From these dread shapes I see
For Athens much advantage. Friends are ye.
Welcome them with true friendship loyally,
So shall your city prosper every way.

CHORUS (*To the Citizens*) Hail, fellow-citizens. We give you joy. 1020
Rejoice, rejoice in all prosperity.
Lovers and well-beloved are ye
Of the Maid enthroned by Zeus. Her children, timely wise,
Sheltered beneath her pinions, ye find favour in the Father's eyes.

ATHENA Joy to you also! By the sacred light 1025
Of these your escort, I will show the road
To the dim chambers of your residence.
Come your ways, by the solemn sacrifice
Attended; pass beneath the earth, to keep
Athens from every harmful influence 1030
Secure, and crown her with glad victory.
While you, my citizens, sons of Cranaos,*
Conduct our guests, as friendly residents
In Athens, and let kind thoughts answer kindness.

CHORUS Rejoice! Again I bid you all rejoice! 1035
All who dwell in Pallas' city, gods and mortals, honouring
The stranger's rights, you shall not find
In all life's fortunes aught unkind.

ATHENA I thank you for your blessing. By the light
Of gleaming torches now to your abode 1040
In caverns neath the earth I will conduct you,
With these my ministers who guard my image—
And rightly—'Tis the apple of the eye
Of Athens. A glorious company
Of children and of women, young and old, 1045
Shall come to drape our guests in crimson robes
Of honour. Let the sacred light lead on,
That so in time to come our guests may prove
Their love by fostering our city's manhood.

CHORUS OF THE ESCORT Daughters of Night, with loving escort tended, 1050
Glorified Spirits, pass on your ways—
Silence all for the holy strain—
Pass to the caverns of earth immemorial,

1032 Son of Kecrops, the mythical founder of Athens.

There to be worshipped with gifts and with praise.
Let all the land in silence yet refrain.   1055
Glad in the light of the torches divine,
Friends to our Athens whose heart you have won—
With Hallelujah crown the festal strain—
Followed by lights and libations, for sign;
Zeus the Allseeing and Fate are at one—   1060
Now, now with Hallelujah crown the festal strain.

Sophocles

*Sophocles (496–401 B.C.) was the most widely acclaimed tragic
writer of his century. He is credited by Aristotle with increasing the
Aeschylean chorus from twelve to fifteen, with introducing
innovations in scene-painting, and with discarding the earlier short
plot for the more ample linear structure exemplified in his surviving
works. His main contribution to the drama of his day was the
introduction of a third actor and the development of the single play
as an independent dramatic unit, as illustrated in plays like* OEDIPUS
REX *and* PHILOCTETES. *This structural model gave him increased
opportunities to represent complex interactions between characters
and a more complicated line of action than earlier forms had.
Altogether, he wrote some 123 plays and won twenty-three prizes.*

Chronology

496 B.C.   Born in the village of Colonus, near Athens, the son of
Sophillus, a wealthy manufacturer
of arms.

c.482   Taught by Lamprus, an out-
standing musician of the day; won
prizes for athletics and fame for
his personal beauty.

480   Led the boys' chorus of thanks-
giving after the victory at Salamis.

468   First entered the contest for tragedy; won his first prize, defeating
Aeschylus in a competition that
aroused great excitement.

c.455   Highly conjectural year for his
production of the *Ajax.*

443–42   Served on the Board of Trea-
surers of the Athenian League.

442   Probable year for his production
of the *Antigone.*

440   Elected one of the ten generals
for the war against Samos.

435–31   Produced *The Women of
Trachis.*

430–29   Produced *Oedipus Rex.*

418–14   Produced *Electra.*

413   Chosen as one of the "ten Coun-
selors" after the disastrous expedition to Sicily.

409   Produced *Philoctetes.*

406   Dressed his chorus in mourning
and led them at the *proagon* (a kind
of preview before the festival pro-
ductions) to announce the death
of Euripides.
Died late in the year.

401   *Oedipus at Colonus* was produced.

Selected Bibliography

Adams, S. M., *Sophocles the Playwright,* Toronto, 1957.
Bowra, C. M., *Sophoclean Tragedy,* Oxford, 1944.

Ehrenberg, Victor, *Sophocles and Pericles,* Oxford, 1954.

Harsh, P. W., "The Role of the Bow in the *Philoctetes* of Sophocles," *American Journal of Philology,* LXXXI (1960), 408–14.

Kirkwood, Gordon M., *A Study of Sophoclean Drama,* Ithaca, N.Y., 1958.

Kitto, H. D. F., *Sophocles: Dramatist and Philosopher,* London, 1958.

Knox, Bernard M. W., *The Heroic Temper, Studies in Sophoclean Tragedy,* Berkeley, Calif., 1964.

———, *Oedipus at Thebes,* New Haven, 1957.

Letters, F. J. H., *The Life and Work of Sophocles,* London, 1953.

Moore, J. A., *Sophocles and Arete,* Cambridge, Mass., 1938.

O'Conner, M. B., *Religion in the Plays of Sophocles,* Menasha, 1923.

Post, C. R., "The Dramatic Art of Sophocles," *Harvard Studies in Classical Philology,* XXIII (1912), 71–127.

Sheppard, J. T., *Aeschylus and Sophocles: their Work and Influence,* 2nd ed., New York, 1946.

———, *The Wisdom of Sophocles,* London, 1947.

Waldock, C. H., *Sophocles the Dramatist,* Cambridge, 1951.

Whitman, Cedric, *Sophocles: a Study in Heroic Humanism,* Cambridge, Mass., 1951.

Tragic mask

OEDIPUS REX

by Sophocles

Translated by Albert Cook

Characters

OEDIPUS, *king of Thebes*
A PRIEST
CREON, *brother-in-law of Oedipus*
CHORUS *of Theban elders*
TEIRESIAS, *a prophet*
JOCASTA, *sister of Creon, wife of Oedipus*
MESSENGER
SERVANT *of Laius, father of Oedipus*
SECOND MESSENGER
(silent) ANTIGONE *and* ISMENE, *daughters of Oedipus*

Before the palace of Oedipus at Thebes. In front of the large central doors, an altar; and an altar near each of the two side doors. On the altar steps are seated suppliants—old men, youths, and young boys—dressed in white tunics and cloaks, their hair bound with white fillets. They have laid on the altars olive branches wreathed with wool-fillets.
The old PRIEST OF ZEUS *stands alone facing the central doors of the palace. The doors open, and* OEDIPUS, *followed by two attendants who stand at either door, enters and looks about.*

OEDIPUS   O children, last born stock of ancient Cadmus,*
What petitions are these you bring to me
With garlands on your suppliant olive branches?
The whole city teems with incense fumes,
Teems with prayers for healing and with groans.   5
Thinking it best, children, to hear all this
Not from some messenger, I came myself,
The world renowned and glorious Oedipus.
But tell me, aged priest, since you are fit
To speak before these men, how stand you here,   10
In fear or want? Tell me, as I desire
To do my all; hard hearted I would be
To feel no sympathy for such a prayer.
PRIEST   O Oedipus, ruler of my land, you see
How old we are who stand in supplication   15

---

[1] The legendary founder of Thebes.

Before your altars here, some not yet strong
For lengthy flight, some heavy with age,
Priests, as I of Zeus, and choice young men.
The rest of the tribe sits with wreathed branches,
In market places, at Pallas' two temples,   20
And at prophetic embers by the river.*
The city, as you see, now shakes too greatly
And cannot raise her head out of the depths
Above the gory swell. She wastes in blight,
Blight on earth's fruitful blooms and grazing flocks,   25
And on the barren birth pangs of the women.
The fever god has fallen on the city,
And drives it, a most hated pestilence
Through whom the home of Cadmus is made empty.
Black Hades is enriched with wails and groans.   30
Not that we think you equal to the gods
These boys and I sit suppliant at your hearth,
But judging you first of men in the trials of life,
And in the human intercourse with spirits: —
You are the one who came to Cadmus' city   35
And freed us from the tribute which we paid
To the harsh-singing Sphinx. And that you did
Knowing nothing else, unschooled by us.*
But people say and think it was some god
That helped you to set our life upright.   40
Now Oedipus, most powerful of all,
We all are turned here toward you, we beseech you,
Find us some strength, whether from one of the gods
You hear an omen, or know one from a man.
For the experienced I see will best   45
Make good plans grow from evil circumstance.
Come, best of mortal men, raise up the state.
Come, prove your fame, since now this land of ours
Calls you savior for your previous zeal.
O never let our memory of your reign   50
Be that we first stood straight and later fell,
But to security raise up this state.
With favoring omen once you gave us luck;
Be now as good again; for if henceforth
You rule as now, you will be this country's king,   55
Better it is to rule men than a desert,

---

21 Divination by burnt offerings was practised at the temple of Apollo on the banks of the Ismenus in
    Thebes.
38 The Sphinx was a winged monster with a woman's head and breasts and a lion's body, and she compelled
    all passers-by to answer her riddle. If they failed to solve it, she killed them. The riddle was this: "What
    animal goes in the morning on four feet, at noon on two, and in the evening on three?" and the correct
    answer is man. When Oedipus gave the correct answer, the Sphinx killed herself, thus freeing Thebes
    of her tyranny.

Since nothing is either ship or fortress tower
Bare of men who together dwell within.

OEDIPUS   O piteous children, I am not ignorant
Of what you come desiring. Well I know   60
You are all sick, and in your sickness none
There is among you as sick as I,
For your pain comes to one man alone,
To him and to none other, but my soul
Groans for the state, for myself, and for you.   65
You do not wake a man who is sunk in sleep;
Know that already I have shed many tears,
And travelled many wandering roads of thought.
Well have I sought, and found one remedy;
And this I did: the son of Menoeceus,   70
Creon, my brother-in-law, I sent away
Unto Apollo's Pythian halls* to find
What I might do or say to save the state.
The days are measured out that he is gone;
It troubles me how he fares. Longer than usual   75
He has been away, more than the fitting time.
But when he comes, then evil I shall be,
If all the god reveals I fail to do.

PRIEST   You speak at the right time. These men just now
Signal to me that Creon is approaching.   80

OEDIPUS   O Lord Apollo, grant that he may come
In saving fortune shining as in eye.

(*Enter* CREON)

PRIEST   Glad news he brings, it seems, or else his head
Would not be crowned with leafy, berried bay.   85

OEDIPUS   We will soon know. He is close enough to hear.—
Prince, my kinsman, son of Menoeceus,
What oracle do you bring us from the god?

CREON   A good one. For I say that even burdens
If they chance to turn out right, will all be well.   90

OEDIPUS   Yet what is the oracle? Your present word
Makes me neither bold nor apprehensive.

CREON   If you wish to hear in front of this crowd
I am ready to speak, or we can go within.

OEDIPUS   Speak forth to all. The sorrow that I bear   95
Is greater for these men than for my life.

CREON   May I tell you what I heard from the god?
Lord Phoebus clearly bids us to drive out,
And not to leave uncured within this country,
A pollution we have nourished in our land.   100

OEDIPUS   With what purgation? What kind of misfortune?

CREON   Banish the man, or quit slaughter with slaughter

⁷² At Delphi.

In cleansing, since this blood rains on the state.

OEDIPUS   Who is this man whose fate the god reveals?

CREON   Laius, my lord, was formerly the guide   105
Of this our land before you steered this city.

OEDIPUS   I know him by hearsay, but I never saw him.

CREON   Since he was slain, the god now plainly bids us
To punish his murderers, whoever they may be.

OEDIPUS   Where are they on the earth? How shall we find   110
This indiscernible track of ancient guilt?

CREON   In this land, said Apollo. What is sought
Can be apprehended; the unobserved escapes.

OEDIPUS   Did Laius fall at home on this bloody end?
Or in the fields, or in some foreign land?   115

CREON   As a pilgrim, the god said, he left his tribe
And once away from home, returned no more.

OEDIPUS   Was there no messenger, no fellow wayfarer
Who saw, from whom an inquirer might get aid?

CREON   They are all dead, save one, who fled in fear   120
And he knows only one thing sure to tell.

OEDIPUS   What is that? We may learn many facts from one
If we might take for hope a short beginning.

CREON   Robbers, Apollo said, met there and killed him
Not by the strength of one, but many hands.   125

OEDIPUS   How did the robber unless something from here
Was at work with silver, reach this point of daring?

CREON   These facts are all conjecture. Laius dead,
There rose in evils no avenger for him.

OEDIPUS   But when the king had fallen slain, what trouble   130
Prevented you from finding all this out?

CREON   The subtle-singing Sphinx made us let go
What was unclear to search at our own feet.

OEDIPUS   Well then, I will make this clear afresh
From the start. Phoebus was right, you were right   135
To take this present interest in the dead.
Justly it is you see me as your ally
Avenging alike this country and the god.
Not for the sake of some distant friends,
But for myself I will disperse this filth.   140
Whoever it was who killed that man
With the same hand may wish to do vengeance on me.
And so assisting Laius I aid myself.
But hurry quickly, children, stand up now
From the altar steps, raising these suppliant boughs.   145
Let someone gather Cadmus' people here
To learn that I will do all, whether at last
With Phoebus' help we are shown saved or fallen.

                    (*Exit* OEDIPUS *and* CREON)

PRIEST Come, children, let us stand. We came here   150
    First for the sake of what this man proclaims.
    Phoebus it was who sent these prophecies
    And he will come to save us from the plague. (*Exeunt*)
               (*Enter* CHORUS *of Elders**)

CHORUS (*Strophe A*) O sweet-tongued voice of Zeus, in what spirit do you   155
                                      come
From Pytho* rich in gold
To glorious Thebes? I am torn on the rack, dread shakes my fearful mind,
Apollo of Delos, hail!
As I stand in awe of you, what need, either new   160
Do you bring to the full for me, or old in the turning times of the year?
Tell me, O child of golden Hope, undying Voice!

(*Antistrophe A*) First on you do I call, daughter of Zeus, undying
                                   Athena
And your sister who guards our land,   165
Artemis, seated upon the throne renowned of our circled Place,*
And Phoebus who darts afar;
Shine forth to me, thrice warder-off of death;
If ever in time before when ruin rushed upon the state,
The flame of sorrow you drove beyond our bounds, come also now.   170

(*Strophe B*) O woe! Unnumbered that I bear
The sorrows are! My whole host is sick, nor is there a sword of thought
To ward off pain. The growing fruits
Of glorious earth wax not, nor women
Withstand in childbirth shrieking pangs.   175
Life on life you may see, which, like the well-winged bird,
Faster than stubborn fire, speed
To the strand of the evening god.*

(*Antistrophe B*) Unnumbered of the city die.
Unpitied babies bearing death lie unmoaned on the ground.   180
Grey-haired mothers and young wives
From all sides at the altar's edge
Lift up a wail beseeching, for their mournful woes.
The prayer for healing shines blent with a grieving cry;
Wherefore, O golden daughter of Zeus,   185
Send us your succour with its beaming face.

(*Strophe C*) Grant that fiery Ares, who now with no brazen shield
Flames round me in shouting attack

---

154 These are men of noble birth.
157 The old name for the district of Delphi.
166 Probably at the market place.
178 That is, to the god of the next world.

May turn his back in running flight from our land,*
May be borne with fair wind   190
To Amphitrite's great chamber*
Or to the hostile port
Of the Thracian surge.*
For even if night leaves any ill undone
It is brought to pass and comes to be in the day.   195
O Zeus who bear the fire
And rule the lightning's might,
Strike him beneath your thunderbolt with death!

(*Antistrophe C*)   O lord Apollo, would that you might come and scatter
                                                     forth   200
Untamed darts from your twirling golden bow;
Bring succour from the plague; may the flashing
Beams come of Artemis,
With which she glances through the Lycian hills.
Also on him I call whose hair is held in gold,   205
Who gives a name to this land,
Bacchus of winy face, whom maidens hail!
Draw near with your flaming Maenad band
And the aid of your gladsome torch
Against the plague, dishonoured among the gods.   210

———————

(*Enter* OEDIPUS)

OEDIPUS   You pray; if for what you pray you would be willing
     To hear and take my words, to nurse the plague,
     You may get succour and relief from evils.
     A stranger to this tale I now speak forth,   215
     A stranger to the deed, for not alone
     Could I have tracked it far without some clue,
     But now that I am enrolled a citizen
     Latest among the citizens of Thebes
     To all you sons of Cadmus I proclaim   220
     Whoever of you knows at what man's hand
     Laius, the son of Labdacus, met his death,
     I order him to tell me all, and even
     If he fears, to clear the charge and he will suffer
     No injury, but leave the land unharmed.   225
     If someone knows the murderer to be an alien
     From foreign soil, let him not be silent;
     I will give him a reward, my thanks besides.
     But if you stay in silence and from fear
     For self or friend thrust aside my command,   230

---

189 Ares, the god of war, is here identified with the plague.
191 The Atlantic.   193 The Black Sea.

Hear now from me what I shall do for this;
I charge that none who dwell within this land
Whereof I hold the power and the throne
Give this man shelter whoever he may be,
Or speak to him, or share with him in prayer   235
Or sacrifice, or serve him lustral rites,*
But drive him, all, out of your homes, for he
Is this pollution on us, as Apollo
Revealed to me just now in oracle.
I am therefore the ally of the god   240
And of the murdered man. And now I pray
That the murderer, whether he hides alone
Or with his partners, may, evil coward,
Wear out in luckless ills his wretched life.
I further pray, that, if at my own hearth   245
He dwells known to me in my own home,
I may suffer myself the curse I just now uttered.
And you I charge to bring all this to pass
For me, and for the god, and for our land
Which now lies fruitless, godless, and corrupt.   250
Even if Phoebus had not urged this affair,
Not rightly did you let it go unpurged
When one both noble and a king was murdered!
You should have sought it out. Since now I reign
Holding the power which he had held before me,   255
Having the selfsame wife and marriage bed—
And if his seed had not met barren fortune
We should be linked by offspring from one mother;
But as it was, fate leapt upon his head.
Therefore in this, as if for my own father   260
I fight for him, and shall attempt all
Searching to seize the hand which shed that blood,
For Labdacus' son, before him Polydorus,
And ancient Cadmus, and Agenor of old.*
And those who fail to do this, I pray the gods   265
May give them neither harvest from their earth
Nor children from their wives, but may they be
Destroyed by a fate like this one, or a worse.
You other Thebans, who cherish these commands,
May Justice, the ally of a righteous cause,   270
And all the gods be always on your side.

CHORUS   By the oath you laid on me, my king, I speak.
     I killed not Laius, nor can show who killed him.
     Phoebus it was who sent this question to us,

And he should answer who has done the deed.   275

OEDIPUS   Your words are just, but to compel the gods
In what they do not wish, no man can do.

CHORUS   I would tell what seems to me our second course.

OEDIPUS   If there is a third, fail not to tell it too.

CHORUS   Lord Teiresias I know, who sees this best   280
Like lord Apollo; in surveying this,
One might, my lord, find out from him most clearly.

OEDIPUS   Even this I did not neglect; I have done it already.
At Creon's word I twice sent messengers.
It is a wonder he has been gone so long.   285

CHORUS   And also there are rumors, faint and old.

OEDIPUS   What are they? I must search out every tale.

CHORUS   They say there were some travellers who killed him.

OEDIPUS   So I have heard, but no one sees a witness.

CHORUS   If his mind knows a particle of fear   290
He will not long withstand such curse as yours.

OEDIPUS   He fears no speech who fears not such a deed.

(*Enter* TEIRESIAS, *led*)

CHORUS   But here is the man who will convict the guilty.
Here are these men leading the divine prophet
In whom alone of men the truth is born.   295

OEDIPUS   O you who ponder all, Teiresias,
Both what is taught and what cannot be spoken,
What is of heaven and what trod on the earth,
Even if you are blind, you know what plague
Clings to the state, and, master, you alone   300
We find as her protector and her saviour.
Apollo, if the messengers have not told you,
Answered our question, that release would come
From this disease only if we make sure
Of Laius' slayers and slay them in return   305
Or drive them out as exiles from the land.
But you now, grudge us neither voice of birds
Nor any way you have of prophecy.
Save yourself and the state; save me as well.   310
Save everything polluted by the dead.
We are in your hands; it is the noblest task
To help a man with all your means and powers.

TEIRESIAS   Alas! Alas! How terrible to be wise,
Where it does the seer no good. Too well I know   315
And have forgot this, or would not have come here.

OEDIPUS   What is this? How fainthearted you have come!

TEIRESIAS   Let me go home; it is best for you to bear
Your burden, and I mine, if you will heed me.

OEDIPUS   You speak what is lawless, and hateful to the state   320
Which raised you, when you deprive her of your answer.

TEIRESIAS   And I see that your speech does not proceed
          In season; I shall not undergo the same.
OEDIPUS   Don't by the gods turn back when you are wise,
          When all we suppliants lie prostrate before you.   325
TEIRESIAS   And all unwise; I never shall reveal
          My evils, so that I may not tell yours.
OEDIPUS   What do you say? You know, but will not speak?
          Would you betray us and destroy the state?
TEIRESIAS   I will not hurt you or me. Why in vain   330
          Do you probe this? You will not find out from me.
OEDIPUS   Worst of evil men, you would enrage
          A stone itself. Will you never speak,
          But stay so untouched and so inconclusive?
TEIRESIAS   You blame my anger and do not see that   335
          With which you live in common, but upbraid me.
OEDIPUS   Who would not be enraged to hear these words
          By which you now dishonor this our city?
TEIRESIAS   Of itself this will come, though I hide it in silence.
OEDIPUS   Then you should tell me what it is will come.   340
TEIRESIAS   I shall speak no more. If further you desire,
          Rage on in wildest anger of your soul.
OEDIPUS   I shall omit nothing I understand
          I am so angry. Know that you seem to me
          Creator of the deed and worker too   345
          In all short of the slaughter; if you were not blind,
          I would say this crime was your work alone.
TEIRESIAS   Really? Abide yourself by the decree
          You just proclaimed, I tell you! From this day
          Henceforth address neither these men nor me.   350
          You are the godless defiler of this land.
OEDIPUS   You push so bold and taunting in your speech;
          And how do you think to get away with this?
TEIRESIAS   I have got away. I nurse my strength in truth.
OEDIPUS   Who taught you this? Not from your art you got it.   355
TEIRESIAS   From you. You had me speak against my will.
OEDIPUS   What word? Say again, so I may better learn.
TEIRESIAS   Didn't you get it before? Or do you bait me?
OEDIPUS   I don't remember it. Speak forth again.
TEIRESIAS   You are the slayer whom you seek, I say.   360
OEDIPUS   Not twice you speak such bitter words unpunished.
TEIRESIAS   Shall I speak more to make you angrier still?
OEDIPUS   Do what you will, your words will be in vain.
TEIRESIAS   I say you have forgot that you are joined
          With those most dear to you in deepest shame   365
          And do not see where you are in sin.
OEDIPUS   Do you think you will always say such things in joy?
TEIRESIAS   Surely, if strength abides in what is true.

OEDIPUS   It does, for all but you, this not for you
    Because your ears and mind and eyes are blind. 370

TEIRESIAS   Wretched you are to make such taunts, for soon
    All men will cast the selfsame taunts on you.

OEDIPUS   You live in entire night, could do no harm
    To me or any man who sees the day.

TEIRESIAS   Not at my hands will it be your fate to fall. 375
    Apollo suffices, whose concern it is to do this.

OEDIPUS   Are these devices yours, or are they Creon's?

TEIRESIAS   Creon is not your trouble; you are yourself.

OEDIPUS   O riches, empire, skill surpassing skill
    In all the numerous rivalries of life, 380
    How great a grudge there is stored up against you
    If for this kingship, which the city gave,
    Their gift, not my request, into my hands—
    For this, the trusted Creon, my friend from the start
    Desires to creep by stealth and cast me out 385
    Taking a seer like this, a weaver of wiles,
    A crooked swindler who has got his eyes
    On gain alone, but in his art is blind.
    Come, tell us, in what clearly are you a prophet?
    How is it, when the weave-songed bitch was here* 390
    You uttered no salvation for these people?
    Surely the riddle then could not be solved
    By some chance comer; it needed prophecy.
    You did not clarify that with birds
    Or knowledge from a god; but when I came, 395
    The ignorant Oedipus, I silenced her,
    Not taught by birds, but winning by my wits,
    Whom you are now attempting to depose,
    Thinking to minister near Creon's throne.
    I think that to your woe you and that plotter 400
    Will purge the land, and if you were not old
    Punishment would teach you what you plot.

CHORUS   It seems to us, O Oedipus our king,
    Both this man's words and yours were said in anger.
    Such is not our need, but to find out 405
    How best we shall discharge Apollo's orders.

TEIRESIAS   Even if you are king, the right to answer
    Should be free to all; of that I too am king.
    I live not as your slave, but as Apollo's.
    And not with Creon's wards shall I be counted. 410
    I say, since you have taunted even my blindness,
    You have eyes, but see not where in evil you are

---

390 The Sphinx was sent to Thebes by Hera, who hated Thebes because she hated Cadmus' daughter
    Semele, the mother of Dionysus. The Sphinx was set like a hound to watch the city, and she chanted
    her riddle to all comers.

Nor where you dwell, nor whom you are living with.
Do you know from whom you spring? And you forget
You are an enemy to your own kin   415
Both those beneath and those above the earth.
Your mother's and father's curse, with double goad
And dreaded foot shall drive you from this land.
You who now see straight shall then be blind,
And there shall be no harbour for your cry   420
With which all Mount Cithaeron soon shall ring,
When you have learned the wedding where you sailed
At home, into no port, by voyage fair.
A throng of other ills you do not know
Shall equal you to yourself and to your children.   425
Throw mud on this, on Creon, on my voice—
Yet there shall never be a mortal man
Eradicated more wretchedly than you.

OEDIPUS   Shall these unbearable words be heard from him?
Go to perdition! Hurry! Off, away,   430
Turn back again and from this house depart.

TEIRESIAS   If you had not called me, I should not have come.

OEDIPUS   I did not know that you would speak such folly
Or I would not soon have brought you to my house.

TEIRESIAS   And such a fool I am, as it seems to you.   435
But to the parents who bore you I seem wise.

OEDIPUS   What parents? Wait! What mortals gave me birth?

TEIRESIAS   This day shall be your birth and your destruction.

OEDIPUS   All things you say in riddles and unclear.

TEIRESIAS   Are you not he who best can search this out?   440

OEDIPUS   Mock, if you wish, the skill that made me great.

TEIRESIAS   This is the very fortune that destroyed you.

OEDIPUS   Well, if I saved the city, I do not care.

TEIRESIAS   I am going now. You, boy, be my guide.

OEDIPUS   Yes, let him guide you. Here you are in the way.   445
When you are gone you will give no more trouble.

TEIRESIAS   I go when I have said what I came to say
Without fear of your frown; you cannot destroy me.
I say, the very man whom you long seek
With threats and announcements about Laius' murder—   450
This man is here. He seems an alien stranger,
But soon he shall be revealed of Theban birth,
Nor at this circumstance shall he be pleased.
He shall be blind who sees, shall be a beggar
Who now is rich, shall make his way abroad   455
Feeling the ground before him with a staff.
He shall be revealed at once as brother
And father to his own children, husband and son
To his mother, his father's kin and murderer.

Go in and ponder that. If I am wrong,
Say then that I know nothing of prophecy.

(*Exit* TEIRESIAS *and then* OEDIPUS)

CHORUS (*Strophe A*)   Who is the man the Delphic rock said with oracular
                                                                        voice
Unspeakable crimes performed with his gory hands?   465
It is time for him now to speed
His foot in flight, more strong
Than horses swift as the storm.
For girt in arms upon him springs
With fire and lightning, Zeus' son   470
And behind him, terrible,
Come the unerring Fates.

(*Antistrophe A*)   From snowy Parnassus just now the word flashed clear
To track the obscure man by every way,
For he wanders under the wild   475
Forest, and into caves
And cliff rocks, like a bull,
Reft on his way, with care on care
Trying to shun the prophecy
Come from the earth's mid-navel,   480
But about him flutters the ever living doom.

(*Strophe B*)   Terrible, terrible things the wise bird-augur stirs.
I neither approve nor deny, at a loss for what to say,
I flutter in hopes and fears, see neither here nor ahead;
For what strife has lain   485
On Labdacus' sons or Polybus'* that I have found ever before
Or now, whereby I may run for the sons of Labdacus
In sure proof against Oedipus' public fame
As avenger for dark death?

(*Antistrophe B*)   Zeus and Apollo surely understand and know   490
The affairs of mortal men, but that a mortal seer
Knows more than I, there is no proof. Though a man
May surpass a man in knowledge,
Never shall I agree, till I see the word true, when men blame Oedipus,
For there came upon him once clear the winged maiden   495
And wise he was seen, by sure test sweet for the state.
So never shall my mind judge him evil guilt.

———————

(*Enter* CREON)

CREON   Men of our city, I have heard dread words
That Oedipus our king accuses me.   500

486 Polybus, the king of Corinth, was thought to be Oedipus' father.

I am here indignant. If in the present troubles
He thinks that he has suffered at my hands
One word or deed tending to injury
I do not crave the long-spanned age of life
To bear this rumor, for it is no simple wrong   505
The damage of this accusation brings me;
It brings the greatest, if I am called a traitor
To you and my friends, a traitor to the state.
CHORUS   Come now, for this reproach perhaps was forced
By anger, rather than considered thought.   510
CREON   And was the idea voiced that my advice
Persuaded the prophet to give false accounts?
CHORUS   Such was said. I know not to what intent.
CREON   Was this accusation laid against me
From straightforward eyes and straightforward mind?   515
CHORUS   I do not know. I see not what my masters do;
(*Enter* OEDIPUS)
But here he is now, coming from the house.
OEDIPUS   How dare you come here? Do you own a face
So bold that you can come before my house   520
When you are clearly the murderer of this man
And manifestly pirate of my throne?
Come, say before the gods, did you see in me
A coward or a fool, that you plotted this?
Or did you think I would not see your wiles   525
Creeping upon me, or knowing, would not ward off?
Surely your machination is absurd
Without a crowd of friends to hunt a throne
Which is captured only by wealth and many men.
CREON   Do you know what you do? Hear answer to your charges   530
On the other side. Judge only what you know.
OEDIPUS   Your speech is clever, but I learn it ill
Since I have found you harsh and grievous toward me.
CREON   This very matter hear me first explain.
OEDIPUS   Tell me not this one thing: you are not false.   535
CREON   If you think stubbornness a good possession
Apart from judgment, you do not think right.
OEDIPUS   If you think you can do a kinsman evil
Without the penalty, you have no sense.
CREON   I agree with you. What you have said is just.   540
Tell me what you say you have suffered from me.
OEDIPUS   Did you, or did you not, advise my need
Was summoning that prophet person here?
CREON   And still is. I hold still the same opinion.
OEDIPUS   How long a time now has it been since Laius—   545
CREON   Performed what deed? I do not understand.
OEDIPUS   —Disappeared to his ruin at deadly hands.

CREON   Far in the past the count of years would run.
OEDIPUS   Was this same seer at that time practising?
CREON   As wise as now, and equally respected.   550
OEDIPUS   At that time did he ever mention me?
CREON   Never when I stood near enough to hear.
OEDIPUS   But did you not make inquiry of the murder?
CREON   We did, of course, and got no information.
OEDIPUS   How is it that this seer did not utter this then?   555
CREON   When I don't know, as now, I would keep still.
OEDIPUS   This much you know full well, and so should speak:—
CREON   What is that? If I know, I will not refuse.
OEDIPUS   This: If he had not first conferred with you
    He never would have said that I killed Laius.   560
CREON   If he says this, you know yourself, I think;
    I learn as much from you as you from me.
OEDIPUS   Learn then: I never shall be found a slayer.
CREON   What then, are you the husband of my sister?
OEDIPUS   What you have asked is plain beyond denial.
CREON   Do you rule this land with her in equal sway?   565
OEDIPUS   All she desires she obtains from me.
CREON   Am I with you two not an equal third?
OEDIPUS   In just that do you prove a treacherous friend.
CREON   No, if, like me, you reason with yourself.   570
    Consider this fact first: would any man
    Choose, do you think, to have his rule in fear
    Rather than doze unharmed with the same power?
    For my part I have never been desirous
    Of being king instead of acting king.   575
    Nor any other man has, wise and prudent.
    For now I obtain all from you without fear.
    If I were king, I would do much unwilling.
    How then could kingship sweeter be for me
    Than rule and power devoid of any pain?   580
    I am not yet so much deceived to want
    Goods besides those I profitably enjoy.
    Now I am hailed and gladdened by all men.
    Now those who want from you speak out to me,
    Since all their chances' outcome dwells therein.   585
    How then would I relinquish what I have
    To get those gains? My mind runs not so bad.
    I am prudent yet, no lover of such plots,
    Nor would I ever endure others' treason.
    And first as proof of this go on to Pytho;   590
    See if I told you truly the oracle.
    Next proof: see if I plotted with the seer;
    If you find so at all, put me to death
    With my vote for my guilt as well as yours.

Do not convict me just on unclear conjecture. 595
It is not right to think capriciously
The good are bad, nor that the bad are good.
It is the same to cast out a noble friend,
I say, as one's own life, which best he loves.
The facts, though, you will safely know in time, 600
Since time alone can show the just man just,
But you can know a criminal in one day.

CHORUS A cautious man would say he has spoken well.
O king, the quick to think are never sure.

OEDIPUS When the plotter, swift, approaches me in stealth 605
I too in counterplot must be as swift.
If I wait in repose, the plotter's ends
Are brought to pass and mine will then have erred.

CREON What do you want then? To cast me from the land?

OEDIPUS Least of all that. My wish is you should die, 610
Not flee to exemplify what envy is.

CREON Do you say this? Will you neither trust nor yield?

OEDIPUS No, for I think that you deserve no trust.

CREON You seem not wise to me.

OEDIPUS   I am for me. 615

CREON You should be for me too.

OEDIPUS   No, you are evil.

CREON Yes, if you understand nothing.

OEDIPUS   Yet I must rule.

CREON Not when you rule badly. 620

OEDIPUS   O city, city!

CREON It is my city too, not yours alone.

(Enter JOCASTA)

CHORUS Stop, princes. I see Jocasta coming
Out of the house at the right time for you. 625
With her you must settle the dispute at hand.

JOCASTA O wretched men, what unconsidered feud
Of tongues have you aroused? Are you not ashamed,
The state so sick, to stir up private ills?
Are you not going home? And you as well? 630
Will you turn a small pain into a great?

CREON My blood sister, Oedipus your husband
Claims he will judge against me two dread ills:
Thrust me from the fatherland or take and kill me.

OEDIPUS I will, my wife; I caught him in the act 635
Doing evil to my person with evil skill.

CREON Now may I not rejoice but die accursed
If ever I did any of what you accuse me.

JOCASTA O, by the gods, believe him, Oedipus.
First, in reverence for his oath to the gods, 640
Next, for my sake and theirs who stand before you.

CHORUS   Hear my entreaty, lord. Consider and consent.

OEDIPUS   What wish should I then grant?

CHORUS   Respect the man, no fool before, who now in oath is strong.

OEDIPUS   You know what you desire? 645

CHORUS   I know.

OEDIPUS   Say what you mean.

CHORUS   Your friend who has sworn do not dishonour
     By casting guilt for dark report.

OEDIPUS   Know well that when you ask this grant from me, 650
     You ask my death or exile from the land.

CHORUS   No, by the god foremost among the gods,
     The Sun, may I perish by the utmost doom
     Godless and friendless, if I have this in mind.
     But ah, the withering earth wears down 655
     My wretched soul, if to these ills
     Of old are added ills from both of you.

OEDIPUS   Then let him go, though surely I must die
     Or be thrust dishonoured from this land by force.
     Your grievous voice I pity, not that man's; 660
     Wherever he may be, he will be hated.

CREON   Sullen you are to yield, as you are heavy
     When you exceed in wrath. Natures like these
     Are justly sorest for themselves to bear.

OEDIPUS   Will you not go and leave me? 665

CREON   I am on my way.
     You know me not, but these men see me just. (*Exit*)

CHORUS   O queen, why do you delay to bring this man indoors?

JOCASTA   I want to learn what happened here.

CHORUS   Unknown suspicion rose from talk, and the unjust devours. 670

JOCASTA   In both of them?

CHORUS   Just so.

JOCASTA   What was the talk?

CHORUS   Enough, enough! When the land is pained
     It seems to me at this point we should stop. 675

OEDIPUS   Do you see where you have come? Though your intent
     Is good, you slacken off and blunt my heart.

CHORUS   O lord, I have said not once alone,
     Know that I clearly would be mad
     And wandering in mind, to turn away 680
     You who steered along the right,
     When she was torn with trouble, our beloved state.
     O may you now become in health her guide.

JOCASTA   By the gods, lord, tell me on what account
     You have set yourself in so great an anger. 685

OEDIPUS   I shall tell you, wife; I respect you more than these men.
     Because of Creon, since he has plotted against me.

JOCASTA   Say clearly, if you can; how started the quarrel?

OEDIPUS He says that I stand as the murderer of Laius.

JOCASTA He knows himself, or learned from someone else?

OEDIPUS No, but he sent a rascal prophet here.
He keeps his own mouth clean in what concerns him.

JOCASTA Now free yourself of what you said, and listen.
Learn from me, no mortal man exists
Who knows prophetic art for your affairs,
And I shall briefly show you proof of this:
An oracle came once to Laius. I do not say
From Phoebus himself, but from his ministers
That his fate would be at his son's hand to die—
A child, who would be born from him and me.
And yet, as the rumor says, they were strangers,
Robbers who killed him where three highways meet.
But three days had not passed from the child's birth
When Laius pierced and tied together his ankles,
And cast him by others' hands on a pathless mountain.
Therein Apollo did not bring to pass
That the child murder his father, nor for Laius
The dread he feared, to die at his son's hand.
Such did prophetic oracles determine.
Pay no attention to them. For the god
Will easily make clear the need he seeks.

OEDIPUS What wandering of soul, what stirring of mind
Holds me, my wife, in what I have just heard!

JOCASTA What care has turned you back that you say this?

OEDIPUS I thought I heard you mention this, that Laius
Was slaughtered at the place where three highways meet.

JOCASTA That was the talk. The rumour has not ceased.

OEDIPUS Where is this place where such a sorrow was?

JOCASTA The country's name is Phocis. A split road
Leads to one place from Delphi and Daulia.

OEDIPUS And how much time has passed since these events?

JOCASTA The news was heralded in the city scarcely
A little while before you came to rule.

OEDIPUS O Zeus, what have you planned to do to me?

JOCASTA What passion is this in you, Oedipus?

OEDIPUS Don't ask me that yet. Tell me about Laius.
What did he look like? How old was he when murdered?

JOCASTA A tall man, with his hair just brushed with white.
His shape and form differed not far from yours.

OEDIPUS Alas! Alas! I think unwittingly
I have just laid dread curses on my head.

JOCASTA What are you saying? I shrink to behold you, lord.

OEDIPUS I am terribly afraid the seer can see.
That will be clearer if you say one thing more.

JOCASTA Though I shrink, if I know what you ask, I will answer.

OEDIPUS   Did he set forth with few attendants then,
        Or many soldiers, since he was a king?
JOCASTA   They were five altogether among them.
        One was a herald. One chariot bore Laius.
OEDIPUS   Alas! All this is clear now. Tell me, my wife,   740
        Who was the man who told these stories to you?
JOCASTA   One servant, who alone escaped, returned.
OEDIPUS   Is he by chance now present in our house?
JOCASTA   Not now. Right from the time when he returned
        To see you ruling and Laius dead,   745
        Touching my hand in suppliance, he implored me
        To send him to fields and to pastures of sheep
        That he might be farthest from the sight of this city.
        So I sent him away, since he was worthy
        For a slave, to bear a greater grant than this.   750
OEDIPUS   How then could he return to us with speed?
JOCASTA   It can be done. But why would you order this?
OEDIPUS   O lady, I fear I have said too much.
        On this account I now desire to see him.
JOCASTA   Then he shall come. But I myself deserve   755
        To learn what it is that troubles you, my lord.
OEDIPUS   And you shall not be prevented, since my fears
        Have come to such a point. For who is closer
        That I may speak to in this fate than you?
        Polybus of Corinth was my father,   760
        My mother, Dorian Merope. I was held there
        Chief citizen of all, till such a fate
        Befell me—as it is, worthy of wonder,
        But surely not deserving my excitement.
        A man at a banquet overdrunk with wine   765
        Said in drink I was a false son to my father.
        The weight I held that day I scarcely bore,
        But on the next day I went home and asked
        My father and mother of it. In bitter anger
        They took the reproach from him who had let it fly.   770
        I was pleased at their actions; nevertheless
        The rumour always rankled; and spread abroad.
        In secret from mother and father I set out
        Toward Delphi. Phoebus sent me away ungraced
        In what I came for, but other wretched things   775
        Terrible and grievous, he revealed in answer;
        That I must wed my mother and produce
        An unendurable race for men to see,
        That I should kill the father who begot me.
        When I heard this response, Corinth I fled   780
        Henceforth to measure her land by stars alone.
        I went where I should never see the disgrace

Of my evil oracles be brought to pass,
And on my journey to that place I came
At which you say this king had met his death.   785
My wife, I shall speak the truth to you. My way
Led to a place close by the triple road.
There a herald met me, and a man
Seated on colt-drawn chariot, as you said.
There both the guide and the old man himself   790
Thrust me with driving force out of the path.
And I in anger struck the one who pushed me,
The driver. Then the old man, when he saw me,
Watched when I passed, and from his chariot
Struck me full on the head with double goad.   795
I paid him back and more. From this very hand
A swift blow of my staff rolled him right out
Of the middle of his seat onto his back.
I killed them all. But if relationship
Existed between this stranger and Laius,   800
What man now is wretcheder than I?
What man is cursed by a more evil fate?
No stranger or citizen could now receive me
Within his home, or even speak to me,
But thrust me out; and no one but myself   805
Brought down these curses on my head.
The bed of the slain man I now defile
With hands that killed him. Am I evil by birth?
Am I not utterly vile if I must flee
And cannot see my family in my flight   810
Nor tread my homeland soil, or else be joined
In marriage to my mother, kill my father,
Polybus, who sired me and brought me up?
Would not a man judge right to say of me
That this was sent on me by some cruel spirit?   815
O never, holy reverence of the gods,
May I behold that day, but may I go
Away from mortal men, before I see
Such a stain of circumstance come to me.

CHORUS   My lord, for us these facts are full of dread.   820
    Until you hear the witness, stay in hope.
OEDIPUS   And just so much is all I have of hope,
    Only to wait until the shepherd comes.
JOCASTA   What, then, do you desire to hear him speak?
OEDIPUS   I will tell you, if his story is found to be   825
    The same as yours, I would escape the sorrow.
JOCASTA   What unusual word did you hear from me?
OEDIPUS   You said he said that they were highway robbers
    Who murdered him. Now, if he still says

The selfsame number, I could not have killed him,   830
Since one man does not equal many men.
But if he speaks of a single lonely traveller,
The scale of guilt now clearly falls to me.

JOCASTA   However, know the word was set forth thus
And it is not in him now to take it back;   835
This tale the city heard, not I alone.
But if he diverges from his previous story,
Even then, my lord, he could not show Laius' murder
To have been fulfilled properly. Apollo
Said he would die at the hands of my own son.   840
Surely that wretched child could not have killed him,
But he himself met death some time before.
Therefore, in any prophecy henceforth
I would not look to this side or to that.

OEDIPUS   Your thoughts ring true, but still let someone go   845
To summon the peasant. Do not neglect this.

JOCASTA   I shall send without delay. But let us enter.
I would do nothing that did not please you. (*Exit* OEDIPUS *and* JOCASTA)

CHORUS (*Strophe A*)   May fate come on me as I bear
Holy pureness in all word and deed,
For which the lofty striding laws were set down,   850
Born through the heavenly air
Whereof the Olympian sky alone the father was;
No mortal spawn of mankind gave them birth,
Nor may oblivion ever lull them down;   855
Mighty in them the god is, and he does not age.

(*Antistrophe A*)   Pride breeds the tyrant.
Pride, once overfilled with many things in vain,
Neither in season nor fit for man,
Scaling the sheerest height   860
Hurls to a dire fate
Where no foothold is found.
I pray the god may never stop the rivalry
That works well for the state.
The god as my protector I shall never cease to hold.   865

(*Strophe B*)   But if a man goes forth haughty in word or deed
With no fear of the Right
Nor pious to the spirits' shrines,
May evil doom seize him
For his ill-fated pride,   870
If he does not fairly win his gain
Or works unholy deeds,
Or, in bold folly lays on the sacred profane hands.
For when such acts occur, what man may boast

Ever to ward off from his life darts of the gods? 875
If practices like these are in respect,
Why then must I dance the sacred dance?

(*Antistrophe B*) Never again in worship shall I go
To Delphi, holy navel of the earth,
Nor to the temple at Abae, 880
Nor to Olympia,
If these prophecies do not become
Examples for all men.
O Zeus, our king, if so you are rightly called,
Ruler of all things, may they not escape 885
You and your forever deathless power.
Men now hold light the fading oracles
Told about Laius long ago
And nowhere is Apollo clearly honored;
Things divine are going down to ruin. 890

———————

(*Enter* JOCASTA)

JOCASTA Lords of this land, the thought has come to me
To visit the spirits' shrines, bearing in hand
These suppliant boughs and offerings of incense.
For Oedipus raises his soul too high 895
With all distresses; nor, as a sane man should,
Does he confirm the new by things of old,
But stands at the speaker's will if he speaks terrors.
And so, because my advice can do no more,
To you, Lycian Apollo—for you are nearest— 900
A suppliant, I have come here with these prayers,
That you may find some pure deliverance for us:
We all now shrink to see him struck in fear,

(*Enter* MESSENGER)

That man who is the pilot of our ship. 905

MESSENGER Strangers, could I learn from one of you
Where is the house of Oedipus the king?
Or best, if you know, say where he is himself.

CHORUS This is his house, stranger; he dwells inside;
This woman is the mother of his children. 910

MESSENGER May she be always blessed among the blest,
Since she is the fruitful wife of Oedipus.

JOCASTA So may you, stranger, also be. You deserve
As much for your graceful greeting. But tell me
What you have come to search for or to show. 915

MESSENGER Good news for your house and your husband, lady.

JOCASTA What is it then? And from whom have you come?

MESSENGER From Corinth. And the message I will tell
    Will surely gladden you—and vex you, perhaps.
JOCASTA What is it? What is this double force it holds?   920
MESSENGER The men who dwell in the Isthmian country
    Have spoken to establish him their king.
JOCASTA What is that? Is not old Polybus still ruling?
MESSENGER Not he. For death now holds him in the tomb.
JOCASTA What do you say, old man? Is Polybus dead?   925
MESSENGER If I speak not the truth, I am ready to die.
JOCASTA O handmaid, go right away and tell your master
    The news. Where are you, prophecies of the gods?
    For this man Oedipus has trembled long,
    And shunned him lest he kill him. Now the man   930
    Is killed by fate and not by Oedipus.

                 (*Enter* OEDIPUS)

OEDIPUS O Jocasta, my most beloved wife,
    Why have you sent for me within the house?
JOCASTA Listen to this man, and while you hear him, think   935
    To what have come Apollo's holy prophecies.
OEDIPUS Who is this man? Why would he speak to me?
JOCASTA From Corinth he has come, to announce that your father
    Polybus no longer lives, but is dead.
OEDIPUS What do you say, stranger? Tell me this yourself.   940
MESSENGER If I must first announce my message clearly,
    Know surely that the man is dead and gone.
OEDIPUS Did he die by treachery or chance disease?
MESSENGER A slight scale tilt can lull the old to rest.
OEDIPUS The poor man, it seems, died by disease.   945
MESSENGER And by the full measure of lengthy time.
OEDIPUS Alas, alas! Why then do any seek
    Pytho's prophetic art, my wife, or hear
    The shrieking birds on high, by whose report
    I was to slay my father? Now he lies   950
    Dead beneath the earth, and here am I
    Who have not touched the blade. Unless in longing
    For me he died, and in this sense was killed by me.
    Polybus has packed away these oracles
    In his rest in Hades. They are now worth nothing.   955
JOCASTA Did I not tell you that some time ago?
OEDIPUS You did, but I was led astray by fear.
JOCASTA Henceforth put nothing of this on your heart.
OEDIPUS Why must I not still shrink from my mother's bed?
JOCASTA What should man fear, whose life is ruled by fate,   960
    For whom there is clear foreknowledge of nothing?
    It is best to live by chance, however you can.
    Be not afraid of marriage with your mother;

Already many mortals in their dreams
Have shared their mother's bed. But he who counts 965
This dream as nothing, easiest bears his life.

OEDIPUS All that you say would be indeed propitious,
If my mother were not alive. But since she is,
I still must shrink, however well you speak.

JOCASTA And yet your father's tomb is a great eye.* 970

OEDIPUS A great eye indeed. But I fear her who lives.

MESSENGER Who is this woman that you are afraid of?

OEDIPUS Merope, old man, with whom Polybus lived.

MESSENGER What is it in her that moves you to fear?

OEDIPUS A dread oracle, stranger, sent by the god. 975

MESSENGER Can it be told, or must no other know?

OEDIPUS It surely can. Apollo told me once
That I must join in intercourse with my mother
And shed with my own hands my father's blood.
Because of this, long since I have kept far 980
Away from Corinth—and happily—but yet
It would be most sweet to see my parents' faces.

MESSENGER Was this your fear in shunning your own city?

OEDIPUS I wished, too, old man, not to slay my father.

MESSENGER Why then have I not freed you from this fear, 985
Since I have come with friendly mind, my lord?

OEDIPUS Yes, and take thanks from me, which you deserve.

MESSENGER And this is just the thing for which I came,
That when you got back home I might fare well.

OEDIPUS Never shall I go where my parents are. 990

MESSENGER My son, you clearly know not what you do.

OEDIPUS How is that, old man? By the gods, let me know.

MESSENGER If for these tales you shrink from going home.

OEDIPUS I tremble lest what Phoebus said comes true.

MESSENGER Lest you incur pollution from your parents? 995

OEDIPUS That is the thing, old man, that always haunts me.

MESSENGER Well, do you know that surely you fear nothing?

OEDIPUS How so? If I am the son of those who bore me.

MESSENGER Since Polybus was no relation to you.

OEDIPUS What do you say? Was Polybus not my father? 1000

MESSENGER No more than this man here but just so much.

OEDIPUS How does he who begot me equal nothing?

MESSENGER That man was not your father, any more than I am.

OEDIPUS Well then, why was it he called me his son?

MESSENGER Long ago he got you as a gift from me. 1005

OEDIPUS Though from another's hand, yet so much he loved me!

MESSENGER His previous childlessness led him to that.

OEDIPUS Had you bought or found me when you gave me to him?

MESSENGER I found you in Cithaeron's folds and glens.

970 That is, a bright comfort [translator's note].

OEDIPUS   Why were you travelling in those regions?
MESSENGER   I guarded there a flock of mountain sheep.
OEDIPUS   Were you a shepherd, wandering for pay?
MESSENGER   Yes, and your saviour too, child, at that time.
OEDIPUS   What pain gripped me, that you took me in your arms?
MESSENGER   The ankles of your feet will tell you that.   1015
OEDIPUS   Alas, why do you mention that old trouble?
MESSENGER   I freed you when your ankles were pierced together.
OEDIPUS   A terrible shame from my swaddling clothes I got.
MESSENGER   Your very name you got from this misfortune.
OEDIPUS   By the gods, did my mother or father do it? Speak.   1020
MESSENGER   I know not. He who gave you knows better than I.
OEDIPUS   You didn't find me, but took me from another?
MESSENGER   That's right. Another shepherd gave you to me.
OEDIPUS   Who was he? Can you tell me who he was?
MESSENGER   Surely. He belonged to the household of Laius.   1025
OEDIPUS   The man who ruled this land once long ago?
MESSENGER   Just so. He was a herd in that man's service.
OEDIPUS   Is this man still alive, so I could see him?
MESSENGER   You dwellers in this country should know best.
OEDIPUS   Is there any one of you who stand before me   1030
        Who knows the shepherd of whom this man speaks?
        If you have seen him in the fields or here,
        Speak forth; the time has come to find this out.
CHORUS   I think the man you seek is no one else
        Than the shepherd you were so eager to see before.   1035
        Jocasta here might best inform us that.
OEDIPUS   My wife, do you know the man we just ordered
        To come here? Is it of him that this man speaks?
JOCASTA   Why ask of whom he spoke? Think nothing of it.
        Brood not in vain on what has just been said.   1040
OEDIPUS   It could not be that when I have got such clues,
        I should not shed clear light upon my birth.
JOCASTA   Don't by the gods, investigate this more
        If you care for your own life. I am sick enough.
OEDIPUS   Take courage. Even if I am found a slave   1045
        For three generations, your birth will not be base.
JOCASTA   Still, I beseech you, hear me. Don't do this.
OEDIPUS   I will hear of nothing but finding out the truth.
JOCASTA   I know full well and tell you what is best.
OEDIPUS   Well, then, this best, for some time now, has given me pain.   1050
JOCASTA   O ill-fated man, may you never know who you are.
OEDIPUS   Will someone bring the shepherd to me here?
        And let this lady rejoice in her opulent birth.
JOCASTA   Alas, alas, hapless man. I have this alone
        To tell you, and nothing else forevermore. (*Exit*)   1055
CHORUS   O Oedipus, where has the woman gone

In the rush of her wild grief? I am afraid
Evil will break forth out of this silence.

OEDIPUS   Let whatever will break forth. I plan to see
The seed of my descent, however small.   1060
My wife, perhaps, because a noblewoman
Looks down with shame upon my lowly birth.
I would not be dishonoured to call myself
The son of Fortune, giver of the good.
She is my mother. The years, her other children,   1065
Have marked me sometimes small and sometimes great.
Such was I born! I shall prove no other man,
Nor shall I cease to search out my descent.

CHORUS (*Strophe*)   If I am a prophet and can know in mind,
Cithaeron,* by tomorrow's full moon   1070
You shall not fail, by mount Olympus,
To find that Oedipus, as a native of your land,
Shall honour you for nurse and mother.
And to you we dance in choral song because you bring
Fair gifts to him our king.   1075
Hail, Phoebus, may all this please you.

(*Antistrophe*)   Who, child, who bore you in the lengthy span of years?
One close to Pan who roams the mountain woods,
One of Apollo's bedfellows?
For all wild pastures in mountain glens to him are dear.   1080
Was Hermes your father, who Cyllene sways,*
Or did Bacchus, dwelling on the mountain peaks,
Take you a foundling from some nymph
Of those by springs of Helicon,* with whom he sports the most?
                    (*Enter* SHEPHERD, *led*)   1085
OEDIPUS   If I may guess, although I never met him,
I think, elders, I see that shepherd coming
Whom we have long sought, as in the measure
Of lengthy age he accords with him we wait for.
Besides, the men who lead him I recognize   1090
As servants of my house. You may perhaps
Know better than I if you have seen him before.

CHORUS   Be assured, I know him as a shepherd
As trusted as any other in Laius' service.

OEDIPUS   Stranger from Corinth, I will ask you first,   1095
Is this the man you said?

MESSENGER   You are looking at him.

1070 A mountain range in Greece where Oedipus was exposed, Pentheus dismembered by the Bacchae,
    and Actaeon transformed into a stag.

1081 Hermes, the son of Maia, was born on Mount Cyllene in Arcadia.

1084 A mountain range in Boeotia, sacred to Apollo and the Muses.

OEDIPUS   You there, old man, look here and answer me
          What I shall ask you. Were you ever with Laius?
SERVANT   I was a slave, not bought but reared at home.   1100
OEDIPUS   What work concerned you? What was your way of life?
SERVANT   Most of my life I spent among the flocks.
OEDIPUS   In what place most of all was your usual pasture?
SERVANT   Sometimes Cithaeron, or the ground nearby.
OEDIPUS   Do you know this man before you here at all?   1105
SERVANT   Doing what? And of what man do you speak?
OEDIPUS   The one before you. Have you ever had congress with him?
SERVANT   Not to say so at once from memory.
MESSENGER   That is no wonder, master, but I shall remind him,
          Clearly, who knows me not; yet well I know   1110
          That he knew once the region of Cithaeron.
          He with a double flock and I with one
          Dwelt there in company for three whole years
          During the six months' time from spring to fall.
          When winter came, I drove into my fold   1115
          My flock, and he drove his to Laius' pens.
          Do I speak right, or did it not happen so?
SERVANT   You speak the truth, though it was long ago.
MESSENGER   Come now, do you recall you gave me then
          A child for me to rear as my own son?   1120
SERVANT   What is that? Why do you ask me this?
MESSENGER   This is the man, my friend, who then was young.
SERVANT   Go to destruction! Will you not be quiet?
OEDIPUS   Come, scold him not, old man. These words of yours
          Deserve a scolding more than this man's do.   1125
SERVANT   In what, most noble master, do I wrong?
OEDIPUS   Not to tell of the child he asks about.
SERVANT   He speaks in ignorance, he toils in vain.
OEDIPUS   If you will not speak freely, you will under torture.
SERVANT   Don't, by the gods, outrage an old man like me.   1130
OEDIPUS   Will someone quickly twist back this fellow's arms?
SERVANT   Alas, what for? What do you want to know?
OEDIPUS   Did you give this man the child of whom he asks?
SERVANT   I did. Would I had perished on that day!
OEDIPUS   You will come to that unless you tell the truth.   1135
SERVANT   I come to far greater ruin if I speak.
OEDIPUS   This man, it seems, is trying to delay.
SERVANT   Not I. I said before I gave it to him.
OEDIPUS   Where did you get it? At home or from someone else?
SERVANT   It was not mine. I got him from a man.   1140
OEDIPUS   Which of these citizens? Where did he live?
SERVANT   O master, by the gods, ask me no more.
OEDIPUS   You are done for if I ask you this again.

SERVANT Well then, he was born of the house of Laius.

OEDIPUS One of his slaves, or born of his own race?   1145

SERVANT Alas, to speak I am on the brink of horror.

OEDIPUS And I to hear. But still it must be heard.

SERVANT Well, then, they say it was his child. Your wife
    Who dwells within could best say how this stands.

OEDIPUS Was it she who gave him to you?   1150

SERVANT   Yes, my lord.

OEDIPUS For what intent?

SERVANT   So I could put it away.

OEDIPUS When she bore him, the wretch.

SERVANT   She feared bad oracles.   1155

OEDIPUS What were they?

SERVANT   They said he should kill his father.

OEDIPUS Why did you give him up to this old man?

SERVANT I pitied him, master, and thought he would take him away
    To another land, the one from which he came.   1160
    But he saved him for greatest woe. If you are he
    Whom this man speaks of, you were born curst by fate.

OEDIPUS Alas, alas! All things are now come true.
    O light, for the last time now I look upon you;
    I am shown to be born from those I ought not to have been.   1165
    I married the woman I should not have married,
    I killed the man whom I should not have killed.

                (*Exit* OEDIPUS *and* SERVANT)

CHORUS (*Strophe A*) Alas, generations of mortal men!
    How equal to nothing do I number you in life!   1170
    Who, O who, is the man
    Who bears more of bliss
    Than just the seeming so,
    And then, like a waning sun, to fall away?
    When I know your example,   1175
    Your guiding spirit, yours, wretched Oedipus,
    I call no mortal blest.

    (*Antistrophe A*) He is the one, O Zeus,
    Who peerless shot his bow and won well-fated bliss,
    Who destroyed the hook-clawed maiden,   1180
    The oracle-singing Sphinx,
    And stood a tower for our land from death;
    For this you are called our king,
    Oedipus, are highest-honoured here,
    And over great Thebes hold sway.   1185

    (*Strophe B*) And now who is more wretched for men to hear,
    Who so lives in wild plagues, who dwells in pains,
    In utter change of life?

Alas for glorious Oedipus!
The selfsame port of rest   1190
Was gained by bridegroom father and his son,
How, O how did your father's furrows ever bear you, suffering man?
How have they endured silence for so long?

(*Antistrophe B*)   You are found out, unwilling, by all seeing Time.
It judges your unmarried marriage where for long   1195
Begetter and begot have been the same.
Alas, child of Laius,
Would I had never seen you.
As one who pours from his mouth a dirge I wail,
To speak the truth, through you I breathed new life,   1200
And now through you I lulled my eye to sleep.

(*Enter* SECOND MESSENGER)

SECOND MESSENGER   O men most honoured always of this land
What deeds you shall hear, what shall you behold!
What grief shall stir you up, if by your kinship   1205
You are still concerned for the house of Labdacus!
I think neither Danube nor any other river
Could wash this palace clean, so many ills
Lie hidden there which now will come to light.
They were done by will, not fate; and sorrows hurt   1210
The most when we ourselves appear to choose them.
CHORUS   What we heard before causes no little sorrow.
What can you say which adds to that a burden?
SECOND MESSENGER   This is the fastest way to tell the tale;
Hear it: Jocasta, your divine queen, is dead.   1215
CHORUS   O sorrowful woman! From what cause did she die?
SECOND MESSENGER   By her own hand. The most painful of the action
Occurred away, not for your eyes to see.
But still, so far as I have memory
You shall learn the sufferings of that wretched woman: 1220
How she passed on through the door enraged
And rushed straight forward to her nuptial bed,
Clutching her hair's ends with both her hands.
Once inside the doors she shut herself in
And called on Laius, who has long been dead,   1225
Having remembrance of their seed of old
By which he died himself and left her a mother
To bear an evil brood to his own son.
She moaned the bed on which by double curse
She bore husband to husband, children to child.   1230
How thereafter she perished I do not know,
For Oedipus burst in on her with a shriek,

And because of him we could not see her woe.
We looked on him alone as he rushed around.
Pacing about, he asked us to give him a sword,   1235
Asked where he might find the wife no wife,
A mother whose plowfield bore him and his children.
Some spirit was guiding him in his frenzy,
For none of the men who are close at hand did so.
With a horrible shout, as if led on by someone,   1240
He leapt on the double doors, from their sockets
Broke hollow bolts aside, and dashed within.
There we beheld his wife hung by her neck
From twisted cords, swinging to and fro.
When he saw her, wretched man, he terribly groaned   1245
And slackened the hanging noose. When the poor woman
Lay on the ground, what happened was dread to see.
He tore the golden brooch pins from her clothes,
And raised them up, and struck his own eyeballs,
Shouting such words as these "No more shall you   1250
Behold the evils I have suffered and done.
Be dark from now on, since you saw before
What you should not, and knew not what you should."
Moaning such cries, not once but many times
He raised and struck his eyes. The bloody pupils   1255
Bedewed his beard. The gore oozed not in drops,
But poured in a black shower, a hail of blood.
From both of them these woes have broken out,
Not for just one, but man and wife together.
The bliss of old that formerly prevailed   1260
Was bliss indeed, but now upon this day
Lamentation, madness, death, and shame—
No evil that can be named is not at hand.
CHORUS   Is the wretched man in any rest now from pain?
SECOND MESSENGER   He shouts for someone to open up the doors   1265
And show to all Cadmeans his father's slayer,
His mother's—I should not speak the unholy word.
He says he will hurl himself from the land, no more
To dwell cursed in the house by his own curse.
Yet he needs strength and someone who will guide him.   1270
His sickness is too great to bear. He will show it to you
For the fastenings of the doors are opening up,
And such a spectacle you will soon behold
As would make even one who abhors it take pity.
                    (*Enter* OEDIPUS)   1275
CHORUS   O terrible suffering for men to see,
Most terrible of all that I
Have ever come upon. O wretched man,

What madness overcame you, what springing daimon*
Greater than the greatest for men   1280
Has caused your evil-daimoned fate?
Alas, alas, grievous one,
But I cannot bear to behold you, though I desire
To ask you much, much to find out,
Much to see,   1285
You make me shudder so!

OEDIPUS   Alas, alas, I am grieved!
Where on earth, so wretched, shall I go?
Where does my voice fly through the air,
O Fate, where have you bounded?   1290

CHORUS   To dreadful end, not to be heard or seen.

(*Strophe A*)

OEDIPUS   O cloud of dark
That shrouds me off, has come to pass, unspeakable,
Invincible, that blows no favoring blast.   1295
Woe,
O woe again, the goad that pierces me,
Of the sting of evil now, and memory of before.

CHORUS   No wonder it is that among so many pains
You should both mourn and bear a double evil.   1300

(*Antistrophe A*)

OEDIPUS   Ah, friend,
You are my steadfast servant still,
You still remain to care for me, blind.
Alas! Alas!   1305
You are not hid from me; I know you clearly,
And though in darkness, still I hear your voice.

CHORUS   O dreadful doer, how did you so endure
To quench your eyes? What daimon drove you on?

(*Strophe B*)   1310

OEDIPUS   Apollo it was, Apollo, friends
Who brought it to pass these evil, evil woes of mine.
The hand of no one struck my eyes but wretched me.
For why should I see,
When nothing sweet there is to see with sight?   1315

CHORUS   This is just as you say.

OEDIPUS   What more is there for me to see,
My friends, what to love,
What joy to hear a greeting?
Lead me at once away from here,   1320
Lead me away, friends, wretched as I am,
Accursed, and hated most
Of mortal to the gods.

¹²⁷⁸ Deity or daemon.

CHORUS   Wretched alike in mind and in your fortune,
How I wish that I had never known you.   1325
(*Antistrophe B*)
OEDIPUS   May he perish, whoever freed me
From fierce bonds on my feet,
Snatched me from death and saved me, doing me no joy.
For if then I had died, I should not be   1330
So great a grief to friends and to myself.
CHORUS   This also is my wish.
OEDIPUS   I would not have come to murder my father,
Nor have been called among men
The bridegroom of her from whom I was born.   1335
But as it is I am godless, child of unholiness,
Wretched sire in common with my father.
And if there is any evil older than evil left,
It is the lot of Oedipus.
CHORUS   I know not how I could give you good advice,   1340
For you would be better dead than living blind.

OEDIPUS   That how things are was not done for the best—
Teach me not this, or give me more advice.
If I had sight, I know not with what eyes
I could ever face my father among the dead,   1345
Or my wretched mother. What I have done to them
Is too great for a noose to expiate.
Do you think the sight of my children would be a joy
For me to see, born as they were to me?
No, never for these eyes of mine to see.   1350
Nor the city, nor the tower, nor the sacred
Statues of gods; of these I deprive myself,
Noblest among the Thebans, born and bred,
Now suffering everything. I tell you all
To exile me as impious, shown by the gods   1355
Untouchable and of the race of Laius.
When I uncovered such a stain on me,
Could I look with steady eyes upon the people?
No, No! And if there were a way to block
The spring of hearing, I would not forbear   1360
To lock up wholly this my wretched body.
I should be blind and deaf.—For it is sweet
When thought can dwell outside our evils.
Alas, Cithaeron, why did you shelter me?
Why did you not take and kill me at once, so I   1365
Might never reveal to men whence I was born?
O Polybus, O Corinth, O my father's halls,
Ancient in fable, what an outer fairness,
A festering of evils, you raised in me.

For now I am evil found, and born of evil. 1370
O the three paths! Alas the hidden glen,
The grove of oak, the narrow triple roads
That drank from my own hands my father's blood.
Do you remember any of the deeds
I did before you then on my way here 1375
And what I after did? O wedlock, wedlock!
You gave me birth, and then spawned in return
Issue from the selfsame seed; you revealed
Father, brother, children, in blood relation,
The bride both wife and mother, and whatever 1380
Actions are done most shameful among men.
But it is wrong to speak what is not good to do.
By the gods, hide me at once outside our land,
Or murder me, or hurl me in the sea
Where you shall never look on me again. 1385
Come venture to lay your hands on this wretched man.
Do it. Be not afraid. No mortal man
                    (*Enter* CREON)
    There is, except myself, to bear my evils.
CHORUS   Here is Creon, just in time for what you ask 1390
    To work and to advise, for he alone
    Is left in place of you to guard the land.
OEDIPUS   Alas, what word, then, shall I tell this man?
    What righteous ground of trust is clear in me,
    As in the past in all I have done him evil? 1395
CREON   Oedipus, I have not come to laugh at you,
    Nor to reproach you for your former wrongs.
    (*To the attendants*)   If you defer no longer to mortal offspring,
    Respect at least the all-nourishing flame
    Of Apollo, lord of the sun. Fear to display 1400
    So great a pestilence, which neither earth
    Nor holy rain nor light will well receive.
    But you, conduct him to the house at once.
    It is most pious for the kin alone
    To hear and to behold the family sins. 1405
OEDIPUS   By the gods, since you have plucked me from my fear,
    Most noble, facing this most vile man,
    Hear me one word—I will speak for you, not me.
CREON   What desire do you so persist to get?
OEDIPUS   As soon as you can, hurl me from this land 1410
    To where no mortal man will ever greet me.
CREON   I would do all this, be sure. But I want first
    To find out from the god what must be done.
OEDIPUS   His oracle, at least, is wholly clear;
    Leave me to ruin, an impious parricide. 1415
CREON   Thus spake the oracle. Still, as we stand

It is better to find out sure what we should do.

OEDIPUS Will you inquire about so wretched a man?

CREON Yes. You will surely put trust in the god.

OEDIPUS I order you and beg you, give the woman   1420
Now in the house such burial as you yourself
Would want. Do last rites justly for your kin.
But may this city never be condemned—
My father's realm—because I live within.
Let me live in the mountains where Cithaeron   1425
Yonder has fame of me, which father and mother
When they were alive established as my tomb.
There I may die by those who sought to kill me.
And yet this much I know, neither a sickness
Nor anything else can kill me. I would not   1430
Be saved from death, except for some dread evil.
Well, let my fate go wherever it may.
As for my sons, Creon, assume no trouble;
They are men and will have no difficulty
Of living wherever they may be.   1435
O my poor grievous daughters, who never knew
Their dinner table set apart from me,
But always shared in everything I touched—
Take care of them for me, and first of all
Allow me to touch them and bemoan our ills.   1440
Grant it, lord,
Grant it, noble. If with my hand I touch them
I would think I had them just as when I could see.
        (*Creon's attendants bring in* ANTIGONE *and* ISMENE)
What's that?   1445
By the gods, can it be I hear my dear ones weeping?
And have you taken pity on me, Creon?
Have you had my darling children sent to me?
Do I speak right?

CREON You do. For it was I who brought them here,   1450
Knowing this present joy your joy of old.

OEDIPUS May you fare well. For their coming may the spirit
That watches over you be better than mine.
My children, where are you? Come to me, come
Into your brother's hands, that brought about   1455
Your father's eyes, once bright, to see like this.
Your father, children, who, seeing and knowing nothing,
Became a father whence he was got himself.
I weep also for you—I cannot see you—
To think of the bitter life in days to come   1460
Which you will have to lead among mankind.
What citizens' gatherings will you approach?
What festivals attend, where you will not cry

When you go home, instead of gay rejoicing?
And when you arrive at marriageable age,   1465
What man, my daughters, will there be to chance you,
Incurring such reproaches on his head,
Disgraceful to my children and to yours?
What evil will be absent, when your father
Killed his own father, sowed seed in her who bore him,   1470
From whom he was born himself, and equally
Has fathered you whence he himself was born.
Such will be the reproaches. Who then will wed you?
My children, there is no one for you. Clearly
You must decay in barrenness, unwed.   1475
Son of Menoeceus—since you are alone
Left as a father to them, for we who produced them
Are both in ruin—see that you never let
These girls wander as beggars without husbands,
Let them not fall into such woes as mine.   1480
But pity them, seeing how young they are
To be bereft of all except your aid.
Grant this, my noble friend, with a touch of your hand.
My children, if your minds were now mature,
I would give you much advice. But, pray this for me,   1485
To live as the time allows, to find a life
Better than that your siring father had.

CREON   You have wept enough here, come, and go inside the house.
OEDIPUS   I must obey, though nothing sweet.
CREON   All things are good in their time.   1490
OEDIPUS   Do you know in what way I go?
CREON   Tell me, I'll know when I hear.
OEDIPUS   Send me outside the land.
CREON   You ask what the god will do.
OEDIPUS   But to the gods I am hated.   1495
CREON   Still, it will soon be done.
OEDIPUS   Then you agree?
CREON   What I think not I would not say in vain.
OEDIPUS   Now lead me away.
CREON   Come then, but let the children go.   1500
OEDIPUS   Do not take them from me.
CREON   Wish not to govern all,
    For what you ruled will not follow you through life.
CHORUS   Dwellers in native Thebes, behold this Oedipus
    Who solved the famous riddle, was your mightiest man.   1505
    What citizen on his lot did not with envy gaze?
    See to how great a surge of dread fate he has come!
    So I would say a mortal man, while he is watching
    To see the final day, can have no happiness
    Till he pass the bound of life, nor be relieved of pain.

Greek terracotta vase (*ca.* 430–420 B.C.) showing Philoctetes wounded, with the bow of Heracles beside him. *The Metropolitan Museum of Art, Fletcher Fund, 1956*

PHILOCTETES

by Sophocles

Translated by Sir George Young

Characters
ODYSSEUS, *prince of Ithaca*
NEOPTOLEMUS, *the young prince of Scyros, son of Achilles*
PHILOCTETES, *prince of Trachis, son of Poias*
A SCOUT *attending on Neoptolemus, afterwards disguised as the master
of a trading vessel*
HERACLES
CHORUS *of Scyrian sailors, followers of* NEOPTOLEMUS
MATE *of the Scyrian crew; Attendants*

Scene, a desert place on the coast of Lemnos; in the background a cave

(*Enter* ODYSSEUS, NEOPTOLEMUS, *and Attendant*)

ODYSSEUS   This is the shore of Lemnos' sea-girt isle,
Untrod by mortals, uninhabited,
Where once, O scion of the first of Greeks,
Achilles' offspring, Neoptolemus,
Under commission from our generals   5
I set on shore the Melian, Poias' son,*
His foot all bleeding with an ulcerous wound;
What time it was not possible for us
To set our hands in peace and quietness
To a drink-offering or burnt-sacrifice,   10
But ever with wild desecrating cries
He kept the whole encampment in distress,
Groaning, lamenting. But why tell this tale?
It is no time for many words from us,
Lest he should learn of my arrival hither,   15
And so the whole contrivance be upset
By which I think to take him presently.
Now you must work, and help to accomplish it;
So look around, where in this neighbourhood
There is a grotto with two entrances,   20
So situate, that at one or other end

---

6 Philoctetes; he has been marooned on the island of Lemnos for ten years, almost the entire duration of
  the Trojan War. He had accompanied the Greek forces as they sailed for Troy, but upon visiting the
  temple of Athena on the island of Chryse he had been bitten severely by the temple's guardian snake.
  His cohorts, repelled by his suppurating wound, abandoned him on Lemnos.

There is a sunny seat when it is cold,
While in the summer time a breeze sends sleep,
Blowing through the tunnelled chamber. And perhaps
A little underneath, on the left hand,   25
You may discover a fresh water-spring,
If it is still in being. Go up thither
Softly, and report if what I say applies
To this same spot, or no; so may you hear
The sequel of my story, and I tell it,   30
And both work on in concert.
NEOPTOLEMUS (*Ascending the rocks*)   King Odysseus,
   Your work lies not far off; for I believe
   I see a cave, such as you say.
ODYSSEUS   High up,   35
   Or low? I cannot mark it.
NEOPTOLEMUS   Here, above;
   And here's a foot-print on the threshold!
ODYSSEUS   See
   That he is not asleep inside!   40
NEOPTOLEMUS   I see
   An empty habitation; tenantless.
ODYSSEUS   Nor any household furniture within?
NEOPTOLEMUS   Yes, flattened leaves, as of some inmate's bed.
ODYSSEUS   And the rest empty, and nothing under-roof?   45
NEOPTOLEMUS   Here is a cup cut out of wood, the work
   Of a rude craftsman; and a pair of flints, too.
ODYSSEUS   What you exhibit is his treasure-heap!
NEOPTOLEMUS   Hilloa! Here are some rags as well, still warm,
   Full of some pestilent unwholesomeness.   50
ODYSSEUS   The man lives in these precincts, it is clear,
   And cannot be far off. How could a man,
   Lame with an old affliction in his limb,
   Walk any distance? But he has gone out,
   Either in quest of food, or of some herb,   55
   If he knows any anodyne. Send therefore
   Your follower to scout, lest unawares
   He fall on me; for he would like to get me,
   Rather than all the Argives, in his power.
NEOPTOLEMUS (*Descending*)   He is going, and the track shall be secured.   60
(*Exit Attendant*)
   Now speak again, and say, what is your pleasure.
ODYSSEUS   Son of Achilles, you must show yourself
   Stout on this errand; not in limbs alone,
   But also in service—if you hear a thing
   Novel, of a kind you have not heard before;   65
   Since you are here to serve.
NEOPTOLEMUS   What are your orders?

ODYSSEUS   You are to inveigle, by the words you utter,
    The spirit of Philoctetes. When he asks   70
    Who and whence are you, say—Achilles' son;
    This is not to be hidden; and you sail homeward,
    Deserting from the Achaians' naval host,*
    Hating them with a mighty hatred; who,
    Sending for you with prayers to come from home,   75
    As their sole means of taking Ilium,
    Thought it not meet to give you, when you came,
    Achilles' armour, which you claimed of them,
    But gave it to Odysseus in your room;
    Saying what you please of evil against me   80
    The extremest of extreme. For by so doing
    You will not hurt me; but if you refuse
    To do this duty, you will bring down trouble
    On all the Argives. For if this man's arrows
    Are not first captured, 'tis impossible   85
    That you should vanquish the Dardanian hold.*
    Now, how that intercourse there cannot be
    With him on my part, while on yours there can,
    Both safe and solid, learn. You have made voyage
    Not under oath to any, nor compelled,   90
    Nor of the army that at first set sail;
    But nought of this can be denied of me;
    Hence, if he sees me, shafts in hand, I perish,
    And shall involve you with me in my ruin.
    This is the thing to be devised, then; how   95
    You shall appropriate the unrivalled weapons.
    Of course I know that it is not your nature
    To say such words, or compass knaveries;
    But, for 'tis sweet to get the gain of winning,
    Dare! In the end, we shall be justified.   100
    Now, for a day's short fragment, lend yourself
    To ruthlessness; and then to after-time
    Be called the most religious of mankind!

NEOPTOLEMUS   The sort of things I chafe to hear prescribed,
    Son of Laertes—these I hate to do;   105
    'Tis not my nature to do ought by guile;
    Not mine, nor, as they say, his who begat me.
    Ready I am to bring the man by force,
    And not by fraud. For he, lame of one foot,
    Will not worst us at force, we being so many.   110
    Nevertheless, being sent to work with you,
    I am averse to be called recreant;

---

[73] That is, the Greeks.

[86] Troy. The arrows are the arrows of Heracles, which, as he was dying in Oeta, he gave to Philoctetes
because Philoctetes alone had dared to follow Heracles' commands and light his funeral pyre.

But I prefer, sir king, rather to fail
In doing well, than to succeed by ill.

ODYSSEUS   Son of an excellent father, I myself   115
Was youthful once, and had a backward tongue,
And an officious hand; but now through trial
I find the words and not the acts of men
Always prevailing.

NEOPTOLEMUS   Why, what else do you bid me   120
But tell a lie?

ODYSSEUS   I tell you by deceit
To capture Philoctetes.

NEOPTOLEMUS   Why by guile
To bring him, rather than persuading him?   125

ODYSSEUS   He cannot be persuaded; and by force
You could not take him.

NEOPTOLEMUS   Has he some resource
Of strength so formidable?

ODYSSEUS   Unerring darts,   130
Whose points are tipped with death.

NEOPTOLEMUS   And is it not
Within a bold man's part, to cope with him?

ODYSSEUS   No, save by guile he take him, as I say.

NEOPTOLEMUS   Do you not think foul shame to say things false?   135

ODYSSEUS   Not when the falsehood brings me safety.

NEOPTOLEMUS   Why,
With what a face could a man blurt it out?

ODYSSEUS   You must not scruple, when you work for gain.

NEOPTOLEMUS   What do I gain, if he should come to Troy?   140

ODYSSEUS   Nought but these shafts take Troy.

NEOPTOLEMUS   And am not I
The man to storm it, as was prophesied?

ODYSSEUS   Not you apart from these, nor these from you.

NEOPTOLEMUS   Well, I may have to seek them, that being so.   145

ODYSSEUS   You will achieve two prizes, if you do it.

NEOPTOLEMUS   Which? If I knew them, I might not refuse.

ODYSSEUS   To be called wise and valiant, both in one.

NEOPTOLEMUS   Go to, I'll do it, and let all shame go by.

ODYSSEUS   Do you remember what I told you?   150

NEOPTOLEMUS   Yes,
Rely on't; I assented once for all.

(Re-enter Attendant)

ODYSSEUS   Do you remain then, and await him here;
But I will hence, lest I should be espied,   155
And send your scout off to the ship again;
Then, if I deem that you are wasting time,
I will send this same fellow back once more,

Disguised like a sea-captain in costume,
That he may not be known; from whom, my son,   160
Gather, as he speaks in parables, whate'er
Has relevancy of his words. Meanwhile
I seek the vessel, and leave this to you;
May Hermes the Conductor* be our guide
In cunning, and the civic Victory,   165
Athena, who preserves me evermore. (*Exeunt* ODYSSEUS *and Attendant*)
                    (*Enter* CHORUS *of Scyrian Sailors*)
                              (*Strophe A*)
CHORUS What, O my master, what should I conceal—
    A stranger on strange soil—and what reveal,   170
        To ears of one inclined suspiciously?
        Tell me: for his art passes other art,
            And counsel other counsel, in whose hand
            Is Jove's Olympian sceptre of command.
        And now to thee   175
            Has come, O son, all this time-honoured sway;
        Wherefore declare what serviceable part
            Thou hast for me to play.
NEOPTOLEMUS Now, for perhaps it pleases you to pry
    In corners, for the spot where he may lie,   180
    Use your eyes with freedom; but whenever
        From these halls shall come a traveller grim,
    To my side step forward, and endeavour
        To afford me help to cope with him.
                              (*Antistrophe A*)   185
CHORUS Master, thou bidd'st me heed, as I did heed,
    To keep an eye on thy most urgent need;
    Now tell me in what sort of habitation,
        And in what quarter, he is wont to dwell;
        That I should know is not unseasonable,   190
        Lest he from somewhere unexpectedly
        Should light on me.
    What is his beat, or what his usual station?
        What errand may he now be going about,
            Within doors or without?   195
NEOPTOLEMUS Thou seest this abode, tunnelled quite through,
    Making a stony resting-place?
1ST SAILOR   And whither
    Has the poor habitant betaken himself?
NEOPTOLEMUS 'Tis plain to me that in his need of food   200
    He is gone gleaning through this neighbourhood.
        For they say it is his way of living,
            Game to shoot with arrows from his bow,

---

164 Hermes, the patron of guile.

                And with grief of sickness ever grieving
                    Still to find no healer for his woe.
                                        (*Strophe B*)   205

CHORUS   Him do I pity! For that he,
                Meeting no eye of sympathy,
                    With not a friend at hand to heed,
                Hapless, alone for evermore,   210
                Is stricken with a disease full sore,
                    Is driven by every passing need.
                How—oh how, thus desolate,
                Bears he up against his fate?
                Woe for the wiles poor mortals plan!   215
                Woe for the hapless tribes of man,
                Whose troubles overfill their vital span!
                                        (*Antistrophe B*)

                He, perchance of no less worth
                Than the men of elder birth,   220
                Destitute of all things good,
                Lies apart, in solitude;
                Harbouring with the shaggy bear,
                Or the pard with spotted hair;
                In disease, in want, forlorn,   225
                Cureless anguish he has borne;
                While Echo on the uplands high,
                Sounding afar, makes low reply,
                With insuppressive voice, to his bitter cry.

NEOPTOLEMUS   None of these things are marvellous to me;   230
        For from above, if I know anything,
        Those sufferings came upon him, by the hand
        Of the hard-hearted Chrysa*; and what now
        He bears of labours, far from comforters,
        Cannot but be by some God's providence,   235
        For that he should not, in assault of Troy,
        Draw to the head the unconquered bolts divine,*
        Before that hour shall come when, we are told,
        It is Troy's fate to be subdued by them.
                                        (*Strophe C*)   240

CHORUS   Hush, my son.
NEOPTOLEMUS   Why?
CHORUS   A sound rose clear
            As of the tramp of a wearied man,
        This way, or that; I hear—I hear   245
                A voice articulate, of one
            Pacing onward, as best he can;
                Yes, the hoarse tone

---

[233] Chryse, at whose temple Philoctetes received his grievous snake bite.
[237] "Divine" because Heracles had received them from Apollo.

That marks a soul worn down with pain,
    From afar I know; 250
For loud and plain
      That note of woe.

(Antistrophe C)

But, my son—

NEOPTOLEMUS   What? 255

CHORUS   Bethink thee anew;
   For the man is not far, but near,
Not, as a shepherd swain might do,
   Piping a tune of merry cheer,
But either, stumbling, he cries perforce 260
   With far-heard shout,
Or viewing the strange unwelcomed course
     Of a ship to ground;
   For he sends out
     A scaring sound. 265

(Enter PHILOCTETES)

PHILOCTETES   Ho strangers, who are you, who have put in
   With galley to this coast—sea without port,
   Shore without shelter? Of what land or race
   Am I to guess you? for your garments' guise 270
   Is Grecian—best beloved of all to me;
   And I would hear you speak. Be not struck dumb
   With terror at the wildness of my looks;
   But pitying an unhappy man—alone—
   Desolate thus and friendless in his wrongs, 275
   If you are come in friendship, speak to me.
   Give me some answer! 'Twere unnatural
   I should lack this from you, or you from me.

NEOPTOLEMUS   Sir stranger, know this first, we are of Greece;
   Since this you fain would learn. 280

PHILOCTETES   O sound most welcome!
   Ah what a thing it is to be addressed,
   After long years, by such a man as you!
   What need, my son, caused you to put in hither—
   To come this way? What impulse? Which of winds 285
   Most friendly? Say all this to me, aloud,
   That I may know your name.

NEOPTOLEMUS   I am by birth
   Of the isle of Scyros; I am sailing home;
   My name's Neoptolemus, Achilles' son; 290
   Now you know all.

PHILOCTETES   O son of sire most dear—
   Sprout from a friendly soil—the foster-child

Of ancient Lycomedes,* on what errand
Made you this land, from what port voyaging?
NEOPTOLEMUS   From Ilium, truly, am I steering now.
PHILOCTETES   How say you? for you did not sail, I know,
With us at first, when we set out for Troy.
NEOPTOLEMUS   Why, were you partner in that enterprise?
PHILOCTETES   O son, do you not know the man you look on?
NEOPTOLEMUS   How should I know a man I never saw?
PHILOCTETES   Nor did you ever hear my name, nor word
Of the afflictions that were killing me?
NEOPTOLEMUS   Nothing of what you ask me do I know
PHILOCTETES   O what a drudge and sport of Gods am I!
Of whose ill plight no whisper ever came
To my own home, or any coast of Greece,
But they who thrust me out unrighteously
Laugh and keep silence, while my sickness ever
Grows on me and increases more and more.
O boy! O son, calling Achilles sire,
I am the man who, may be, thou hast heard
Was master of the arms of Heracles,
The son of Poias, Philoctetes! whom
The Captains twain and the Cephallenite king*
Cast out thus shamefully—deserted—sick
Of a consuming wound—pierced through and through
By the destroying viper's venomous fangs;
And in this plight, boy, they exposed me here,
Left me, and went! when from the Chrysean coast
They put in hither with their navy, straight,
Soon as they saw me sleeping on the beach,
Tired with long tossing, in a sheltered cave,
They laughed, they went, they left me! casting me
A few mean rags, a beggar's garniture,
And some poor pittance, too, of nourishment,
Such as, I pray, be theirs! O then, my son,
What sort of waking, think you, from that sleep
Had I when they were gone! How did I weep,
How did I wail, for my calamities!
Seeing the ships which I was leader of
All gone away, and no man in the place
Who should suffice me, or should comfort me
In the disease of which I laboured; yea
Though I sought everywhere, nothing I found
Left to me, save my anguish; and, my son,
Of that no lack indeed! Hour after hour
Passed by me; and I must needs make shift alone,

294 Neoptolemus was brought up by Lycomedes, his maternal grandfather.
315 Agamemnon, Menelaus, and Odysseus.

Under this scanty shelter. For my food,
This quiver sought out what supplied my need,　　　　340
Hitting the doves on wing; then to the mark
Of the shot bolt I had to crawl, with pain,
Dragging a wounded foot. If upon this
I wanted to get anything to drink,
Or, as in winter when the hoar frost lay,　　　　345
To break some sticks to burn, this, creeping forth,
I had to manage, in my misery.
Then there would be no fire; but striking hard
With flint on flint I struck out painfully
An obscure spark, which keeps me still alive.　　　　350
Thus shelter overhead, not without fire,
Furnishes all, save healing of my sore.—
Come now and hear about the isle, my son;
No sailor willingly approaches it;
For anchorage there is not, or a port　　　　355
Whither a man might sail, and make his mart
By traffic, or find welcome; prudent men
Do not make voyage here. Some one, perhaps,
Might land against his will; for these things oft
Will happen in the long-drawn life of men;　　　　360
But such, my son, when they do come, in words
Pity me, and in compassion give me, say
Some morsel of food, or matter of attire;
But that thing no man, when I hint it, will do—
Take me safe home; but this tenth year already　　　　365
In hunger and distress I pine and perish,
Feeding the gnawing tooth of my disease.
The Atreidæ, and Odysseus' violence,
Have done me all this wrong; the like of which,
O boy, may the Olympian Gods give them　　　　370
One day to suffer, in revenge for me!
1ST SAILOR　　I feel I pity thee, O Poias' son,
As much as any of thy visitors.
NEOPTOLEMUS　And I myself, in witness to this tale,
Can swear 'tis true; for I have felt their malice—　　　　375
The Atreidæ—and Odysseus' violence.
PHILOCTETES　Have you a feud, too, with the villain sons
Of Atreus, and are furious, at your griefs?
NEOPTOLEMUS　I wish my hand could some day satisfy
The measure of my fury, that Mycenæ　　　　380
And Sparta, both, might know, how Scyros also
Is mother of stout hearts!
PHILOCTETES　　　　　　Well said, my son!
What do you charge them with? what is the cause
Of your deep anger? why have you come hither?　　　　385

NEOPTOLEMUS O son of Poias, I will tell you—yet
 I hardly shall know how—what injuries
 They did me when I came. After Fate brought
 Achilles to his end—

PHILOCTETES   O woe is me!   390
 Tell me no more, till I have learnt this first,
 If Peleus' son is dead?

NEOPTOLEMUS   Yes, he is dead;
 Killed by no man, but by a God; subdued
 By Phœbus, as they tell me; arrow-slain.   395

PHILOCTETES Well, noble was the slayer, and the slain.
 O son, I know not whether I shall first
 Explore your grievance, or lament for him.

NEOPTOLEMUS Poor soul, I should have thought your own enough
 For you to mourn, without your neighbours' troubles!   400

PHILOCTETES You have said right; therefore begin once more
 Your story of the way they injured you.

NEOPTOLEMUS There came for me, in a fine painted vessel,
 The great Odysseus, and the foster-sire
 Of my own father,* saying, (either in sooth   405
 Or, perhaps, feigning,) that is was forbidden
 Now that my sire had fallen, that any man
 Other than I should storm the towers of Troy.
 This tale propounding, in this sort, sir friend,
 They did not let me linger very long,   410
 Before I straight embarked; urged most of all
 By yearning for the dead, that I might see him
 Before they buried him; for I never saw him;
 And then the tale, no doubt, made for my honour,
 That I should take the Towers, if I went.   415
 Well, after two days' voyage I arrived
 At black Sigeum, with a gale astern;
 And forthwith in a circle all the host
 Hailed me as I stepped on shore; swearing they saw
 The dead Achilles come to life again.   420
 All the same, dead he lay; and I, poor fool,
 When I had mourned him, after no long space,
 Going to the Atreidæ, (friends, belike, of mine,)
 Claimed my sire's arms and other property.
 But they put forth—oh, a most pitiful tale!   425
 "O offspring of Achilles, all the rest
 That was your father's you may take, and welcome!
 But those arms own another master now,
 Laertes' son." I burst out weeping straight,

---

405 Phoenix, the son of the king of Argos, offended his father and fled to the court of Peleus, who showed
 him favor. In gratitude Phoenix took up the tuition of Peleus' son Achilles, whom he accompanied to
 Troy.

And stood up in deep wrath, and spake with anguish; 430
"You villain, did you dare to give my arms
Without my leave to any man but me?"
Then said Odysseus, who was standing by,
"Yea my son, rightly have they given them,
For, on a time, he owed his life to me." 435
I, in a rage, straightway belaboured them
With all sorts of abuse, sparing for nought,
If that man was to snatch my arms from me!
Who, being thus driven, although not choleric,
Cut to the heart at what he heard me say, 440
Retorted thus; "You were not with us! You
Were absent from your duty! and, since you come
To bluster, you shall never sail off with them
To Scyros!" After flouts and injuries
Of such a nature, I am steering home; 445
Spoiled by Odysseus, basest, and base-born,
Of what is mine. Still, him I do not blame
Like those in power. For a city all
Follows its leaders; a whole host, the same;
And men who are unruly become bad 450
By force of teaching.—All my tale is told.
May whosoever is the Atreidæ's foe
Be dear to Heaven, as he must be to me.

CHORUS (1)   O Mother, thou who gavest birth
 To Zeus himself! Silvan Earth, 455
  Who fillest all with bread;
    Who dost control
    The floods that roll
  Over Pactolus' golden bed;
On thee we cried, Mother adored, 460
When on this man was outpoured
  All the Atreidæ's pride;
    What time they gave
    Harness and glaive,
  His father's—setting him aside: 465
Immortal Queen, thee we invoked,
Who behind thy lions yoked,
  Slayers of the herd, dost ride!*
    There was won
    For Laertes' son 470
  Glory surpassing all beside.

PHILOCTETES   Strangers, you seem to have sailed here to me
With a clear passport, in your injuries
Not dissonant with mine; I recognize
The Atreidæ's doings, and Odysseus' hand. 475

468 Rhea, who is invoked here, was usually represented as riding in a chariot drawn by lions.

For I am certain he would have a voice
In every evil word and wickedness,
And that thereout he is not like to bring
Anything just to pass. I wonder, though,
Never at this—but that the greater Ajax,   480
If present, seeing it done, permitted it.

NEOPTOLEMUS   He was no more, my friend; had he been living,
I never should have been so plundered.

PHILOCTETES   How?
What did you say? Is he too dead and gone?   485

NEOPTOLEMUS   He walks no more on earth.

PHILOCTETES   O woe is me!
But not the son of Tydeus!* Not that son
Of Sisyphus, palmed on Laertes!* They
Will not have died! Pity they were ever born!   490

NEOPTOLEMUS   Not they, you may be certain; they are now
Flourishing right bravely in the Argive host.

PHILOCTETES   And what of him, old, valiant and my friend,
Nestor of Pylos? He was wont to avert
With wise advice the mischiefs of their doing.   495

NEOPTOLEMUS   Badly he fares, indeed; since he has lost
Antilochus, a son of his, by death.

PHILOCTETES   Alas! You tell me two calamities
In the same breath! of two, who least of any
I could have wished to hear were dead! Good lack,   500
What must we look to, when such men have perished,
The while Odysseus still survives, when he,   c
Instead of them, ought rather to have been
Reported slain!

NEOPTOLEMUS   A clever gamester he.   505
But, Philoctetes! even clever plans
Are sometimes foiled.

PHILOCTETES   Now tell me in Heaven's name,
Where did you leave Patroclus all this while,
Who was your father's darling?   510

NEOPTOLEMUS   He had died, too.
And, in short compass I may say to you—
War never slays a bad man in its course,
But the good always!

PHILOCTETES   I can bear you out.   515
And while we talk of it, I will enquire
After a man—unworthy indeed, but shrewd
And apt of speech—what is become of him.

NEOPTOLEMUS   Who but Odysseus is it whom you mean?

---

488 Diomed, the son of Tydeus, often worked closely with Odysseus.

489 This phrase refers to Odysseus. Anticlea, the wife of Sisyphus, was pregnant with Odysseus when she
married Laertes.

PHILOCTETES   I did not speak of him; but there was one 520
    Thersites, who was always trying to speak,
    By no means only once—where none would have him;
    Know you if he still lives?
NEOPTOLEMUS   I never saw him
    But I did hear that he is yet alive. 525
PHILOCTETES   He may well be so! Nothing ever died
    That was pernicious; but the Deities
    Foster it well; yea, they delight to turn
    All that is profligate and villainous
    Backward from Hades, while the good and just 530
    They speed on their way ever. In what light
    Must we regard these things? how praise them? when
    Praising things heavenly, I find faults in Heaven!
NEOPTOLEMUS   I, O thou son of an Œtæan sire,*
    Shall take good care henceforward to survey 535
    Ilium and the Atreidæ from afar;
    And where the mean are mightier than the brave,
    And goodness withers, and the coward bears rule,
    I never will approve such company;
    But rock-bound Scyros shall suffice for me 540
    Henceforward, and contentment with my home.
    Now to my ship I go; farewell to thee,
    Thou son of Poias; may you fare right well!
    And may the Powers restore you from disease
    According to your wish. Let us be going; 545
    That whensoever Heaven vouchsafes us means
    Of sailing, we may start.
PHILOCTETES   Already, son,
    Are you afoot?
NEOPTOLEMUS   Yes, we must time our voyage 550
    By watching from hard by, not out of sight.
PHILOCTETES   Now for your sire's, your mother's sake, O son,
    And any dear one's whom you have at home,
    Suppliant I beg, leave me not here alone,
    Abandoned to such evils as you see, 555
    And all you have heard I dwell in! Stow me, say
    For ballast! The discomfort well I know,
    Is much, of such a cargo; bear it, though!
    To noble natures shame is odious; while
    Kindness brings honour. And to you, my son, 560
    There were foul shame in leaving this undone;
    But in the doing the fullest meed of praise,
    Should I come living to the Œtæan land.
    Come now, the trouble will not last a day
    Venture it! Take me, throw me where you please, 565

534 Oeta was the mountainous country over which Poias ruled.

Into the hold, into the bows, the stern,
Wherever I shall plague my mates the least!
Consent, my son, yea by prayer-answering Jove!
Hearken, I beseech you at your knees—although
A hapless wretch, being lame; ah leave me not   570
Forsaken here, where is no trace of men!
But either take me safe to your own dwelling,
Or to Chalcodon's* homesteads, in Eubœa;
And thence to Œta, and Cape Trachis, and
Sperchius' fair stream will not be far to go.   575
So shall you bring me to my father's arms,
For whom 'tis long that I have been afraid
He has already died; for oftentimes
By those who have come did I send to him, with prayers
That he would send and fetch me safe again;   580
But either he is dead, or I suppose
My emissaries, as is natural,
Making small count of what was due to me,
Pushed on their voyage home. But now—for you
I come to as conductor, equally   585
And messenger yourself—pity me, and save me;
Seeing how on all sides danger lies in wait,
And 'tis by hazard that mortality
Fare well, or fare not well; and to his danger
A man should look, who is untouched by trouble,   590
And when he lives at ease then most of all
Watch, lest destruction take him unawares.
CHORUS (2)   Have compassion, O my chief!
He has told of many a grief,
   Many a painful care;   595
      Such load of woes
      May none of those
   Whom I cherish have to bear!
But if, sir king, thou hatest thus
The bitter sons of Atreus,   600
   Hear what my sentence is;
      Change the bane
      Into gain,
   Bane they meant, to gain of his;
To the home he longed for so,   605
Swiftly embarking, let us go;
   Our ship is tight and yare;
      Thus would I
      In safety fly
From the revenge the Gods prepare.   610
NEOPTOLEMUS   Take care you do not play at being kind

573 An ancient king of Euboea.

Now, but as soon as you are overwhelmed
By the proximity of his disease,
No longer seem the same, as you now promise.

1ST SAILOR   No fear of that. It is impossible   615
That you shall ever have this stone to cast,
With right, at me.

NEOPTOLEMUS   Well, it were shame indeed
That I should seem reluctant, more than you,
In labour for a stranger at his need.   620
Come then; if you think fit, let us set sail.
Let him start quickly; for the ship shall take him,
And none shall say him nay. Heaven only guide us
Safe from this land, thither, where we would go!

PHILOCTETES   O day most happy! O most welcome face!   625
O sailors dear! How shall I prove indeed
What debt of gratitude you lay on me!
Let us be going, my son; first taking leave
Of the unhomelike home that is within,
That you may learn what sort of life I lived,   630
And what stout heart I kept. For I suppose
No other beside me, seeing the sight
With his eyes, merely, would have borne it all;
While I was taught by long necessity
To be resigned to ills.   635

1ST SAILOR   Stay, let us listen;
Two persons, one a sailor from your ship,
And one a stranger, are approaching us;
Hear what they say before you go within.

        (*Enter* SCOUT *disguised as a trading captain, and Mate*)   640

SCOUT   Son of Achilles, this your shipmate, who
With other two kept guard over your vessel,
I bade inform me in what place you tarried,
Since I have crossed you, not intending it,
But by chance, somehow, having come to moor   645
At the same ground. Sailing as shipmaster
With a small convoy home from Ilium
To Peparethus, famed for grape-clusters,
When I had heard the sailors, one and all,
Were of the crew that had embarked with you,   650
I thought it better not to hold my peace,
Nor to make sail till I had spoken with you,
And been rewarded, as is fair. Perhaps
You have heard nothing of your own concerns—
The new designs the Argives have on you?   655
Nor mere designs, but deeds, now in the doing,
No longer loitered over.

NEOPTOLEMUS   Truly, sir,

The merit of your forethought must secure
My gratitude, if I am no churl born.   660
But tell me what you mean; that I may learn
What last new scheme you know of from the host.

SCOUT   Old Phœnix and the sons of Theseus
Are gone, with galleys, in pursuit of you.

NEOPTOLEMUS   To bring me back by parley, or perforce?   665

SCOUT   I know not. What I heard I come to tell you.

NEOPTOLEMUS   Is it for the Atreidæ Phœnix and his mates
Are taking this in hand so hastily?

SCOUT   Be sure 'tis doing, and that without delay.

NEOPTOLEMUS   How was it Odysseus was not prompt to sail,   670
As his own post, in this? Did some fear stay him?

SCOUT   He and the son of Tydeus were just starting
After another, when I put to sea.

NEOPTOLEMUS   Who could that be, for whom Odysseus' self
Would have embarked?   675

SCOUT   Well, he said—somebody;
But tell me first, who is this personage?
And do not speak out loud.

NEOPTOLEMUS   This, stranger, is
The famous Philoctetes!   680

SCOUT   Then don't ask me
Anything more, but with what speed you may
Take yourself off, out of this land, and sail.

PHILOCTETES   What says he, boy? Why does the shipman talk
Aside to you, making his trade of me?   685

NEOPTOLEMUS   I do not know as yet; what he would say
He must speak out to you, to these, and me.

SCOUT   Seed of Achilles, do not tell of me,
For saying what I ought not, to the host;
Many are the friendly acts they do to me,   690
And I to them, such as a poor man may.

NEOPTOLEMUS   I am the Atreidæ's enemy; and he,
Hating the Atreidæ, is my greatest friend.
If, as you say, you came to do me good,
No word you have heard must you conceal from us.   695

SCOUT   My son, mind what you are doing.

NEOPTOLEMUS   So I do.

SCOUT   I shall hold you accountable for this.

NEOPTOLEMUS   Do, but say on.

SCOUT   I will. The two you wot of,   700
The son of Tydeus and Odysseus, sail
To arrest this man; and they have sworn an oath
To bring him, either by persuading him
With oratory, or else by dint of force.
So all the Achaians heard Odysseus say   705

Openly; for he had full confidence,
More than the other, to accomplish it.

NEOPTOLEMUS And for what cause did the Atreidæ turn
After so long so vehemently to him
Whom all this while they had kept in banishment? ₇₁₀
What remorse touched them, or what Nemesis
And force of Gods who punish wickedness?

SCOUT All this, for you perhaps have heard it not,
I will explain. There was a high-born seer,
A son of Priam's, Helenus by name, ₇₁₅
Whom he we speak of, he we call—the knave—
By all disgraceful and vile epithets,
Odysseus—sallying forth by night, alone,
Captured, and bound; and brought him, and displayed
Amidst the Achaian ranks, a goodly prize! ₇₂₀
Who gave them oracles of all beside,
And that they never would be conquerers
Of Troia's towers, unless they could persuade
And bring this person from the island here
Where he dwells now. This when Laertes' son ₇₂₅
Heard the seer say, he undertook forthwith
To fetch the man to the Achaians' presence;
He rather thought, taking him willingly;
But if reluctant, then against his will;
Which if he failed of doing, he staked his head ₇₃₀
To be cut off by any man who pleased!
My son, you have heard all; my counsel is,
For you and him and any other man
For whom you have regard, to lose no time.

PHILOCTETES Me miserable! Did he, the utter pest, ₇₃₅
Swear to cajole and fetch me to the host?
I am as likely to come up to light,
When dead, from Hades, as his father did!*

SCOUT Of that I know not. Now to my ship I go.
To the best ends may Heaven attend you both! (*Exit*) ₇₄₀

PHILOCTETES Is it not monstrous that Laertes' son
Should ever hope, boy, with soft soothing words
To take me, and to show me from his vessel
To all the mob of Argives? He, than whom
I easier would hearken to the snake— ₇₄₅
The abhorred snake, which has thus made me lame!
But there is nothing which he will not say,
Nothing he dares not do! And now, I know
That he will come; well, my son, let us go;
So that a breadth of sea may sunder us ₇₅₀

---

⁷³⁸ Before his death Sisyphus instructed his wife to leave him unburied; then when he died, he obtained permission to return to earth to rebuke her impiety, in this way achieving a second term of life.

Far from Odysseus' vessel! Let us hence;
A timely haste is the right means to afford
Sleep and refreshment when our toil is past.

NEOPTOLEMUS   Were it not well, when the head-wind shall cease,
Then to set sail? for it is adverse now.   755

PHILOCTETES   Winds are fair always, when you fly from harm.

NEOPTOLEMUS   Nay but this gale is adverse to them also!

PHILOCTETES   No gale blows adversely to plunderers,
When robbery and rapine are in hand.

NEOPTOLEMUS   Well then, if you think fit, let us be off;   760
And take, out of your dwelling, anything
For which you have most use, and most desire.

PHILOCTETES   Some things I need, though from a scanty store.

NEOPTOLEMUS   What is there, which is not on board my vessel?

PHILOCTETES   A herb I have, with which I always lull   765
This ulcer best, and soothe the pain away.

NEOPTOLEMUS   Well, bring it forth. What would you take beside?

PHILOCTETES   If any of my arrows have been dropped
Unheeded, that I should not leave them here
For any man to gather.   770

NEOPTOLEMUS   What, are those
The famous bow and arrows in your hand?

PHILOCTETES   These and no other are they, which I carry.

NEOPTOLEMUS   May I look at them close, and handle them,
And do them worship, as a god?   775

PHILOCTETES   Both this,
My son, and anything besides of mine
Is at your service, which may profit you.

NEOPTOLEMUS   I have the longing; but no more than thus—
I would, an if I might; if not, no matter.   780

PHILOCTETES   Modestly spoken! Yes my son, that may you,
You who alone have given me to behold
This light of day—to see the Œtæan soil—
My aged sire—my friends! who set me up,
From underneath, over my enemies!   785
They shall be yours to touch and give me back
At pleasure; and to boast that, for your merit,
Alone of mortals you laid hand to them.
'Twas in return for kindness I first got them.

1ST SAILOR   To see you, and to have you for a friend,   790
Pleases me well; for he that knows the way
To return good for good, must be a friend
Better than all possessions.

NEOPTOLEMUS   Now go in.

PHILOCTETES   That will I, and take you with me; for my ailment   795
Craves to have you for an auxiliary.

(*Exeunt* PHILOCTETES *and* NEOPTOLEMUS)

CHORUS (*Strophe A*) I have heard the tale that was told—
    I did not behold—
      What by Cronos' invincible son*   800
        To Ixion was done,
    Who approached Jove's bed, whom he bound
      To a wheel whirled round;
  But I know of no other, by hearing or seeing, that is,
  No mortal, tied to a loathlier fate than his,   805
Who for no violent deed, or stain of fraud on his name,
But being as good as the good are, perishes here in shame.
    At this, too, I wonder,
      How, listening to the shock
    Of the surges' thunder   810
      About his lonely rock,
  Still, still he endured the continual cares and fears
      Of a life, all tears!

(*Antistrophe A*) Where none but himself to greet—
    No use of his feet—   815
    Nor any neighbour he found,
      Of the region round,
      In whose compassionate ears
        To bewail, with tears,
  His raw deep-festering sore—who might stay the flood, 820
  From wounds of his raging foot, of the fevered blood,
When a fit came on, with soothing herbs, the growth of the soil;
But hither and thither ever, hobbling along with toil,
    He would crawl, where healing
      Might be found for his journey's pain—   825
    Like an infant feeling
      For its nurse's arms in vain—
  Whensoever the soul-consuming Fury's force
      Had out-spent its course;
(*Strophe B*) Raising no seed   830
  Out of the hallowed lap of earth, for food;
    Nor aught beside of good,
  Such as the cunning spirit achieves of men;
    But only now and then
  What he might hit, with arrows from the string 835
      Sped on swift wing
    His appetite to feed.
  Poor soul, that never in a ten years' space

---

800 Zeus or Jove. When Ixion had been purified of his father-in-law's blood by Zeus, he ungratefully
attempted Hera's honor; for this offense Zeus bound him to a perpetually revolving wheel in Hades.

Revelled in one full draught of wine outpoured,
But ever had to journey with set face   840
    To any standing pool he had explored!

(*Antistrophe B*)   But met withal
Now by a child of warriors, his allies,
    He shall at length arise,
Happy, out of woes, and magnified by them.   845
    Who with sea-traversing stem,
The tale of many months being complete,
        Conducts his feet
    Back to his fathers' hall,
Where dwell the Meliad Nymphs—and to the banks   850
    Of Spherchius; where, with fire of Heaven all-bright,
The brazen-shielded Hero joins the ranks
    Of all the Gods, high o'er Mount Œta's height.*

————————————

(*Enter* NEOPTOLEMUS *and* PHILOCTETES)

NEOPTOLEMUS   Move forward, if you will. Why, without reason,   855
    Are you so silent? Why stand thus aghast?
PHILOCTETES   Eh, eh!
NEOPTOLEMUS   What is it?
PHILOCTETES   Nothing serious. On, my son.
NEOPTOLEMUS   Are you in pain, from your unhealed disease?   860
PHILOCTETES   No, not at all; I think 'tis better now.
    O Heavens!
NEOPTOLEMUS   Why do you groan, and call on Heaven?
PHILOCTETES   To come and save me, and be good to me.
    Eh, eh!   865
NEOPTOLEMUS   What is the matter? Won't you tell me?
    Must you be silent thus? You seem in pain.
PHILOCTETES   I am ruined, my son, and shall not have the power
    To hide my anguish from you. Well a day!
    It goes through me, it goes through me! Woe is me!   870
    I am ruined, my son; I am gnawed, my son. Alack,
    Alack the day! Alack, alack the day!
    For Heaven's sake, if you have a sword, my son,
    Ready to hand, smite me upon the foot,
    Cut it off quickly! Spare not for my life!   875
    Quick, boy!
NEOPTOLEMUS   What is it, thus suddenly begun,
    For which you moan so, and bewail yourself?
PHILOCTETES   You know, my son.
NEOPTOLEMUS   What is it?   880
PHILOCTETES   You know, boy!

[853] This passage alludes to the apotheosis of Heracles in Oeta.

NEOPTOLEMUS   What?
  I know not!

PHILOCTETES   How, you know not? Lack, alack-a-day!

NEOPTOLEMUS   Truly the stress is dreadful of your sickness.   885

PHILOCTETES   Yes, dreadful beyond utterance; pity me!

NEOPTOLEMUS   What must I do?

PHILOCTETES   Do not betray me, in terror;
  For it is come, after an interval,
  By winding ways; as it was gorged before,   890
  So now, it seems, the same.

NEOPTOLEMUS   Alas, poor wretch—
  Wretch that you seem, truly, for all your troubles!
  Would you I should touch you, and take hold of you?

PHILOCTETES   Not that, by any means; but take this bow,   895
  As you were asking me but now, and keep
  And guard it, till this spasm of my disease,
  Now present, slackens. For sleep seizes me
  After this agony has run its course;
  It cannot end before; but you must leave me   900
  To sleep in quiet. And if in the meanwhile
  Those men arrive, I charge you in Heaven's name,
  That neither freely nor against your will,
  Nor any how, you suffer them to get it;
  Lest you become the slayer of your own self,   905
  And of me too, who am your supplicant.

NEOPTOLEMUS   Take heart; so far as foresight can ensure,
  It shall not pass, save to your hands and mine.
  Hand it to me, and luck go with it!

PHILOCTETES (*Giving the bow and arrows*)   Here,   910
  Take it, my son; but adore, first, the Power
  Whose name is Jealousy; so may it prove
  To thee not baneful, as it was to me
  And him who was its owner ere my time.

NEOPTOLEMUS   Heaven grant it so to us! and grant us, too,   915
  A favourable and swift passage thither,
  Where God ordains, and whither we are bound.

PHILOCTETES   Ah but I fear, my son, your prayers are vain;
  For here again are welling drops of blood,
  Red from the wound, and I expect some change.   920
  Alack, fie on it! Alack again, my foot,
  What evil you will work me! It grows upon me;
  It comes on close. O wretched that I am!
  You know the worst; pray do not go away!
  O well-a-day!   925
  Thou man of Cephallenia,* would this pang
  Could grip thy breast, right through thee! Fie, alack!

926 Odysseus.

Alack once more! O you two generals,
Agamemnon and Menelaus, would that you
Might have this plague to bear, instead of me,   930
As long a time as I! O me, woe's me!
O Death, kind Death, how is it that always called,
Thus, every day, thou canst not ever come?
O youth, good youth, good now, take hold of me,
And burn me in that thrice welcome Lemnian flame,*   935
As on a time unto Jove's offspring I,
Earning those weapons, which you carry now,
Thought it no sin to do! What say you, son?
What do you say?
Why are you silent? What are you about?   940

NEOPTOLEMUS   Why, I was sighing with grief, at your distress.

PHILOCTETES   Nay my son, all the same, do not lose courage;
For it comes sharply, and goes away with speed.
Only I entreat, do not abandon me!

NEOPTOLEMUS   Fear not, we will remain.   945

PHILOCTETES   Will you remain?

NEOPTOLEMUS   Be assured I will.

PHILOCTETES   I do not think it meet
To put you on your oath, my son.

NEOPTOLEMUS   Why no;   950
Since I may not arrive without you!

PHILOCTETES   Reach
Your hand, for pledge.

NEOPTOLEMUS   I pledge it, to remain.

PHILOCTETES   Yonder now, yonder—   955

NEOPTOLEMUS   Whither say you?

PHILOCTETES   Above—

NEOPTOLEMUS   What do you rave of now? Why do you stare
At the orb above us?

PHILOCTETES   Let me, let me go.   960

NEOPTOLEMUS   Let you go—whither?

PHILOCTETES   Let me be awhile.

NEOPTOLEMUS   Leave hold I will not.

PHILOCTETES   You will kill me, if
You touch me!   965

NEOPTOLEMUS   I quit hold then, if indeed
You are more sober now.

PHILOCTETES   Take me, O Earth,
Dying, as I am! for my infirmity
No longer lets me keep myself upright. (*Throws himself on the ground*)   970

NEOPTOLEMUS   It seems he will be fast asleep, ere long;
For see, his head sinks backward. How the sweat
Stands over all his frame! and a black vein

935 The volcano on Mount Moschylus on Lemnos.

Has opened on the surface of his foot,
Discharging blood. Well, let us leave him, friends,
In quietness, till he has fallen asleep.

CHORUS   Sleep, thou that know'st not pain,
      That know'st not care,
  Blest and twice blest again,
      Come, with soft air!
  Keep from his eyes this light,
  Which overspreads our sight
  Now, of the noonday bright;
      Come, saviour fair!

1ST SAILOR   Look, my son; where standest thou?
      How wilt thou proceed?
  What shall be thy study now?
      Dost thou see, and heed?
  Wherefore are we lingering?
  Time, that orders everything,
  To our very feet doth bring
      Power for all our need.

NEOPTOLEMUS   He hears no sound, indeed; but this is plain,
  For us to have his weapons is no gain,
      Sailing without himself. Him God bade bring;
  His is the garland; and to boast in vain,
      And lie, and fail, is a disgraceful thing.

CHORUS   God will provide a way;
      But as for thee,
  Low, low, my son, convey
      Thy words to me;
  For of all souls that weep,
  Stricken with sickness deep,
  Their sleep, which is not sleep,
      Is quick to see.

2D SAILOR   Now, so far as thou hast power,
      Stealthily, my son,
  This examine, this explore,
      How it shall be done:
  For—thou knowest whom I would name—
  If your counsels are the same,
  There await you bale and blame
      Your prudence cannot shun.

CHORUS   The breeze blows fair, the breeze blows fair, my King;
      And without help, and without sight,
      Stretched out he lies, as in the night,
      (Sleep is good in the warm sun-light.)
  Powerless of hand and foot and everything!
  He sees not, looks not, answers not with speech.
      More than the dead who are beneath at rest;

975

980

985

990

995

1000

1005

1010

1015

1020

My son, so far as my poor thoughts can reach,
    The toil that has no risk is best.
NEOPTOLEMUS Peace, I say, and be careful; for the man
  Opens his eyes, and raises up his head.
PHILOCTETES O daylight, that receivest me from sleep!   1025
  O sojourn unexpected of these strangers!
  I never could have boasted, O my son,
  That you would bear to abide my sufferings,
  With such compassion tarrying at my side
  To afford help. Not so complacently   1030
  Did the Atreidæ, our brave generals,
  Bear to endure this plague! but, son of mine,
  For noble is your nature and your birth,
  You, though oppressed with noise and noisomeness,
  Made light of all these ills! And now, my son,   1035
  Since of my torment there does seem to be
  Some respite, some oblivion, raise me up
  With your own hand; set me upon my feet;
  So that, as soon as numbness gives me leave,
  We may proceed on board, and straightway sail.   1040
NEOPTOLEMUS I am right glad to see you beyond hope
  Awake and still alive and without pain;
  For you did seem, being so far gone already,
  To all appearance, a dead man. But now
  Raise yourself; or if you prefer it, these   1045
  Shall carry you; for they will not grudge the trouble,
  When you and I both choose to have it so.
PHILOCTETES I thank you, son; raise me, as you are minded;
  But let these be, lest they be overcome,
  Before they need, with noisomeness. Enough   1050
  The task for them, to live with me on board.
NEOPTOLEMUS So be it. But stand upright and take fast hold.
PHILOCTETES Fear not. The old exercise will straighten me.
NEOPTOLEMUS Alack! What next, in the world, am I to do?
PHILOCTETES What is it, boy? what were you going to say?   1055
NEOPTOLEMUS I do not know what way I ought to turn
  My perplexed speech.
PHILOCTETES   But what perplexes you?
  Do not talk thus, my son!
NEOPTOLEMUS   Only already   1060
  I have gone too far to help it.
PHILOCTETES   It is not
  The offence of my disease induces you
  Now to refuse to take me in your crew?
NEOPTOLEMUS All is offence, when any man forsakes   1065
  His proper self, to do what fits him not,

PHILOCTETES   But you, in aiding a good man, do nothing,
  Say nothing, to bely your parentage.
NEOPTOLEMUS   I shall be shamed. That is what tortures me.
PHILOCTETES   Never, by what you are doing! What you say   1070
  Causes me fear.
NEOPTOLEMUS   O Heavens, what shall I do?
  Must I be proved twice base, both hiding that
  I should not hide, and saying what is most shameful?
PHILOCTETES   If I am not a fool, this fellow seems   1075
  Like to betray me, leave me, and so set sail!
NEOPTOLEMUS   Leave you? Oh no! Rather what tortures me
  Is that I am conveying you, to your sorrow!
PHILOCTETES   What say you, son? I do not understand.
NEOPTOLEMUS   I will hide nothing from you; 'tis to Troy   1080
  You are to sail, to the Achaians, and
  The Atreidæ's fleet.
PHILOCTETES   Woe's me! what did you say?
NEOPTOLEMUS   Do not cry out, before you are informed—
PHILOCTETES   Informed! of what? What would you do to me?   1085
NEOPTOLEMUS   First cure you of this disease, and afterwards,
  Along with you, when I get there, storm Troy!
PHILOCTETES   And do you really mean to do it?
NEOPTOLEMUS   'Tis ruled
  By strong Necessity; pray, be not angry!   1090
PHILOCTETES   I am undone, unhappy! I am betrayed!
  O stranger-guest, what hast thou done to me?—
  Give back my bow at once!
NEOPTOLEMUS   That cannot be;
  For duty and advantage both oblige me   1095
  To obey those in power.
PHILOCTETES   O thou fire!
  Thou universal horror! Masterpiece
  Abominable, of monstrous villainy!
  What hast thou done to me? How hast thou cheated me!   1100
  Art not ashamed, O rogue, to look at me
  Thy supplicant, me thy petitioner?
  Thou hast robbed me of my life, taking my bow.
  Give it back, I beg thee! Give it back, I pray!
  By our father's gods, son, do not take my life!   1105
  Woe's me! he does not even answer me!
  He means to keep it—see, he turns away!
  You bays, you promontories, O you haunts
  Of mountain brutes, O cliffs precipitous,
  To you—for other hearers have I none—   1110
  Present, my old familiars, I appeal;
  See how Achilles' son is wronging me!

Swearing to take me home, to Troy he drags me;
And pledging his right hand, he has obtained—
Relic of Jove-born Heracles—my bow, 1115
Meaning in the Argives' sight to flourish it;
Like some strong prisoner, by force he drags me,
And knows not he is killing a dead man,
A vapour's shadow, an unsubstantial shade!
For in full strength he never had captured me, 1120
Since even thus he had not, save by guile;
But now, unhappy, I have been deceived.
What must I do? Nay, give it back to me;
Nay, even yet, be thy true self once more;
What say'st thou? Thou art dumb! I am lost, unhappy! 1125
O double-portalled frontal of the rock,
Back, once again, I come and enter thee,
Bare, without means of life; but I shall starve
Here, in the fields alone; not killing now
Winged bird, or silvan quarry, with my bow, 1130
But I myself, wretched, when I am dead,
Yielding a meal to things on which I fed.
Creatures I chased before will now chase me;
And I shall pay for bloodshed with my blood,
By practice of a seeming innocent! 1135
O may'st thou perish!—not yet, until I know
Whether thou wilt repent, and change thy purpose;
But if thou wilt not, evil be thine end!

(*Enter* ODYSSEUS, *behind*)

1ST SAILOR   What shall we do? For us to embark, sir king, 1140
Or yield to this man's prayers, now lies with you.

NEOPTOLEMUS   A strange compassion has come over me,
Not now at first, but some time since, for him.

PHILOCTETES   Pity me, O boy, for Heaven's sake! Publish not
Your own shame to the world, in cheating me! 1145

NEOPTOLEMUS   O what am I to do? Would I had never
Left Scyros! These things are so hard for me.

PHILOCTETES   You are not vile; but you have come, 'tis plain,
Primed with disgraceful teaching, from the vile.
Now take to other leaders, as is meet, 1150
And give me up my weapons, and set sail.

NEOPTOLEMUS   O men, what shall we do?

ODYSSEUS (*Advancing*)   What are you doing?
You wicked knave! Come back! Give me that bow!

PHILOCTETES   O who is this? Odysseus do I hear? 1155

ODYSSEUS   Yes, to be sure, Odysseus; I am here.

PHILOCTETES   O, I am bought and sold! I am undone!
Then it was he who was my kidnapper,
Who robbed me of my weapons!

ODYSSEUS　　　　　　　　　　Doubtless, I; 　　　　　1160
None else; that I avow.

PHILOCTETES　　　　　　Give back my bow,
Give it me, boy!

ODYSSEUS　　　　That shall he never do,
Even if he would. Now, you must march with these, 　　1165
Or they shall force you.

PHILOCTETES　　　　　　They—by force—take me,
O vilest and most impudent of men!

ODYSSEUS　　If you will not go freely.

PHILOCTETES　　　　　　　　O thou soil 　　　1170
Of Lemnos! O thou all-subduing flame
Lit by Hephaistus! Is it to be borne,
That he should force me from your borders?

ODYSSEUS　　　　　　　　　　Zeus
It is, if you would know—Zeus, this land's master— 　　1175
Zeus, who has willed these things. His servant I.

PHILOCTETES　　Caitiff, what words dost thou devise to say?
Alleging Gods, thou makest thy gods liars!

ODYSSEUS　　Not so, but faithful. You are bound to go.

PHILOCTETES　　No. 　　　　　　　　　　1180

ODYSSEUS　　　　Yes, I say; you must obey me, here.

PHILOCTETES　　Me miserable! my father, it appears,
Gat me no freeman, but a bond-slave!

ODYSSEUS　　　　　　　　　　Nay,
Peer of the best, with whom it is your fate 　　　1185
To storm Troy's walls, and to demolish them.

PHILOCTETES　　No ever, even in extremity,
While this firm steep of earth remains to me.

ODYSSEUS　　What would you?

PHILOCTETES　　　　　　Leap head-foremost off the rock, 　1190
From the top to the bottom, and dash out my brains!

ODYSSEUS　　Seize him! don't let him do it. (PHILOCTETES *is seized*)

PHILOCTETES　　　　　　O you hands,
How are you abused, for lack of your old string,
Made prisoners by this fellow! Thou, whose thoughts 　1195
Are nowise wholesome, nowise generous,
How hast thou supplanted me! How hast thou stalked me!
Employing as a cover for thyself
This youth, unknown to me, unmeet for thee,
But meet, indeed, for me; who nothing knew, 　　1200
Save to perform what was commanded him,
And even now feels manifest remorse
At his own errors, and my sufferings.
But thy base soul, peering through crannies ever,
Well, although simple and without his will, 　　1205
Instructed him in evil, to be wise.

And now thou think'st to bind and carry me,
Wretch! from this beach, on which thou didst expose me
Friendless, forsaken, homeless, a dead corpse
Among the living. Ah, perdition on thee! 1210
Not seldom have I prayed that prayer for thee.
But—for the Gods allot me no good fortune—
Thou livest to rejoice, and I to grieve
At this same thing, that amid many ills
I live, unhappy, laughed to scorn by thee, 1215
And the two captains, sons of Atreus,
Of whom, in this, thou art the minister.
Yet thou through trickery and by force constrained
Did'st sail with them*; while I, thrice miserable,
Who volunteered, and brought seven ships with me, 1220
Dishonoured am cast out—by them, thou sayest—
They say by thee! And now, why do you hale me?
Why carry me away? To what end? Me,
Who nothing am, and am long dead, to you?
Abhorred of Heaven! How is it I am not now 1225
Lame, and of evil savour? If I sail with you,
How will you manage to burn sacrifice
And pour libations any more to Heaven?
It was your pretext, in extruding me.
Perdition overwhelm you! As it will, 1230
If Gods love justice, for your wrongs to me.
And I am sure they do; for never else
Would you have sailed after a beggar thus;
But some remorse on my account, from Heaven,
Goaded you on. But O my native land, 1235
And you, regarding Gods! sooner or late,
If you have any pity left for me,
Grant vengeance, vengeance, vengeance on them all!
Miserable indeed I am; but I should feel
Cured of my plague, if I could see their fall! 1240

1ST SAILOR   Odysseus, sorely angered is the man;
And sore the word which he has uttered here,
And unsubmissive to adversity.

ODYSSEUS   I might say much in answer, had I time;
Now, I am master of one thing to say: 1245
Where such-an-one is needed, such am I!
Where there is trial who is just, who brave,
You will not find a man more scrupulous.
No doubt, by nature I am covetous
Of success everywhere; but not with you; 1250
Now, willingly, I will give place to you;

1219 Odysseus had attempted to evade the war by pretending madness; but when he was detected in the
ruse by Palamedes, he was forced to go.

Yes, let him go; do not keep hold of him;
Let him stay here. We have no use for you,
Now we have got these arms; for we have Teucer*
Among us, who has learnt this mystery   1255
And I, too, think that I can draw the string
And point the arrow just as well as you.
What need of you, then? To your heart's content
Pace Lemnos up and down! But let us go;
And your reward, it may be, shall confer   1260
Honour on me, which was by rights your own.

PHILOCTETES   What shall I do? Alas, shall you be seen
Graced with my arms among the Argives?
ODYSSEUS   Nay,
Make me no answer; I am going, I say.   1265
PHILOCTETES   Seed of Achilles, will you go away
Thus? Shall I never hear your accents more?
ODYSSEUS   Go forward. Though you be magnanimous,
Regard him not, lest you should spoil our luck.
PHILOCTETES   O sirs, shall I be left here desolate   1270
By you as well? Will not you pity me?
1ST SAILOR   Our captain is this youth; all that he tells you,
That we say also.
NEOPTOLEMUS   By Odysseus here
I shall be told that I am pitiful;   1275
Nevertheless, if this man wishes it,
Until the crew have got the ship's gear ready,
And we have offered up our prayers to Heaven,
Tarry; meantime, perhaps he may take thought
More kindly on us. Now let us twain set forward;   1280
Do you make haste to follow, when we call.
            (*Exeunt* ODYSSEUS *and* NEOPTOLEMUS)
                        (*Strophe A*)
PHILOCTETES   Thou nook of the rock—thou cave,
            Now sultry, now icy chill,
        Was it fated never to be   1285
        That I might depart from thee?
            Must thou hold to me still
        In dying, and be my grave?
        Say, O thou dolorous lair
        That rang to my despair,   1290
            Where now shall I seek for store?
            How get my daily bread?
            Ye flutterers overhead,
        Fly on, through whistling air!   1295
        I stay you now no more.
CHORUS   Surely thyself, thyself would have it so,

1254 The greatest archer among the Greeks.

O victim of the curse!
Not from without, not from a stronger foe
    Does this mischance arise,
When, having it in thy power to be wise,
Thou turnest from the better lot to what is worse!
                    (*Antistrophe A*)

PHILOCTETES   Ah wretched—wretched indeed,
        Toilworn and pitiful I,
    Who henceforth tarrying here,
    Without one comrade near,
        Must live on ever, and die!
    Bringing home no game at need,
    None, on wings of the bow,
    By mastering hands laid low;
        But a tale of cunning design,
            Close hidden, unscanned by me,
            Beguiled me! O might I see
    That trickster doomed to a woe
        As long, as cruel as mine!

CHORUS   Destiny, destiny brought thee to this end,
        Sent by the powers divine;
    Thou wert defrauded by no hand of mine;
        Keep thou for others, friend,
    Thy bitter boding curse; for as for me,
This is my care, that thou repel not amity.
                    (*Strophe B*)

PHILOCTETES   Somewhere now, seated by the sea
        Upon the foam-white strand,
    He mocks at me—Ah woe is me!
        And tosses in his hand
    What no man ever took away—
    What gave me meat from day to day.

    O bow of mine, from hands of mine
        Ravished—how pityingly,
    Surely, thou must thy gaze incline—
        If thou hast sense—toward me,
    The friend of Heracles of yore,
    Me, that may use thee now no more!

    Now thou art handled in my place
        By a right cunning lord,
    And viewest his deceits how base,
        And him, the foe abhorred,
    By whose unworthy arts arose
    For me—O Zeus! a thousand woes.

CHORUS   He acts a manly part

Who justifies whatever makes for gain,
   And, while so doing, yet refrains to dart
A tongue of malice forth, to inflict pain.   1345
Chosen out of many for the task, that king,
     In following the behest
Of those who sent him, was accomplishing
     Succour for all the rest.
                       (*Antistrophe B*)   1350
PHILOCTETES   Come hither you wild feathered brood,
       And tribes of fierce-eyed beasts,
   Who on these mountains seek your food,
       Whom this lone island feasts;
   No longer from your lairs take flight;   1355
   I wield no more those shafts of might.

   Alas for my unhappy lot!
      No longer need you fear;
   Weak is the watch that guards this spot;
      Now is your time! Draw near,   1360
   Avenge you, glut you, freely dine
   On this infected flesh of mine!

   My breath of life is well nigh spent;
      Whence shall I get me bread?
   What mortal can find nourishment   1365
      Merely by breezes fed,
   Of nothing, henceforth, making spoil
   In all the foison of the soil?
CHORUS   If thou at all hold dear
   The friendly stranger, who in all good will   1370
     Draws near to thee, prythee do thou draw near;
   Learn, and learn well, 'tis not beyond thy skill
   To turn thy back upon this destiny,
      So piteous to sustain,
   So checkless of the manifold misery   1375
      That follows in its train.
                     (*Strophe C*)
PHILOCTETES   Again, again
   Thou dost remind me of mine ancient pain,
     O best of all who have been here as yet!
      Ah, why would'st thou undo me?   1380
      Oh what hast thou done to me?
1ST SAILOR   Why say'st thou this?
PHILOCTETES   Because thy hopes are set
   On carrying me to that same Trojan land   1385
   Which I detest!
1ST SAILOR   Yea, for I think that best,

PHILOCTETES   Begone at once! Leave me behind!

1ST SAILOR   Welcome, right welcome to me is this command,
    Which I right gladly obey.   1390
    Away, away,
    Let us aboard, each to his place assigned.

PHILOCTETES   For God's sake, I adjure you, leave me not!
    Nay I beseech you!

1ST SAILOR   Soft!   1395

PHILOCTETES   O strangers, stay,
    In Heaven's name!

1ST SAILOR   What
    Criest thou?

PHILOCTETES   Alas, destiny, destiny!   1400
    O foot, my foot, what shall I do with thee
    In all my after life? O woe is me!
    O strangers, come, come back, come back again!

1ST SAILOR   What, to do something different
    From that thou didst set forth as thine intent   1405

PHILOCTETES   Let it not give offence
    That reeling under a tempestuous pain
    I cry aloud, words without sense!

                        (*Strophe D*)

1ST SAILOR   Come, poor sufferer, as we counsel thee.   1410

PHILOCTETES   Never, never, know it for certainty!
        Not though he, whose hand
        Wields the lightning brand,
        With its meteor rays
        Should set me all ablaze!   1415
        Down with Troy—with all
        Those beneath its wall—
        All who had the heart
        To banish far apart
        This limb—this foot of mine!   1420
        But O my friends, incline
        One boon to accord, I pray!

1ST SAILOR   What would'st thou really say?

PHILOCTETES   Reach me, if you have it, here
        A sword, an axe, or spear.   1425

1ST SAILOR   So you may do—what violent deed, I wonder?

PHILOCTETES   Cut flesh from bone—hew joint from joint asunder!
        Death—death is my desire.

1ST SAILOR   How so?

PHILOCTETES   Seeking my sire.   1430

1ST SAILOR   Where, on earth?

PHILOCTETES   In the Grave.
        For now no more, I know,
        Lives he beneath the sun.—

> O city, O native city,
> Might I but see thee, I, the man they pity,
> Who left thy sacred wave,
> And went as aider to the Danaan foe!*
> —My days are done. (*Retires*)

1ST SAILOR By this you would have seen me, some time since,
Marching to join my ship, but that I marked
Odysseus coming, and Achilles' son
Drawing nigh toward us.

(*Enter* ODYSSEUS *and* NEOPTOLEMUS)

ODYSSEUS   Will you not declare
Upon what errand you are creeping back,
Hastening so eagerly?

NEOPTOLEMUS   Yes, to undo
The wrong I did before.

ODYSSEUS   Monstrous! What wrong?

NEOPTOLEMUS That at your word and the whole host's—

ODYSSEUS   You did
A deed—of what kind, unbecoming you?

NEOPTOLEMUS Catching a man by shameful frauds and tricks—

ODYSSEUS What man? O Heavens! have you some new design—

NEOPTOLEMUS No, nothing new; to Poias' offspring, though—

ODYSSEUS What will you do? Truly I am afraid—

NEOPTOLEMUS From whom I had these weapons, back once more—

ODYSSEUS O Zeus, what will you say? You do not mean,
Surely, to yield them?

NEOPTOLEMUS   Yes, for shamefully
And against justice I gat hold of them.

ODYSSEUS 'Fore Heaven, do you say this to outrage me?

NEOPTOLEMUS If to speak truth is outrage?

ODYSSEUS   What is this,
Achilles' son? What have you said?

NEOPTOLEMUS   Desire you
I should repeat the same words twice and thrice?

ODYSSEUS I should have wished to hear them not at all!

NEOPTOLEMUS Be well assured, you have heard me out.

ODYSSEUS   There is—
There is a man to stop your doing so.

NEOPTOLEMUS   What!
Who is there who will stop my doing it?

ODYSSEUS The whole Achaian people, I for one.

NEOPTOLEMUS Wise as you are, you utter nothing wise.

ODYSSEUS You neither say nor seek to do things wise.

NEOPTOLEMUS If acts are just, they are better than if wise.

[1438] Danaus was a legendary king of Argos; thus "Danaan" means Greek.

ODYSSEUS   How just—what by my counsels you obtained,
That to surrender back?

NEOPTOLEMUS   The sin I sinned
To my own shame, I will essay to mend.

ODYSSEUS   And in so doing not fear the Achaian host?

NEOPTOLEMUS   Being in the right, I quail not at your menace.
It is no force of yours which I obey,
Thus acting.

ODYSSEUS   Not the Trojans, then, but you
Will I assail in fight!

NEOPTOLEMUS   Come what come may!

ODYSSEUS   See you this right hand feeling for the hilt?

NEOPTOLEMUS   Ay? You will find me playing at that same game,
And ready, too!

ODYSSEUS   Nay, I will let you be.
Rather I will depart and tell the tale
To the whole army, which shall punish you. (*Retires*)

NEOPTOLEMUS   You are discreet; and if you prove as wise
Always, perhaps you will escape scot-free.
Thou son of Poias, Philoctetes! Ho!
Come out, and leave this rock-built tenement!

PHILOCTETES (*Within*)   What new alarm is thundering at my cave?
What would you, sirs? Why do you call me forth?
(*Entering*) Ha, 'tis ill done! Are you not come to add
Some heavy suffering to my sufferings?

NEOPTOLEMUS   Nay,
Fear nothing; hear the words I am come to say.

PHILOCTETES   I am afraid; I trusted you before,
And through fair words fared foully.

NEOPTOLEMUS   Is it not
Within the bounds, that one may turn again?

PHILOCTETES   Just such you were when you purloined my weapons,
In language honest, secretly my bane.

NEOPTOLEMUS   But not so now. Still, I would hear from you
Whether you are minded to persist in staying,
Or to set sail with us.

PHILOCTETES   Stop, say no more;
For all that you can say will be in vain.

NEOPTOLEMUS   So resolved are you?

PHILOCTETES   As I say, and more so.

NEOPTOLEMUS   I wish you would have hearkened to my words;
But if I am not speaking seasonably,
I have done.

PHILOCTETES   Yes, all you say will be in vain;
For you shall never find me favourable,
Who have by guile robbed me of my livelihood,
And after, come to give advice to me—

Offspring most vile, of a most worthy sire!
Destruction seize you all! the Atreidæ first,
Next Laertes' son, and you!

NEOPTOLEMUS   Curse us no further;
But come and take your weapons from my hand.   1530

PHILOCTETES   What? Am I being beguiled a second time?

NEOPTOLEMUS   The holy majesty of Jove most high
Bear witness—no!

PHILOCTETES   O sayer of sweetest things—
If you speak truth!   1535

NEOPTOLEMUS (*Giving the bow and arrows*)   The deed shall testify.
Stretch out your hand, and repossess your weapons.

ODYSSEUS (*Advancing*)   In the Atreidæ's name, and the whole host's,
That I forbid! Be the Gods witnesses!

PHILOCTETES   Whose voice—was it Odysseus—that I heard,   1540
My son?

ODYSSEUS   Doubt it not! and you see me ready
To pack you off, by force, to Troia's shores,
Whether Achilles' son consents, or no.

PHILOCTETES   At your cost be it, unless this dart go wrong!   1545

NEOPTOLEMUS   Nay, by no means! For Heaven's sake do not shoot!

PHILOCTETES   Let go my hand, dear boy, for Heaven's sake!

NEOPTOLEMUS   No,
I will not. (*Exit* ODYSSEUS)

PHILOCTETES   Oh, why did you frustrate me   1550
In slaying an adversary and enemy
With my own shafts?

NEOPTOLEMUS   Because 'twere honourable
Neither for you nor me.

PHILOCTETES   Of this, at least,   1555
Be certain; that the army's foremost men,
The falsehood-mongers of the Achaian host,
Are brave in words, but cowards at the steel!

NEOPTOLEMUS   So be it. You have your bow, and need not, now,
Feel indignation or despite at me.   1560

PHILOCTETES   Yes, you have shown the nature, O my child,
From which you sprang; no son of Sisyphus,
But of Achilles, who was praised the most
Among the living, when he was alive,
And is, among the dead.   1565

NEOPTOLEMUS   It pleases me
That you should praise my father, and myself;
Still, hear what I would have you do for me;
There is necessity for men to endure
The fortunes given from Heaven; but whosoe'er   1570
Lies under voluntary miseries,
As you do, it is right that none on such

Should bestow pardon, or should pity them.
But you are savage, and reject advice,
If a man warn you kindly; deeming him,   1575
For very hate, an adversary and foe.
Yet I will speak, yea, and by Zeus I swear it;
And know this well, and write it on your heart;
I tell you, you are sick of this disease
By Heaven's decree, for coming near the guard   1580
Who watches over the hypæthral close
Of Chrysa—the concealed snake-sentinel;*
And you shall never find a cure, be certain,
Of your sore malady, while the same sun
Rises on this side and on that goes down,   1585
Till of your own will you shall come to Troy,
And meet Asclepius' sons*, who are in our ranks,
And so be lightened of your plague, and then
With these your arrows, and with me to aid,
Conquer the city's towers before them all!   1590
How do I know all this? Why, I will tell you;
There is a man of Troy prisoner to us,
Helenus, a seer of seers; and he says plainly
That these things so must be; and furthermore
That it is doomed, by the next harvest-time,   1595
All Troy should fall; else, if he lie in this,
He is willing to pay forfeit by his death.
Now you know all, choose to agree with us!
For honourable is the accruing gain,
If you, being singled out for the Greeks' champion,   1600
Should come to healing hands, and therewithal,
Win glory in the highest, by taking Troy,
That city of many woes!

PHILOCTETES   Detested life!
Why dost thou hold me above ground, yet seeing,—   1605
O why not let me go, down to the grave?
Alas, what shall I do? How can I be
Deaf to his words, my friendly counsellor?
Am I to yield, then? How, an if I do,
Shall I go forth—wretch—in the face of day?   1610
With whom shall I consort? How, O you eyes,
The witnesses of all things done to me,
Will you endure my having fellowship
With Atreus' offspring, who destroyed me? How
With the pernicious son of Laertes?   1615
For it is not the pain of what is past

1582 The serpent placed as guard in the roofless treasure room in the temple of Athena Chrysa; a frequent
   practice.
1587 Asclepius was the god of medical art.

That galls me; but I fancy I foresee
What at their hands I needs must yet endure.
For those who have begotten evil deeds
Of their own minds, are by their own minds trained 1620
In all things else to evil. And in this
I am surprised at you; for it was right
That you should never go to Troy, yourself,
Nay, should keep me away; and, for the men
Who wronged you, spoiling you of your father's treasure, 1625
Who judged the hapless Ajax* not so worthy
Of your sire's weapons, as Odysseus—what!
Will you join league with them, and force me to it?
Not so my son! but as you sware to me,
Carry me home; stay you in Scyros; leave 1630
Wretches like them to perish wretchedly!
So will you gain a twofold gratitude,
From me and from my father, and not come,
Through helping villains, to resemble them.

NEOPTOLEMUS All that you say is fair; still, I desire 1635
That trusting to the Gods, and to my story,
You would consent to sail, and leave this land,
Under my friendly convoy.

PHILOCTETES   What, to Troy?
To the detested son of Atreus? 1640
With this unlucky foot?

NEOPTOLEMUS   Rather, to those
Who shall relieve you and this ulcerous limb
From torment, and redeem you from disease.

PHILOCTETES O sayer of strange things, what words are these? 1645

NEOPTOLEMUS What will end well, I know, for both of us.

PHILOCTETES And in saying this have you no dread of Heaven?

NEOPTOLEMUS What dread should a man have, of profiting?

PHILOCTETES Profit to me, or the Atreidæ?

NEOPTOLEMUS   Why 1650
To you; being friendly, and my advice the same.

PHILOCTETES Friendly, and want to give me to my foes?

NEOPTOLEMUS O sir, learn to be prudent, in your troubles.

PHILOCTETES I know that you will ruin me, by this tale.

NEOPTOLEMUS I shall not; but I say, you grow no wiser. 1655

PHILOCTETES Do I not know the Atreidæ cast me out?

NEOPTOLEMUS But how if they will bring you safely back?

PHILOCTETES To behold Troy? Never, with my good will!

NEOPTOLEMUS Then what is to be done, if I in talk
Fail to persuade you to do aught I say? 1660
'Twere easiest I should cease from words, and you

1626 Son of Telamon, king of Salamis, second only to Achilles in bravery and strength; when Agamemnon
    awarded Achilles' arms to Odysseus, Ajax died of rage.

Live on, as now, without deliverance.

PHILOCTETES Leave me to suffer that which I must suffer.
But what you promised, giving me your hand,
To send me home—this, my son, do, I pray you;   1665
And do not linger, or take further thought
On Troy; Troy has made sorrow enough for me.

NEOPTOLEMUS If you will, let us be going.

PHILOCTETES   O well said, at length

NEOPTOLEMUS Lean on me as you are walking.   1670

PHILOCTETES   Yea, with all my strength.

NEOPTOLEMUS But how shall I avoid the Greeks' anger?

PHILOCTETES   Never care!

NEOPTOLEMUS What if they lay waste my country?

PHILOCTETES   Shall not I be there?   1675

NEOPTOLEMUS What assistance will you bring us?

PHILOCTETES   With Heracles' bow—

NEOPTOLEMUS How say you?

PHILOCTETES   I will repel them.

NEOPTOLEMUS   Kiss the soil, here, and go.   1680
                    (*Enter* HERACLES, *above*)

HERACLES Nay, not yet; first hear my precepts,
Child of Poias! It is thy privilege
Thou should'st list to Alcides'* accents,
Thou should'st see him! I come, forsaking   1685
Seats ethereal, for thy benefit,
Merely to tell thee Jove's high counsel,
Merely to hinder
That mad course thou followest. Do thou
Give good heed to the words I say.—   1690

And first I will inform thee of my fortunes,
How after all my labours past and done
I have attained to immortality,
As thou may'st witness. And thyself, be sure,
Must go through this experience, and so make,   1695
By these thy labours, thy life glorious.
Go with this man to Troy; there first of all
Thou shalt be healed of pitiful disease,
And chosen first in prowess of the host,
Shalt deprive Paris with my shafts of life,   1700
The causer of these ills; and shalt take Troy,
And to thy halls send booty, by the host
Awarded thee for prize, to thy sire's dwelling,
Poias, in Œta's upland, thine own land.
And of what spoils that host shall give thee, bring,   1705
For my bow's work, a tribute to my pyre.

[1684] Another name for Heracles.

—You too, son of Achilles, I exhort;
For neither have you power to capture Troy
Without his aid, nor he apart from you;
But like two lions ranging side by side   1710
Each be the other's guard.
(*To Philoctetes*)   —Lo, I will send
Asclepius to Troy, to cure your sickness;
For needs must Ilium a second time
Fall by my arrows.* But remember well,   1715
When you lay waste the land, to have respect
For what is due to Heaven; for all things else
Stand in the counsels of our father Jove
Second to this. The praise of piety
Cleaves to a mortal in his hour of death,   1720
Nor perishes, whether he die or live.

PHILOCTETES   O thou whose accents, long desired, I hear,
   Whose face, though late, I see, unto thy precepts
   I will not be rebellious.

NEOPTOLEMUS   No, nor I.   1725

HERACLES   No longer, then, delay to accomplish them;
   Time and the wind astern urge on to sail. (*Disappears*)

PHILOCTETES   One greeting to the country, ere I go.

   Farewell to the old familiar cave,
   To the roaring bass of the breaking wave   1730
      And the Naiads of the dale!
   Where many a time my hair was wet,
   Deep in the inmost nook beset,
      Lashed by a southern gale!
   Where often the voice of my lament   1735
   Amid the storm was backward sent,
      Echoed from Hermes' brow;
   O springs, with your liquid Lycian freight,
   Never expecting a joy so great,
      I leave you—I leave you now!   1740
   Farewell to the sea-girt Lemnian land!
   Give us good convoy from the strand,
      Where friendly counsels lead,
   And the prevailing word of Doom,
   And the all-mastering Power, by whom   1745
      These issues were decreed.

CHORUS   All together on our way
   Let us to the Sea Nymphs pray
   To prosper our return this day. (*Exeunt omnes*)

1715 Heracles had sacked Troy before, when Laomedon had refused to give him the horses he had promised
in return for ridding the city of a monster.

Euripides

Euripides (484–406 B.C.) *was the youngest of the great tragic writers of his age and the least popular in his own time. More critical in temper and impatient with the values of his society than Aeschylus or Sophocles, Euripides is thought to have been an embittered and unhappy man. Altogether, he wrote ninety-two plays, of which nineteen are extant, and won five prizes. Although he introduced no conspicuous innovations in theatrical method, he profoundly modified the Sophoclean single-play form by drawing characters of notably human, unheroic dimensions and by using materials and themes that have prompted critics to call many of his plays tragicomedies. While plays like* ALCESTIS *and* ANDROMACHE *illustrate this new Euripidean form, plays like* THE TROJAN WOMEN *and* THE BACCHAE *reflect his debt to older models.*

Chronology

484 B.C.   Born, probably on the Athenian island of Salamis, the son of Muesarchus, in a well-to-do, but not eminent family.

455   First entered the contest for tragedy.

441   Won his first prize.

*c.*440   The general period of his *Cyclops,* the only complete extant satyr play.

438   Produced *Alcestis.*

431   Produced *Medea.*

428   Produced *Hippolytus.*

415   Produced *The Trojan Women,* the third play of his only known trilogy, of which other member plays were the lost *Alexander* and *Palamedes.*

412   Produced *Helen.*

408   Produced *Orestes.*
Journeyed to the court of Archelaus, the king of Macedonia.

406   Died in Macedonia.

405   *The Bacchae* was produced.

Selected Bibliography

Appleton, R. B., *Euripides the Idealist,* London, 1927.
Bates, W. N., *Euripides: a Student of Human Nature,* Philadelphia, 1930.
Blaiklock, E. M., *The Male Characters of Euripides. A Study in Realism,* Wellington, N.Z., 1930.
Carpenter, R., *The Ethics of Euripides,* New York, 1916.
Decharmé, P., *Euripides and the Spirit of his Drama,* New York, 1906.
Greenwood, L. H. G., *Aspects of Euripidean Tragedy,* Cambridge, 1953.
Grube, F. M. A., *The Drama of Euripides,* 2nd ed., London, 1961.
Jones, W H. S., *The Moral Standpoint of Euripides,* London, 1906.
Lucas, F. L., *Euripides and his Influence,* Boston, 1928.

Murray, Gilbert, *Euripides and his Age,* Oxford, 1946.
Norwood, Gilbert, *Essays on Euripidean Drama,* Cambridge, 1954.
Verral, A. W., *Euripides the Rationalist,* Cambridge, 1913.
Zuntz, G., *The Political Plays of Euripides,* Manchester, 1953.

Vase painting showing a performance of a post-Euripidean version of *Medea*. The pedestals at left and right suggest the limits of the *orchestra*. 4th century B.C. *Photo Historical Pictures Service—Chicago*

THE
TROJAN WOMEN

by Euripides

Translated by Edith Hamilton

Characters
POSEIDON, *god of the sea*
ATHENA, *daughter of Zeus and patroness of Athens*
HECUBA, *queen of Troy*
TALTHYBIUS, *the Greek herald*
CASSANDRA, *a daughter of Hecuba*
ANDROMACHE, *the widow of Hector*
MENELAUS, *the king of Sparta*
HELEN, *his wife*
ASTYANAX, *the son of Hector*
Soldiers, guards, and attendants

The scene is a space of waste ground except for a few huts to right and left, where the women selected for the Greek leaders are housed; far in the background Troy, the wall in ruins, is slowly burning, as yet more smoke than flame; in front a woman with white hair lies on the ground; it is just before dawn; a tall dim figure is seen, back of the woman.

POSEIDON   I am the sea god. I have come
up from the salt sea depths of the Aegean,
from where the sea nymphs' footsteps fall,
weaving the lovely measures of the dance.
For since that day I built the towers of stone   5
around this town of Troy, Apollo with me,
—and straight we raised them, true by line and plummet—
good will for them has never left my heart,
my Trojans and their city.
City? Smoke only—all is gone,   10
perished beneath Greek spears.
A horse was fashioned, big with arms.
Parnassus was the workman's home,
in Phocia, and his name Epeius.
The skill he had Athena gave him.   15
He sent it through the walls—it carried death.
The wooden horse, so men will call it always,

which held and hid those spears.
A desert now where groves were. Blood drips down
from the gods' shrines. Beside his hearth 20
Priam lies dead upon the altar steps
of Zeus, the hearth's protector.
While to the Greek ships pass the Trojan treasure,
gold, gold in masses, armor, clothing,
stripped from the dead. 25
The Greeks who long since brought war to the town,
—ten times the seed was sown before Troy fell—
wait now for a fair wind for home,
the joyful sight of wife and child again.
Myself defeated by the Argive goddess 30
Hera and by Athena, both in league together—
I too must take my leave of glorious Troy,
forsake my altars. When a town is turned
into a desert, things divine fall sick.
Not one to do them honor. 35
Scamander's stream is loud with lamentation,
so many captive women weeping.
Their masters drew lots for them. Some will go
to Arcady and some to Thessaly.
Some to the lords of Athens, Theseus' sons. 40
Huts here hold others spared the lot, but chosen
for the great captains.
With them, like them a captive of the spear,
the Spartan woman, Helen.
But if a man would look on misery, 45
it is here to see—Hecuba lies there
before the gates. She weeps.
Many tears for many griefs.
And one still hidden from her.
But now upon Achilles' grave her daughter 50
was killed—Polyxena. So patiently she died.
Gone is her husband, gone her sons, all dead.
One daughter whom the Lord Apollo loved,
yet spared her wild virginity, Cassandra,
Agamemnon, in the dark, will force upon his bed. 55
No thought for what was holy and was God's.
O city happy once, farewell.
O shining towers, crumbling now
beneath Athena's hand, the child of God,
or you would still stand firm on deep foundations. (*As he turns to go the* 60
goddess PALLAS ATHENA *enters*)

ATHENA   Am I allowed to speak to one who is
my father's nearest kinsman,*

[63] Poseidon was Zeus' brother.

a god among gods honored, powerful?
If I put enmity aside, will he?   65

POSEIDON   He will, most high Athena. We are kin,
old comrades too, and these have magic power.

ATHENA   Thanks for your gentleness. What I would say
touches us both, great king.

POSEIDON   A message from the gods? A word from Zeus?   70
Some spirit, surely?

ATHENA   No, but for Troy's sake, where we stand, I seek
your power to join my own with it.

POSEIDON   What! Now—at last? Has that long hatred left you?
Pity—when all is ashes—burned to ashes?   75

ATHENA   The point first, please. Will you make common cause
with me? What I wish done will you wish, too?

POSEIDON   Gladly. But what you wish I first must know.
You come to me for Troy's sake or for Greece?

ATHENA   I wish to make my Trojan foes rejoice,   80
and give the Greeks a bitter home-coming.

POSEIDON   The way you change! Here—there—then back again.
Now hate, now love—not limit ever.

ATHENA   You know how I was outraged and my temple.

POSEIDON   Oh that—when Ajax dragged Cassandra out?   85

ATHENA   And not one Greek to punish him—not one to blame him.

POSEIDON   Even though your power ruined Troy for them.

ATHENA   Therefore with you I mean to hurt them.

POSEIDON   Ready for all you wish. But—hurt them? How?

ATHENA   Give them affliction for their coming home.   90

POSEIDON   Held here, you mean? Or out on the salt sea?

ATHENA   Whenever the ships sail.
Zeus shall send rain, unending rain, and sleet,
and darkness blown from heaven.
He will give me—he has promised—his thunderbolt,   95
to strike the ships with fire. They shall burn.
Your part, to make your sea-roads roar—
wild waves and whirlwinds,
while dead men choke the winding bay.
So Greeks shall learn to reverence my house   100
and dread all gods.

POSEIDON   These things shall be. No need of many words
to grant a favor. I will stir the sea,
the wide Aegean. Shores and reefs and cliffs
will hold dead men, bodies of many dead.   105
Off to Olympus with you now, and get
those fiery arrows from the hand of Zeus.
Then when a fair wind sends the Greeks to sea,
watch the ships sail. (*Exit* ATHENA)
Oh, fools, the men who lay a city waste,   110

giving to desolation temples, tombs,
the sanctuaries of the dead—so soon
to die themselves. (*Exit* POSEIDON)

———————————

(*The two gods have been talking before daylight, but now the day begins to dawn
and the woman lying on the ground in front moves. She is* HECUBA, *the aged*   115
queen of Troy)

HECUBA   Up from the ground—O weary head, O breaking neck.
This is no longer Troy. And we are not
the lords of Troy.
Endure. The ways of fate are the ways of the wind.   120
Drift with the stream—drift with fate.
No use to turn the prow to breast the waves.
Let the boat go as it chances.
Sorrow, my sorrow.
What sorrow is there that is not mine,   125
grief to weep for.
Country lost and children and husband.
Glory of all my house brought low.
All was nothing—nothing, always.
Keep silent? Speak?   130
Weep then? Why? For what? (*She begins to get up*)
Oh, this aching body—this bed—
it is very hard. My back pressed to it—
Oh, my side, my brow, my temples.
Up! Quick, quick. I must move.   135
Oh, I'll rock myself this way, that way,
to the sound of weeping, the song of tears,
dropping down forever.
The song no feet will dance to ever,
for the wretched, the ruined.   140

O ships, O prows, swift oars,
out from the fair Greek bays and harbors,
over the dark shining sea,
you found your way to our holy city,
and the fearful music of war was heard,   145
the war song sung to flute and pipe,
as you cast on the shore your cables,
ropes the Nile dwellers twisted and coiled,
and you swung, oh, my grief, in Troy's waters.

What did you come for? A woman?   150
A thing of loathing, of shame,
to husband, to brother, to home.
She slew Priam, the king,

father of fifty sons,
she wrecked me upon   155
the reef of destruction.

Who am I that I wait*
here at a Greek king's door?
A slave that men drive on,
an old gray woman that has no home.   160
Shaven head brought low in dishonor.
O wives of the bronze-armored men who fought,
and maidens, sorrowing maidens,
plighted to shame,
see—only smoke left where was Troy.   165
Let us weep for her.
As a mother bird cries to her feathered brood,
so will I cry.
Once another song I sang
when I leaned on Priam's scepter,   170
and the beat of dancing feet
marked the music's measure.
Up to the gods
the song of Troy rose at my signal. (*The door of one of the huts opens and a
                    woman steals out, then another, and another*)   175

FIRST WOMAN   Your cry, O Hecuba—oh, such a cry—
    What does it mean? There in the tent
    we heard you call so piteously,
    and through our hearts flashed fear.
    In the tent we were weeping, too,   180
    for we are slaves.
HECUBA   Look, child, there where the Greek ships lie—
ANOTHER WOMAN   They are moving. The men hold oars.
ANOTHER   O God, what will they do? Carry me off
    over the sea in a ship far from home?   185
HECUBA   You ask and I know nothing,
    but I think ruin is here.
ANOTHER WOMAN   Oh, we are wretched. We shall hear the summons.
    Women of Troy, go forth from your home,
    for the Greeks set sail.   190
HECUBA   But not Cassandra, oh, not her.
    She is mad—she has been driven mad. Leave her within.
    Not shamed before the Greeks—not that grief too.
    I have enough.
        O Troy, unhappy Troy, you are gone   195
    and we, the unhappy, leave you,
    we who are living and we who are dead.

---

[157] This is the way Professor Murray translates the line and the one following. The translation is so simple
    and beautiful, I cannot bear to give it up for a poorer one of my own [trans. note].

(More women now come out from a second hut)

A WOMAN   Out of the Greek king's tent
   trembling I come, O Queen,   200
   to hear my fate from you.
   Not death—They would not think of death
   for a poor woman.

ANOTHER   The sailors—they are standing on the prow.
   Already they are running out the oars.   205

ANOTHER   *(She comes out of a third hut and several follow her)*
   It is so early—but a terror woke me.
      My heart beats so.

ANOTHER   Has a herald come from the Greek camp?
   Whose slave shall I be? I—bear that?   210

HECUBA   Wait for the lot drawing. It is near.

ANOTHER   Argos shall it be, or Phthia?*
      or an island of the sea?
      A Greek soldier lead me there,
   far, far from Troy?   215

HECUBA   And I a slave—to whom—where—how?
   You old gray woman, patient to endure,
   you bee without a sting,
   only an image of what was alive.
      or the ghost of one dead.   220
   I watch a master's door?
      I nurse his children?
      Once I was queen in Troy.

ONE WOMAN TO ANOTHER   Poor thing. What are your tears
   to the shame before you?   225

THE OTHER   The shuttle will still pass through my hands,
   but the loom will not be in Troy.

ANOTHER   My dead sons. I would look at them once more.
   Never again.

ANOTHER   Worse to come.   230
   A Greek's bed—and I—

ANOTHER   A night like that? Oh, never—
   oh, no—not that for me.

ANOTHER   I see myself a water carrier,
   dipping my pitcher in the great Pierian spring.   235

ANOTHER   The land of Theseus, Athens, it is known
   to be a happy place. I wish I could go there.

ANOTHER   But not to the Eurotas, hateful river,
   where Helen lived. Not there, to be a slave
   to Menelaus who sacked Troy.   240

ANOTHER   Oh, look. A man from the Greek army—
   a herald. Something strange has happened,
   he comes so fast. To tell us—what?

212 Phthia was a city in Thessaly; the birthplace of Achilles.

What will he say? Only Greek slaves are here,
waiting for orders. 245
(Enter TALTHYBIUS *with soldiers)*
TALTHYBIUS You know me, Hecuba. I have often come
with messages to Troy from the Greek camp.
Talthybius—these many years you've known me.
I bring you news. 250
HECUBA It has come, women of Troy. Once we only feared it.
TALTHYBIUS The lots are drawn, if that is what you feared.
HECUBA Who—where? Thessaly? Phthia? Thebes?
TALTHYBIUS A different man takes each. You're not to go together.
HECUBA Then which takes which? Has any one good fortune? 255
TALTHYBIUS I know, but ask about each one, not all at once.
HECUBA My daughter, who—who drew her? Tell me—
Cassandra. She has had so much to bear.
TALTHYBIUS King Agamemnon chose her out from all.
HECUBA Oh! but—of course—to serve his Spartan wife? 260
TALTHYBIUS No, no—but for the king's own bed at night.
HECUBA Oh, never. She is God's, a virgin, always.
That was God's gift to her for all her life.
TALTHYBIUS He loved her for that same strange purity.*
HECUBA Throw away, daughter, the keys of the temple. 265
Take off the wreath and the sacred stole.
TALTHYBIUS Well, now—a king's bed is not so bad.
HECUBA My other child you took from me just now?
TALTHYBIUS *(Speaking with constraint)* Polyxena, you mean? Or someone
else? 270
HECUBA Her. Who drew her?
TALTHYBIUS They told her off to watch Achilles' tomb.
HECUBA To watch a tomb? My daughter?
That a Greek custom?
What strange ritual is that, my friend? 275
TALTHYBIUS *(Speaking fast and trying to put her off)* Just think of her as happy
—all well with her.
HECUBA Those words—Why do you speak like that?
She is alive?
TALTHYBIUS *(Determined not to tell her)* What happened was—well, she is 280
free from trouble.
HECUBA *(Wearily giving the riddle up)* Then Hector's wife—my Hector, wise
in war—
Where does she go, poor thing—Andromache?
TALTHYBIUS Achilles' son took her. He chose her out. 285
HECUBA And I, old gray head, whose slave am I,
creeping along with my crutch?
TALTHYBIUS Slave of the king of Ithaca, Odysseus.
HECUBA Beat, beat my short head! Tear, tear my cheek!

[264] This line, too, is Professor Murray's, and retained here for the reason given above [trans. note].

lis slave—vile lying man. I have come to this— 290
'here is nothing good he does not hurt—a lawless beast.
Ie twists and turns, this way and that, and back again.
ι double tongue, as false in hate as false in love.
ℑity me, women of Troy,
    have gone. I am lost—oh, wretched. 295
Λn evil fate fell on me,
ι lot the hardest of all.

ℑMAN   You know what lies before you, Queen, but I—
What man among the Greeks owns me?

THYBIUS (*To the soldiers*)   Off with you. Bring Cassandra here. Be quick, 300
you fellows. We must give her to the chief,
into his very hand. And then these here
to all the other generals. But what's that—
that flash of light inside there?

            (*Light shines through the crevices of one of the huts*) 305
Set fire to the huts—is that their plan,
these Trojan women? Burn themselves to death
rather than sail to Greece. Choosing to die instead.
How savagely these days the yoke bears down
on necks so lately free. 310
Open there, open the door. (*Aside*) As well for them perhaps,
but for the Greeks—they'd put the blame on me.

CUBA   No, no, there is nothing burning. It is my daughter,
Cassandra. She is mad.

(CASSANDRA *enters from the hut dressed like a priestess, a wreath in her hair,* 315
            a torch in her hand. She does not seem to see anyone)

ΛSSANDRA   Lift it high—in my hand—light to bring.
I praise him. I bear a flame.
With my torch I touch to fire
this holy place. 320
    Hymen, O Hymen.
    Blessed the bridegroom,
    blessed am I
to lie with a king in a king's bed in Argos.
    Hymen, O Hymen. 325
Mother, you weep
tears for my father dead,
mourning for the beloved
    country lost.
I for my bridal here 330
lift up the fire's flame
to the dawn, to the splendor,
to you, O Hymen.
Queen of night,
give your starlight 335
to a virgin bed,

as of old you did.
Fly, dancing feet.
Up with the dance.
   Oh, joy, oh, joy!
Dance for my father dead,
   most blest to die.
Oh, holy dance!
Apollo—you?
Lead on then.
There in the laurel grove
I served your altar.
   Dance, Mother, come.
   Keep step with me.
Dear feet with my feet
   tracing the measure
   this way and that.
Sing to the Marriage god,
oh, joyful song.
Sing for the bride, too,   355
joyously all.
Maidens of Troy,
dressed in your best,
honor my marriage.
Honor too him   360
whose bed fate drives me to share.

A WOMAN   Hold her fast, Queen, poor frenzied girl.
She might rush straight to the Greek camp.

HECUBA   O fire, fire, when men make marriages
you light the torch, but this flame flashing here   365
is for grief only. Child, such great hopes once I had.
I never thought that to your bridal bed
Greek spears would drive you.
Give me your torch. You do not hold it straight,
you move so wildly. Your sufferings, my child,   370
have never taught you wisdom.
You never change. Here! someone take the torch
into the hut. This marriage needs no songs,
but only tears.

CASSANDRA   O Mother, crown my triumph with a wreath.   375
Be glad, for I am married to a king.
Send me to him, and if I shrink away,
drive me with violence. If Apollo lives,
my marriage shall be bloodier than Helen's.
Agamemnon, the great, the glorious lord of Greece—   380
I shall kill him, Mother, lay his house as low
as he laid ours, make him pay for all
he made my father suffer, brothers, and—

But no. I must not speak of that—that axe
which on my neck—on others' too—   385
nor of that murder of a mother.
All, all because he married me and so
pulled his own house down.
But I will show you. This town now, yes, Mother,
is happier than the Greeks. I know that I am mad,   390
but Mother, dearest, now, for this one time
I do not rave.
One woman they came hunting, and one love,
Helen, and men by tens of thousands died.
Their king, so wise, to get what most he hated   395
destroyed what most he loved,
his joy at home, his daughter, killing her
for a brother's sake, to get him back a woman
who had fled because she wished—not forced to go.
And when they came to the banks of the Scamander   400
those thousands died. And why?
No man had moved their landmarks
or laid siege to their high-walled towns.
But those whom war took never saw their children.
No wife with gentle hands shrouded them for their grave.   405
They lie in a strange land. And in their homes
are sorrows, too, the very same.
Lonely women who died, old men who waited
for sons that never came—no son left to them
to make the offering at their graves.   410
That was the glorious victory they won.
But we—we Trojans died to save our people,
no glory greater. All those the spear slew,
friends bore them home and wrapped them in their shroud
with dutiful hands. The earth of their own land   415
covered them. The rest, through the long days they fought,
had wife and child at hand, not like the Greeks,
whose joys were far away.
And Hector's pain—your Hector. Mother, hear me.
This is the truth: he died, the best, a hero.   420
Because the Greeks came, he died thus.
Had they stayed home, we never would have known him.
This truth stands firm: the wise will fly from war.
But if war comes, to die well is to win
the victor's crown.   425
The only shame is not to die like that.
So, Mother, do not pity Troy,
or me upon my bridal bed.

TALTHYBIUS (*He has been held awestruck through all this, but can bear no more*)
    Now if Apollo had not made you mad   430

I would have paid you for those evil words,
bad omens, and my general sailing soon.
(*Grumbles to himself*) The great, who seem so wise, have no more sense
than those who rank as nothing.
Our king, the first in Greece, bows down   435
before this mad girl, loves her, chooses her
out of them all. Well, I am a poor man,
but I'd not go to bed with her.
(*Turns to* CASSANDRA) Now you—you know your mind is not quite right.
So all you said against Greece and for Troy,   440
I never heard—the wind blew it away.
Come with me to the ship now.
(*Aside*) A grand match for our general, she is.
(*To* HECUBA, *gently*) And you, do follow quietly when Odysseus' men
                                                come   445
His wife's a good, wise woman, so they say.

CASSANDRA (*Seeming to see* TALTHYBIUS *for the first time and looking him over*
    haughtily)   A strange sort of slave, surely.
Heralds such men are called,
hated by all, for they are tyrants' tools.   450
You say my mother goes to serve Odysseus?
(*She turns away and speaks to herself*) But where then is Apollo's word,
                                                made clear
to me, that death will find her here?
And—no, that shame I will not speak of.   455
Odysseus! wretched—but he does not know.
   Soon all these sorrows, mine and Troy's, will seem
compared to his like golden hours.
Ten years behind him here, ten years before him.
Then only, all alone, will he come home,   460
and there find untold trouble has come first.
But his cares—why let fly one word at him?
Come, let us hasten to my marriage.
We two shall rest, the bridegroom and the bride,
within the house of death.   465
O Greek king, with your dreams of grandeur yet to come,
vile as you are, so shall your end be,
in darkness—all light gone.
And me—a cleft in the hills,
washed by winter rains,   470
his tomb near by.
There—dead—cast out—naked—
and wild beasts seeking food—
It is I there—I myself—Apollo's servant.
O flowers of the God I love, mysterious wreaths,   475
away. I have forgotten temple festival,
I have forgotten joy.

Off. I tear them from my neck.
Swift winds will carry them
up to you, O God of truth.
My flesh still clean, I give them back to you.   480
Where is the ship? How do I go on board?
Spread the sail—the wind comes swift.
Those who bring vengeance—three are they,
And one of them goes with you on the sea.   485
Mother, my Mother, do not weep. Farewell,
dear City. Brothers, in Troy's earth laid, my father,
a little time and I am with you.
You dead, I shall come to you a victor.
Those ruined by my hand who ruined us. (*She goes out with* TALTHYBIUS   490
        and the soldiers. HECUBA, *motionless for a moment, falls*)

A WOMAN   The Queen! See—see—she is falling.
Oh, help! She cannot speak.
Miserable slaves, will you leave her on the ground,
old as she is. Up—lift her up.   495
HECUBA   Let me be. Kindness not wanted is unkindness.
I cannot stand. Too much is on me.
Anguish here and long since and to come—
O God—Do I call you? You did not help.
But there is something that cries out for God   500
when trouble comes.
Oh, I will think of good days gone,
days to make a song of,
crowning my sorrow by remembering.
We were kings and a king I married.   505
Sons I bore him, many sons.
That means little—but fine, brave lads.
They were the best in all Troy.
No woman, Trojan, Greek, or stranger,
had sons like mine to be proud of.   510
I saw them fall beneath Greek spears.
My hair I shore at the grave of the dead.
Their father—I did not learn from others
that I must weep for him—these eyes beheld him.
I, my own self, saw him fall murdered   515
upon the altar, when his town was lost.
My daughters, maidens reared to marry kings,
are torn from me. For the Greeks I reared them.
All gone—no hope that I shall look upon
their faces any more, or they on mine.   520
And now the end—no more can lie beyond—
an old gray slave woman I go to Greece.

The tasks they know for my age hardest, mine.
The door to shut and open, bowing low
—I who bore Hector—meal to grind; upon   525
the ground lay this old body down that once
slept in a royal bed; torn rags around me,
torn flesh beneath.
And all this misery and all to come
because a man desired a woman.   530
Daughter, who knew God's mystery and joy,
what strange chance lost you your virginity?
And you, Polyxena—where are you gone?
No son, no daughter, left to help my need,
and I had many, many—   535
Why lift me up? What hope is there to hold to?
   This slave that once went delicately in Troy,
take her and cast her on her bed of clay,
rocks for her pillow, there to fall and die,
wasted with tears. Count no one happy,   540
however fortunate, before he dies.

CHORUS   Sing me, O Muse, a song for Troy,
   a strange song sung to tears,
   a music for the grave.
   O lips, sound forth a melody   545
      for Troy.

A four-wheeled cart brought the horse to the gates,
brought ruin to me,
   captured, enslaved me.
Gold was the rein and the bridle,   550
deadly the arms within,
and they clashed loud to heaven as the threshold was passed.

High on Troy's rock the people cried,
"Rest at last, trouble ended.
Bring the carven image in.   555
Bear it to Athena,
fit gift for the child of God."

Who of the young but hurried forth?
Who of the old would stay at home?
With song and rejoicing they brought death in,   560
treachery and destruction.

All that were in Troy,
hastening to the gate,
drew that smooth-planed horse of wood
carven from a mountain pine,   565

where the Greeks were hiding,
where was Troy's destruction,
gave it to the goddess,
gift for her, the virgin,
driver of the steeds that never die.   570

With ropes of twisted flax,
as a ship's dark hull is drawn to land,
they brought it to her temple of stone,
to her floor that soon would run with blood,
   to Pallas Athena.   575

   On their toil and their joy
the dark of evening fell,
but the lutes of Egypt still rang out
   to the songs of Troy.

And girls with feet light as air   580
dancing, sang happy songs.
The houses blazed with light
through the dark splendor,
   and sleep was not.

A GIRL I was among the dancers.   585
   I was singing to the maiden of Zeus,
   the goddess of the hills.*
   A shout rang out in the town,
   a cry of blood through the houses,
   and a frightened child caught his mother's skirt   590
   and hid himself in her cloak.
   Then War came forth from his hiding place—
   Athena, the virgin, devised it.
   Around the altars they slaughtered us.
   Within on their beds lay headless men,   595
   young men cut down in their prime.
   This was the triumph-crown of Greece.
   We shall bear children for her to rear,
   grief and shame to our country.
   (*A chariot approaches, loaded with spoils. In it sits a woman and a child*) 600

A WOMAN Look, Hecuba, it is Andromache.
   See, in the Greek car yonder.
   Her breast heaves with her sobs and yet
   the baby sleeps there, dear Astyanax,
   the son of Hector.   605

ANOTHER Most sorrowful of women, where do you go?
   Beside you the bronze armor that was Hector's,
   the spoil of the Greek spear, stripped from the dead.

587 Artemis.

Will Achilles' son use it to deck his temples?

ANDROMACHE I go where my Greek masters take me. 610

HECUBA Oh, our sorrow—our sorrow.

ANDROMACHE Why should you weep? This sorrow is mine.

HECUBA O God—

ANDROMACHE What has come to me is mine.

HECUBA My children— 615

ANDROMACHE Once we lived, not now.

HECUBA Gone—gone—happiness—Troy—

ANDROMACHE And you bear it.

HECUBA Sons, noble sons, all lost.

ANDROMACHE Oh, sorrow is here. 620

HECUBA For me—for me.

ANDROMACHE For the city, in its shroud of smoke.
Come to me, O my husband.

HECUBA What you cry to lies in the grave.
My son, wretched woman, mine. 625

ANDROMACHE Defend me—me, your wife.

HECUBA My son, my eldest son,
whom I bore to Priam,
whom the Greeks used shamefully,
come to me, lead me to death. 630

ANDROMACHE Death—oh, how deep a desire.

HECUBA Such is our pain—

ANDROMACHE For a city that has fallen, fallen.

HECUBA For anguish heaped upon anguish.

ANDROMACHE For the anger of God against Paris, 635
your son, who fled from death,
who laid Troy's towers low
  to win an evil love.
Dead men—bodies—blood—
vultures hovering— 640
Oh, Athena the goddess is there, be sure,
and the slave's yoke is laid upon Troy.

HECUBA O country, desolate, empty.

ANDROMACHE My tears fall for you.

HECUBA Look and see the end— 645

ANDROMACHE Of the house where I bore my children.

HECUBA O children, your mother has lost her city,
and you—you have left her alone.
Only grief is mine and mourning.
Tears and more tears, falling, falling. 650
The dead—they have forgotten their pain.
They weep no more.

A WOMAN (*Aside to another*) Tears are sweet in bitter grief,
and sorrow's song is lamentation.

ANDROMACHE Mother of him whose spear of old brought death 655 to Greeks unnumbered, you see what is here.

HECUBA   I see God's hand that casts the mighty down
and sets on high the lowly.

ANDROMACHE   Driven like cattle captured in a raid,
my child and I—the free changed to a slave.   660
Oh, changed indeed.

HECUBA   It is fearful to be helpless. Men just now
have taken Cassandra—forced her from me.

ANDROMACHE   And still more for you—more than that—

HECUBA   Number my sorrows, will you? Measure them?   665
One comes—the next one rivals it.

ANDROMACHE   Polyxena lies dead upon Achilles' tomb,
a gift to a corpse, to a lifeless thing.

HECUBA   My sorrow! That is what Talthybius meant—
I could not read his riddle. Oh, too plain.   670

ANDROMACHE   I saw her there and left the chariot
and covered her dead body with my cloak,
and beat my breast.

HECUBA   Murdered—my child. Oh, wickedly!
Again I cry to you. Oh, cruelly slain!   675

ANDROMACHE   She has died her death, and happier by far
dying than I alive.

HECUBA   Life cannot be what death is, child.
Death is empty—life has hope.

ANDROMACHE   Mother, O Mother, hear a truer word.   680
Now let me bring joy to your heart.
I say to die is only not to be,
and rather death than life with bitter grief.
They have no pain, they do not feel their wrongs.
But the happy who has come to wretchedness,   685
his soul is a lost wanderer,
the old joys that were once, left far behind.
She is dead, your daughter—to her the same
as if she never had been born.
She does not know the wickedness that killed her.   690
While I—I aimed my shaft at good repute.
I gained full measure—then missed happiness.
For all that is called virtuous in a woman
I strove for and I won in Hector's house.
Always, because we women, whether right or wrong,   695
are spoken ill of
unless we stay within our homes, my longing
I set aside and kept the house.
Light talk, glib women's words,
could never gain an entrance there.   700
My own thoughts were enough for me,
best of all teachers to me in my home.

Silence, a tranquil eye, I brought my husband,
knew well in what I should rule him,
and when give him obedience. 705
And this report of me came to the Greeks
for my destruction. When they captured me
Achilles' son would have me.
I shall be a slave to those who murdered—
O Hector, my beloved—shall I thrust him aside, 710
open my heart to the man that comes to me,
and be a traitor to the dead?
And yet to shrink in loathing from him
and make my masters hate me—
One night, men say, one night in a man's bed 715
will make a woman tame—
Oh, shame! A woman throw her husband off
and in a new bed love another—
Why, a young colt will not run in the yoke
with any but her mate—not a dumb beast 720
that has no reason, of a lower nature.
O Hector, my beloved, you were all to me,
wise, noble, mighty, in wealth, in manhood, both.
No man had touched me when you took me,
took me from out my father's home 725
and yoked a girl fast to you.
And you are dead, and I, with other plunder,
am sent by sea to Greece. A slave's yoke there.
Your dead Polyxena you weep for,
what does she know of pain like mine? 730
The living must have hope. Not I, not any more.
I will not lie to my own heart. No good will ever come.
But oh, to think it would be sweet.

A WOMAN We stand at the same point of pain. You mourn your ruin,
and in your words I hear my own calamity. 735

HECUBA Those ships—I never have set foot on one,
but I have heard of them, seen pictures of them.
I know that when a storm comes which they think
they can ride out, the sailors do their best,
one by the sail, another at the helm, 740
and others bailing.
But if great ocean's raging overwhelms them,
they yield to fate.
They give themselves up to the racing waves.
So in my many sorrows I am dumb. 745
I yield, I cannot speak.
The great wave from God has conquered me.
But, O dear child, let Hector be,
and let be what has come to him.

Your tears will never call him back.   750
Give honor now to him who is your master.
Your sweet ways—use them to allure him.
So doing you will give cheer to your friends.
Perhaps this child, my own child's son,
you may rear to manhood and great aid for Troy,   755
and if ever you should have more children,
they might build her again. Troy once more be a city!
Oh—one thought leads another on.
But why again that servant of the Greeks?
I see him coming. Some new plan is here.   760
(*Enter* TALTHYBIUS *with soldiers. He is troubled and advances hesitatingly*)

TALTHYBIUS Wife of the noblest man that was in Troy,
O wife of Hector, do not hate me.
Against my will I come to tell you.
The people and the kings have all resolved—   765
ANDROMACHE What is it? Evil follows words like those.
TALTHYBIUS This child they order—Oh, how can I say it—
ANDROMACHE Not that he does not go with me to the same master—
TALTHYBIUS No man in Greece shall ever be his master.
ANDROMACHE But—leave him here—all that is left of Troy?   770
TALTHYBIUS I don't know how to tell you. What is bad,
words can't make better—
ANDROMACHE I feel you kind. But you have not good news.
TALTHYBIUS Your child must die. There, now you know
the whole, bad as it is.   775
ANDROMACHE Oh, I have heard an evil worse
than a slave in her master's bed.
TALTHYBIUS It was Odysseus had his way. He spoke
to all the Greeks.
ANDROMACHE O God. There is no measure to my pain.   780
TALTHYBIUS He said a hero's son must not grow up—
ANDROMACHE God, on his own sons may that counsel fall.
TALTHYBIUS —but from the towering wall of Troy be thrown.
Now, now—let it be done—that's wiser.
Don't cling so to him. Bear your pain   785
the way a brave woman suffers.
You have no strength—don't look to any help.
There's no help for you anywhere. Think—think.
The city gone—your husband too. And you
a captive and alone, one woman—how   790
can you do battle with us? For your own good
I would not have you try, and draw
hatred down on you and be shamed.
Oh, hush—never a curse upon the Greeks.
If you say words that make the army angry   795
the child will have no burial, and without pity—

Silence now. Bear your fate as best you can.
So then you need not leave him dead without a grave,
and you will find the Greeks more kind.

ANDROMACHE Go die, my best beloved, my own, my treasure,   800
in cruel hands, leaving your mother comfortless.
Your father was too noble. That is why
they kill you. He could save others,
he could not save you for his nobleness.
My bed, my bridal—all for misery—   805
when long ago I came to Hector's halls
to bear my son—oh, not for Greeks to slay,
but for a ruler over teeming Asia.
Weeping, my little one? There, there.
You cannot know what waits for you.   810
Why hold me with your hands so fast, cling so fast to me?
You little bird, flying to hide beneath my wings.
And Hector will not come—he will not come,
up from the tomb, great spear in hand, to save you.
Not one of all his kin, of all the Trojan might.   815
How will it be? Falling down—down—oh, horrible.
And his neck—his breath—all broken.
And none to pity. You little thing,
curled in my arms, you dearest to your mother,
how sweet the fragrance of you.   820
All nothing then—this breast from where
your baby mouth drew milk, my travail too,
my cares, when I grew wasted watching you.
Kiss me—Never again. Come, closer, closer.
Your mother who bore you—put your arms around my neck.   825
Now kiss me, lips to lips.
O Greeks, you have found out ways to torture
that are not Greek.
A little child, all innocent of wrong—
you wish to kill him.   830
O Helen, evil growth, that was sown by Tyndareus,
you are no child of Zeus, as people say.
Many the fathers you were born of,
Madness, Hatred, Red Death, whatever poison
the earth brings forth—no child of Zeus,   835
but Greece's curse and all the world's.
God curse you, with those beautiful eyes
that brought to shame and ruin
Troy's far-famed plains.
Quick! take him—seize him—cast him down—   840
if so you will. Feast on his flesh.
God has destroyed me, and I cannot—
I cannot save my child from death.

Oh hide my head for shame and fling me
into the ship. (*She falls, then struggles to her knees*)   845
My fair bridal—I am coming—
Oh, I have lost my child, my own.

A WOMAN   O wretched Troy, tens of thousands lost
for a woman's sake, a hateful marriage bed.

TALTHYBIUS   (*Drawing the child away*)   Come, boy, let go. Unclasp those   850
                                   loving hands,
poor mother.
Come now, up, up, to the very height,
where the towers of your fathers crown the wall,
and where it is decreed that you must die.   855
(*To the soldiers*) Take him away.
A herald who must bring such orders
should be a man who feels no pity,
and no shame either—not like me.

HECUBA   Child, son of my poor son, whose toil was all in vain,   860
we are robbed, your mother and I, oh, cruelly—
robbed of your life. How bear it?
What can I do for you, poor piteous child?
Beat my head, my breast—all I can give you.
Troy lost, now you—all lost.   865
The cup is full. Why wait? For what?
Hasten on—swiftly on to death. (*The soldiers, who have waited while*
HECUBA *speaks, go out with the child and* TALTHYBIUS. *One of them takes*
        ANDROMACHE *to the chariot and drives off with her*)

CHORUS   The waves make a ring around Salamis.   870
The bees are loud in the island.
King Telamon built him a dwelling.
It fronted the holy hills,
where first the gray gleaming olive
Athena showed to men,   875
the glory of shining Athens,
her crown from the sky.
He joined himself to the bowman,
the son of Alcmena, for valorous deeds.
Troy, Troy he laid waste, my city,   880
long ago when he went forth from Greece.
When he led forth from Greece the bravest
in his wrath for the steeds* withheld,
and by fair-flowing Simois stayed his oar
that had brought him over the sea.   885
Cables there made the ship fast.
In his hand was the bow that never missed.

883 When Troy was destroyed the first time, the reason was that the Trojan king had promised two immortal horses to Heracles ("the son of Alcmena") but did not give them to him. Heracles in revenge
ruined the city. The son of this king was Ganymede, cup-bearer to Zeus [trans. note].

It brought the king to his death.*
Walls of stone that Phoebus had built
he wrecked with the red breath of fire.   890
He wasted the plain of Troy.
Twice her walls have fallen. Twice
a blood-stained spear struck her down,
  laid her in ruin.

In vain, O you who move   895
with delicate feet where the wine-cups are gold,
son of that old dead king,
who fill with wine the cup Zeus holds,
service most fair—
she who gave you birth is afire.   900
The shores of the sea are wailing for her.
As a bird cries over her young,
women weep for husbands, for children,
for the old, too, who gave them birth.
Your dewy baths are gone,   905
and the race-course where you ran.
Yet your young face keeps the beauty of peace
in joy, by the throne of Zeus.
While Priam's land
lies ruined by Greek spearsmen.   910

Love, O Love,
once you came to the halls of Troy,
and your song rose up to the dwellers in heaven.
How did you then exalt Troy high,
binding her fast to the gods, by a union—   915
No—I will not speak blame of Zeus.*
But the light of white-winged Dawn, dear to men,
is deadly over the land this day,
shining on fallen towers.
And yet Dawn keeps in her bridal bower   920
her children's father, a son of Troy.*
Her chariot bore him away to the sky.
It was gold, and four stars drew it.
Hope was high then for our town.
But the magic that brought her the love of the gods   925
has gone from Troy. (*As the song ends* MENELAUS *enters with a bodyguard
                              of soldiers*)

---

888 This king was Laomedon.
916 An allusion to Zeus' infatuation with the boy Ganymede.
921 This passage alludes to the story of Tithonus, the consort of Eos, or Dawn, or Aurora, and another
   son of Laomedon. At Eos' request Tithonus was granted immortality, though not permanent youth.

MENELAUS How bright the sunlight is today—
　　　this day, when I shall get into my power
　　　Helen, my wife. For I am Menelaus,　　　　　　　　　　930
　　　the man of many wrongs.
　　　I came to Troy and brought with me my army,
　　　not for that woman's sake, as people say,
　　　but for the man who from my house,
　　　and he a guest there, stole away my wife.　　　　　　935
　　　Ah, well, with God's help he has paid the price,
　　　he and his country, fallen beneath Greek spears.
　　　I am come to get her—wretch—I cannot speak her name
　　　who was my wife once.
　　　In a hut here, where they house the captives,　　　940
　　　she is numbered with the other Trojan women.
　　　The men who fought and toiled to win her back,
　　　have given her to me—to kill, or else,
　　　if it pleases me, to take her back to Argos.
　　　And it has seemed to me her death in Troy　　　945
　　　is not the way. I will take her overseas,
　　　with swift oars speeding on the ship,
　　　and there in Greece give her to those to kill
　　　whose dearest died because of her.
　　　(*To his men*) Attention! Forward to the huts.　　　950
　　　Seize her and drag her out by that long blood-drenched hair—
　　　　　　　　(*Stops suddenly and controls himself*)
　　　And when fair winds come, home with her to
　　　Greece. (*Soldiers begin to force the door of one of the huts*)
HECUBA (*Comes slowly forward*) O thou who dost uphold the world,　　　955
　　　whose throne is high above the world,
　　　thou, past our seeking hard to find, who art thou?
　　　God, or Necessity of what must be,
　　　or Reason of our reason?
　　　Whate'er thou art, I pray to thee,　　　　　　　　960
　　　seeing the silent road by which
　　　all mortal things are led by thee to justice.
MENELAUS What have we here? A queer prayer that.
HECUBA (*She comes still nearer to him and he recognizes her*) Kill her, Menelaus?
　　　You will? Oh, blessings on you!　　　　　　　　965
　　　But—shun her, do not look at her.
　　　Desire for her will seize you, conquer you.
　　　For through men's eyes she gets them in her power.
　　　She ruins them and ruins cities too.
　　　Fire comes from her to burn homes,　　　　　　970
　　　magic for death. I know her—so do you,
　　　and all these who have suffered.
　　　　(HELEN *enters from the hut. The soldiers do not touch her. She is very gentle
　　　　　　　　and undisturbed*)

HELEN (*With sweet, injured dignity; not angry at all*) Menelaus, these things 975
    might well make a woman fear.
  Your men with violence have driven me from my room,
  have laid their hands upon me.
  Of course I know—almost I know—you hate me,
  but yet I ask you, what is your decision, 980
  yours and the Greeks? Am I to live or not?
MENELAUS Nothing more clear. Unanimous, in fact.
  Not one who did not vote you should be given me,
  whom you have wronged, to kill you.
HELEN Am I allowed to speak against the charge? 985
  To show you if I die that I shall die
  most wronged and innocent?
MENELAUS I have come to kill you, not to argue with you.
HECUBA Oh, hear her. She must never die unheard.
  Then, Menelaus, let me answer her. 990
  The evil that she did in Troy, you do not know.
  But I will tell the story. She will die.
  She never can escape.
MENELAUS That means delay. Still—if she wants to speak,
  she can. I grant her this because of what you say, 995
  not for her sake. She can be sure of that.
HELEN And perhaps, no matter if you think I speak
  the truth or not, you will not talk to me,
  since you believe I am your enemy.
  Still, I will try to answer what I think 1000
  you would say if you spoke your mind,
  and my wrongs shall be heard as well as yours.
  First: who began these evils? She, the day
  when she gave birth to Paris. Who next was guilty?
  The old king who decreed the child should live, 1005
  and ruined Troy and me—Paris, the hateful,
  the firebrand.*
  What happened then? Listen and learn.
  This Paris—he was made the judge for three,
  all yoked together in a quarrel—goddesses. 1010
  Athena promised he should lead the Trojans
  to victory and lay all Greece in ruins.
  And Hera said if he thought her the fairest
  she would make him lord of Europe and of Asia.
  But Aphrodite—well, she praised my beauty— 1015
  astonishing, she said—and promised him
  that she would give me to him if he judged
  that she was loveliest. Then, see what happened.

1007 Just before Paris' birth, Hecuba dreamed she gave birth to a firebrand.

She won, and so my bridal brought all Greece
great good. No strangers rule you,   1020
no foreign spears, no tyrant.
Oh, it was well for Greece, but not for me,
sold for my beauty and reproached besides
when I deserved a crown.
But—to the point. Is that what you are thinking?   1025
Why did I go—steal from your house in secret?
That man, Paris, or any name you like to call him,
his mother's curse—oh, when he came to me
a mighty goddess walked beside him.
And you, poor fool, you spread your sails for Crete,   1030
left Sparta—left him in your house.
Ah well—Not you, but my own self I ask,
what was there in my heart that I went with him,
a strange man, and forgot my home and country?
Not I, but Aphrodite. Punish her,   1035
be mightier than Zeus who rules
the other gods, but is her slave.
She is my absolution—
One thing with seeming justice you might say.
When Paris died and went down to the grave,   1040
and when no god cared who was in my bed,
I should have left his house—gone to the Greeks.
Just what I tried to do—oh, many times.
I have witnesses—the men who kept the gates,
the watchmen on the walls. Not once, but often   1045
they found me swinging from a parapet,
a rope around this body, stealthily
feeling my way down.
The Trojans then no longer wanted me,
but the man who next took me—and by force—   1050
would never let me go.
My husband, must I die, and at your hands?
You think that right? Is that your justice?
I was forced—by violence. I lived a life
that had no joy, no triumph. In bitterness   1055
I lived a slave.
Do you wish to set yourself above the gods?
Oh, stupid, senseless wish!

A WOMAN   O Queen, defend your children and your country.
Her soft persuasive words are deadly.   1060
She speaks so fair and is so vile.
A fearful thing.

HECUBA   Her goddesses will fight on my side while
I show her for the liar that she is.
Not Hera, not virgin Athena, do I think   1065

would ever stoop to folly great enough
to sell their cities. Hera sell her Argos,
Athena Athens, to be the Trojan's slave!
playing like silly children there on Ida,
and each one in her insolence demanding 1070
the prize for beauty. Beauty—why was Hera
so hot for it? That she might get herself
a better mate than Zeus?
Athena—who so fled from marriage that she begged
one gift from Zeus, virginity. 1075
But she would have the prize, you say. And why?
To help her hunt some god to marry her?
Never make gods out fools to whitewash your own evil.
No one with sense will listen to you.
And Aphrodite, did you say—who would not laugh? 1080
—must take my son to Menelaus' house?
Why? Could she not stay quietly in heaven
and send you on—and all your town—to Troy?
My son was beautiful exceedingly.
You saw him—your own desire was enough. 1085
No need of any goddess.
Men's follies—they are Aphrodite.
She rose up from the sea-foam; where the froth
and foam of life are, there she is.
It was my son. You saw him in his Eastern dress 1090
all bright with gold, and you were mad with love.
Such little things had filled your mind in Argos,
busied with this and that.
Once free of Sparta and in Troy where gold,
you thought, flowed like a river, you would spend 1095
and spend, until your spendthrift hand
had drowned the town.
Your luxuries, your insolent excesses,
Menelaus' halls had grown too small for them.
Enough of that. By force you say he took you? 1100
You cried out? Where? No one in Sparta heard you.
Young Castor was there and his brother too,
not yet among the stars.
And when you came to Troy and on your track the Greeks,
and death and agony in battle, 1105
if they would tell you, "Greece has won today,"
you would praise this man here, Menelaus,
to vex my son, who feared him as a rival.
Then Troy had victories, and Menelaus
was nothing to you. 1110
Looking to the successful side—oh yes,
you always followed there.

There was no right or wrong side in your eyes.
And now you talk of ropes—letting your body down
in secret from the wall, longing to go.   1115
Who found you so?
Was there a noose around your neck?
A sharp knife in your hand? Such ways
as any honest woman would have found,
who loved the husband she had lost?   1120
Often and often I would tell you, Go,
my daughter. My sons will find them other wives.
I will help you. I will send you past the lines
to the Greek ships. Oh, end this war
between our foes and us. But this was bitter to you.   1125
In Paris' house you had your insolent way.
You liked to see the Eastern men fall at your feet.
These were great things to you.
Look at the dress you wear, your ornaments.
Is that the way to meet your husband?   1130
You should not dare to breathe the same air with him.
Oh, men should spit upon you.
Humbly, in rags, trembling and shivering,
with shaven head—so you should come,
with shame at last, instead of shamelessness,   1135
for all the wickedness you did.
King, one word more and I am done.
Give Greece a crown, be worthy of yourself.
Kill her. So shall the law stand for all women,
that she who plays false to her husband's bed,   1140
shall die.
A WOMAN   O son of an ancient house, O King, now show
that you are worthy of your fathers.
The Greeks called you a woman, shamed you
with that reproach. Be strong. Be noble. Punish her.   1145
MENELAUS (*Impatiently*)   I see it all as you do. We agree.
She left my house because she wanted to—
went to a stranger's bed. Her talk of Aphrodite—
big words, no more. (*Turns to* HELEN) Go. Death is near.
Men there are waiting for you. In their hands are stones.   1150
Die—a small price for the Greeks' long suffering.
You shall not any more dishonor me.
HELEN (*Kneeling and clinging to him*)   No! No! Upon my knees—see, I am
                                             praying to you.
It was the gods, not me. Oh, do not kill me.   1155
Forgive.
HECUBA   The men she murdered. Think of those
who fought beside you—of their children too.
Never betray them. Hear that prayer.

MENELAUS (*Roughly*) Enough, old woman. She is nothing to me.   1160
  Men, take her to the ships and keep her safe
  until she sails. (*The soldiers lead* HELEN *out*)
HECUBA But not with you! She must not set foot on your ship.
MENELAUS (*Bitterly*) And why? Her weight too heavy for it?
HECUBA A lover once, a lover always.   1165
MENELAUS (*Pauses a moment to think*) Not so when what he loved has gone.
  But it shall be as you would have it.
  Not on the same ship with me. The advice is good.
  And when she gets to Argos she shall die
  a death hard as her heart.   1170
  So in the end she will become a teacher,
  teach women chastity—no easy thing,
  but yet her utter ruin will strike terror
  into their silly hearts,
  even women worse than she. (*He goes*)   1175
CHORUS And so your temple in Ilium,
  your altar of frankincense,
  are given to the Greek,
  the flame from the honey, the corn and the oil,
  the smoke from the myrrh floating upward,   1180
  the holy citadel.
  And Ida, the mountain where the ivy grows,
  and rivers from the snows rush through the glens,
  and the boundary wall of the world
  where the first sunlight falls,   1185
  the blessed home of the dawn.

  The sacrifice is gone, and the glad call
  of dancers, and the prayers at evening to the gods
  that last the whole night long.
  Gone too the golden images,   1190
  and the twelve Moons, to Trojans holy.
  Do you care, do you care, do you heed these things,
  O God, from your throne in high heaven?
  My city is perishing,
  ending in fire and onrushing flame.   1195
A WOMAN O dear one, O my husband,
  you are dead, and you wander
  unburied, uncared for, while over-seas
  the ships shall carry me,
  swift-winged ships darting onward,   1200
  On to the land the riders love,
  Argos, where the towers of stone
  built by giants reach the sky.
ANOTHER Children, our children.
  At the gate they are crying, crying,   1205

calling to us with tears,
Mother, I am all alone.
They are driving me away
To a black ship, and I cannot see you.

ANOTHER Where, oh where? To holy Salamis,   1210
    with swift oars dipping?
    Or to the crest of Corinth,
    the city of two seas,
    where the gates King Pelops built
    for his dwelling stand?   1215

ANOTHER Oh, if only, far out to sea,
    the crashing thunder of God
    would fall down, down on Menelaus' ship,
    crashing down upon her oars,
    the Aegean's wild-fire light.   1220
    He it was drove me from Troy.
    He is driving me in tears
    over to Greece to slavery.

ANOTHER And Helen, too, with her mirrors of gold,
    looking and wondering at herself,   1225
    as pleased as a girl.
    May she never come to the land of her fathers,
    never see the hearth of her home,
    her city, the temple with brazen doors
    of goddess Athena.   1230
    Oh, evil marriage that brought
    shame to Greece, the great,
    and to the waters of Simois
    sorrow and suffering. (TALTHYBIUS *approaches with a few soldiers. He is*
                        carrying the dead child)   1235

ANOTHER WOMAN Before new sufferings are grown old
    come other new.
    Look, unhappy wives of Troy,
    the dead Astyanax.
    They threw him from the tower as one might pitch a ball. 1240
    Oh, bitter killing.
    And now they have him there.

TALTHYBIUS (*He gives the body into* HECUBA'S *arms*) One ship is waiting,
        Hecuba, to take aboard
    the last of all the spoil Achilles' son was given,   1245
    and bear it with the measured beat of oars
    to Thessaly's high headlands.
    The chief himself has sailed because of news
    he heard, his father's father
    driven from his land by his own son.   1250
    So, more for haste even than before,
    he went and with him went Andromache.

She drew tears from me there upon the ship
mourning her country, speaking to Hector's grave,
begging a burial for her child, your Hector's son, 1255
who thrown down from the tower lost his life.
And this bronze-fronted shield, the dread of many a Greek,
which Hector used in battle,
that it should never, so she prayed,
hang in strange halls, her grief before her eyes, 1260
nor in that bridal chamber where she must be a wife,
Andromache, this dead boy's mother.
She begged that he might lie upon it in his grave,
instead of cedar wood or vault of stone.
And in your arms she told me I must lay him, 1265
for you to cover the body, if you still
have anything, a cloak left—
And to put flowers on him if you could,
since she has gone. Her master's haste
kept her from burying her child. 1270
So now, whenever you have laid him out,
we'll heap the earth above him, then
up with the sails!
Do all as quickly as you can. One trouble
I saved you. When we passed Scamander's stream 1275
I let the water run on him and washed his wounds.
I am off to dig his grave now, break up the hard earth.
Working together, you and I,
will hurry to the goal, oars swift for home.

HECUBA   Set the shield down—the great round shield of Hector. 1280
I wish I need not look at it. (TALTHYBIUS *goes out with the soldiers*)
You Greeks, your spears are sharp but not your wits.
You feared a child. You murdered him.
Strange murder. You were frightened, then? You thought
he might build up our ruined Troy? And yet 1285
when Hector fought and thousands at his side,
we fell beneath you. Now, when all is lost,
the city captured and the Trojans dead,
a little child like this made you afraid.
The fear that comes when reason goes away— 1290
Myself, I do not wish to share it. (*She dismisses the Greeks and their ways*)
Beloved, what a death has come to you.
If you had fallen fighting for the city,
if you had known strong youth and love
and godlike power, if we could think 1295
you had known happiness—if there is
happiness anywhere—
But now—you saw and knew, but with your soul
you did not know, and what was in your house

you could not use.   1300
Poor little one. How savagely our ancient walls,
Apollo's towers, have torn away the curls
your mother's fingers wound and where she pressed
her kisses—here where the broken bone grins white—
Oh no—I cannot—   1305
Dear hands, the same dear shape your father's had,
how loosely now you fall. And dear proud lips
forever closed. False words you spoke to me
when you would jump into my bed, call me sweet names
and tell me, Grandmother, when you are dead,   1310
I'll cut off a great lock of hair and lead my soldiers all
to ride out past your tomb.
Not you, but I, old, homeless, childless,
must lay you in your grave, so young,
so miserably dead.   1315
Dear God. How you would run to greet me.
And I would nurse you in my arms, and oh,
so sweet to watch you sleep. All gone.
What could a poet carve upon your tomb?
"A child lies here whom the Greeks feared and slew."   1320
Ah, Greece should boast of that.
Child, they have taken all that was your father's,
but one thing, for your burying, you shall have,
the bronze-barred shield.
It kept safe Hector's mighty arm, but now   1325
it has lost its master.
The grip of his own hand has marked it—dear to me then—
His sweat has stained the rim. Often and often
in battle it rolled down from brows and beard
while Hector held the shield close.   1330
Come, bring such covering for the pitiful dead body
as we still have. God has not left us much
to make a show with. Everything I have
I give you, child.
    O men, secure when once good fortune comes—   1335
fools, fools. Fortune's ways—
here now, there now. She springs
away—back—and away, an idiot's dance.
No one is ever always fortunate. (*The women have come in with coverings
    and garlands*)   1340
A WOMAN Here, for your hands, they bring you clothing for the dead,
    got from the spoils of Troy.
HECUBA (*Shrouding the body and putting garlands beside it*) Oh, not because
    you conquered when the horses raced,
    or with the bow outdid your comrades,
    your father's mother lays these wreaths beside you,   1345

and of all that was yours, gives you this covering.
A woman whom God hates has robbed you,
taken your life, when she had taken your treasure
and ruined all your house.   1350
A WOMAN   Oh, my heart! As if you touched it—touched it.
Oh, this was once our prince, great in the city.
HECUBA   So on your wedding day I would have dressed you,
the highest princess of the East your bride.
Now on your body I must lay the raiment,   1355
all that is left of the splendor that was Troy's.
And the dear shield of Hector, glorious in battle,
mother of ten thousand triumphs won,
it too shall have its wreath of honor,
undying it will lie beside the dead.   1360
More honorable by far than all the armor
Odysseus won, the wicked and the wise.
A WOMAN   You, O child, our bitter sorrow,
earth will now receive.
Mourn, O Mother.   1365
HECUBA   Mourn, indeed.
A WOMAN   Weeping for all the dead.
HECUBA   Bitter tears.
A WOMAN   Your sorrows that can never be forgotten. (*The Funeral rite is now
begun,* HECUBA *symbolically healing the wounds*)   1370
HECUBA   I heal your wounds; with linen I bind them.
Ah, in words only, not in truth—
a poor physician.
But soon among the dead your father
will care for you.   1375
A WOMAN   Beat, beat your head.
Lift your hands and let them fall,
moving in measure.
HECUBA   O Women. Dearest—
A WOMAN   Oh, speak to us. Your cry—what does it mean?   1380
HECUBA   Only this the gods would have,
pain for me and pain for Troy,
those they hated bitterly.
Vain, vain, the bulls we slew.*
And yet—had God not bowed us down,   1385
not laid us low in dust,
none would have sung of us or told our wrongs
in stories men will listen to forever.
Go: lay our dead in his poor grave,
with these last gifts of death given to him.   1390
I think those that are gone care little
how they are buried. It is we, the living,

1384 As sacrifices.

our vanity. (*Women lift the shield with the body on it and carry it out*)

A WOMAN   Poor mother—her high hopes were stayed on you
and they are broken.   1395
They called you happy at your birth,
a good man's son.
Your death was miserable exceedingly.

ANOTHER   Oh, see, see—
On the crested height of Troy   1400
fiery hands. They are flinging torches.
Can it be
some new evil?
Something still unknown?

TALTHYBIUS (*He stops as he enters and speaks off stage*)   Captains, attention.   1405
You have been given charge
to burn this city. Do not let your torches sleep.
Hurry the fire on.
When once the town is level with the ground
then off for home and glad goodbye to Troy.   1410
And you, you Women—I will arrange for you
as well, one speech for everything—
whenever a loud trumpet-call is sounded,
go to the Greek ships, to embark.
Old woman, I am sorriest for you,   1415
follow. Odysseus' men are here to get you.
He drew you—you must leave here as his slave.

HECUBA   The end then. Well—the height of sorrow, I stand there.
Troy is burning—I am going.
But—hurry, old feet, if you can,   1420
a little nearer—here, where I can see
my poor town, say goodbye to her.
You were so proud a city, in all the East
the proudest. Soon your name the whole world knew,
will be taken from you. They are burning you   1425
and leading us away, their slaves.
O God—What makes me say that word?
The gods—I prayed, they never listened.
Quick, into the fire—Troy, I will die with you.
Death then—oh, beautiful.   1430

TALTHYBIUS   Out of your head, poor thing, with all you've suffered.
Lead her away—Hold her, don't be too gentle.
She must be taken to Odysseus.
Give her into his hands. She is his— (*Shakes his head*)
his prize. (*It grows darker*)   1435

A WOMAN   Ancient of days, our country's Lord,
Father, who made us,
You see your children's sufferings.
Have we deserved them?

ANOTHER   He sees—but Troy has perished, the great city. ¹⁴⁴⁰
   No city now, never again.

ANOTHER   Oh, terrible!
   The fire lights the whole town up.
   The inside rooms are burning.
   The citadel—it is all flame now. ¹⁴⁴⁵

ANOTHER   Troy is vanishing.
   War first ruined her.
   And what was left is rushing up in smoke,
   the glorious houses fallen.
   First the spear and then the fire. ¹⁴⁵⁰

HECUBA (*She stands up and seems to be calling to someone far away*)   Children,
   hear, your mother is calling.

A WOMAN (*Gently*)   They are dead, those you are speaking to.

HECUBA   My knees are stiff, but I must kneel.
   Now, strike the ground with both my hands— ¹⁴⁵⁵

A WOMAN   I too, I kneel upon the ground.
   I call to mine down there.
   Husband, poor husband.

HECUBA   They are driving us like cattle—taking us away.

A WOMAN   Pain, all pain. ¹⁵⁶⁰

ANOTHER   To a slave's house, from my country.

HECUBA   Priam, Priam, you are dead,
   and not a friend to bury you.
   The evil that has found me—
   do you know? ¹⁵⁶⁵

A WOMAN   No. Death has darkened his eyes.
   He was good and the wicked killed him.

HECUBA   O dwellings of the gods and O dear city,
   the spear came first and now
   only the red flame lives there. ¹⁵⁷⁰

A WOMAN   Fall and be forgotten. Earth is kind.

ANOTHER   The dust is rising, spreading out like a great wing of smoke.
   I cannot see my house.

ANOTHER   The name has vanished from the land,
   and we are gone, one here, one there. ¹⁵⁷⁵
   And Troy is gone forever. (*A great crash is heard*)

HECUBA   Did you hear? Did you know—

A WOMAN   The fall of Troy—

ANOTHER   Earthquake and flood and the city's end—

HECUBA   Trembling body—old weak limbs, ¹⁵⁸⁰
   you must carry me on to the new day of slavery. (*A trumpet sounds*)

A WOMAN   Farewell, dear city.
   Farewell, my country, where once my children lived.
   On to the ships—
   There below, the Greek ships wait. (*The trumpet sounds again and the* ¹⁵⁸⁵
                                    women pass out)

Agave brandishing the head of Pentheus, and Bacchae. Roman stucco relief, *ca.* 1st century A.D.
Courtesy German Archaeological Institute, Rome

THE BACCHAE

by Euripides

Translated by Margaret Kinmont Tennant

Characters
DIONYSUS, *divine son of Zeus and Semele*
CADMUS, *formerly king of Thebes, father of Semele*
PENTHEUS, *king of Thebes, grandson of Cadmus*
AGAVE, *mother of Pentheus, daughter of Cadmus*
TEIRESIAS, *an aged seer*
CHORUS *of Bacchantes*
A soldier of Pentheus' guard
Two Messengers

(*Enter* DIONYSUS *in fox-skin cap, with thyrsus. He has the majesty of a wild animal, a beautiful and dreadful innocence*)

DIONYSUS   I am here on Theban soil, the son of Zeus,
Dionysus, born of Semele, Cadmus' child,
When death descended charioted by fire.*
I in the likeness of a mortal stand
Where flows Ismenus, and by Dirce's well.   5
   There, by the walls, my mother lies entombed
Our Lady of Thunders: in her ruined bower
The smouldering fires of Zeus are yet alive,
As Hera still triumphs in her revenge.*
But blest be Cadmus for this hallowed plot,   10
His daughter's precinct. I have wreathed it round
With the luxuriance of my clustered vine.
   Now have I passed the Lydian fields of gold,
Phrygia, and sunburnt glens of Persia,
The Bactrian fastnesses, the highland snows   15
Of Ecbatana, Araby the Blest,
And Asian coasts, where on frequented ways
The Hellene mingling with barbarian keeps
Fair towered cities built by the salt sea;
And Thebes out of all Hellas I elect,   20
While other lands in my solemnities

---

[3] At Semele's request that Zeus appear to her in all his heavenly splendor, he appeared as a column of fire and consumed her. Of this union Dionysus was born. To conceal him from Hera, Zeus encased the child in his thigh.

[9] That is, through Semele's consummation.

Dance, that I be revealed to man as God.
And first in Thebes, my chosen one, I wed
The fawn-skin to their flesh; wake the wild cry,
And arm them with the ivy-tressèd spear*;   25
Since her own sisters, whom it least became,
Declared Dionysus was no son of Zeus;
But Semele, fallen to some mortal love,
Made Zeus the author of her shame, forsooth:
A lying trick of Cadmus; for whose lie,   30
They say, she took her chastisement by fire.*
Wherefore I lashed them out of hearth and home,
Who now inhabit the bare mountain-side,
Wandering, and, perforce, my vestments wear.
And all Cadmean women, that were past   35
Their childhood, I afflicted and drove out;
And rich and poor sit under the stone-pines
With Cadmus' daughters, on the roofless rocks.
For so this people, though my mysteries
For them be veiled, whether they will or no,   40
Shall know my mother's champion, who is risen,
The Immortal One she bare to Supreme God.
   Cadmus has now resigned his sovereignty.
Pentheus, his grandson and his heir, defies
The god in me, and in his litanies   45
My name is unremembered, and my peace
He scorns. But I will show myself as God
To him, and to all Thebes. It it be well
With Thebes, I go my way to consummate
My revelation. If they arm their wrath   50
To drive my Mænads from the mountain, I
Defend my own, and lead my host to war.
To this end have I hid my face divine,
Veiled in the semblance of mortality.

   Ye women, ye my worshippers, who come   55
In my communion and my embassy
From Tmolus, rampart of the Lydian plain,
Take the drum, racy of the Phrygian soil,
The instrument of Cybele's riot and mine,
And with its menace be the royal halls   60
Besieged, that all the City of Cadmus see;
While on the ridges of Cithæron, where
My Mænads are, I weave my mystery. (*Exit*)
   (*Enter* CHORUS *as* DIONYSUS *leaves. The leader bears the Winnowing-fan,
   the mystic cradle of Dionysus, laden with the fruits of earth*)   65

---

25 The thyrsus, a staff tipped with ivy leaves and sometimes used as a javelin.
31 Semele's sisters thought that the story of her union with Zeus was invented by Cadmus.

CHORUS   From afar, from afar . . . .
    I am swept here from the cold mountains of Tmolus,
        By a child of the Thunder;
    And with labour that is heart's ease
        And with awe worship his name;   70
        Who is there? Who is there? Who
        On the road? Way for the Bacchus!
            And in silence
        Let him pass! Hear me with chaste lips
            In the rites ancient and holy   75
                Dionysus, I'll chant thee.

    Happy the one whose soul resteth
    In the gods, a pure Mænad,
        In the Mystic Way walking;
    Purging her sins with long vigil   80
        On the Blessèd Hills; dancing
        That her soul be kept holy,
    When the Great Mother of Ida
    In procession goes to the Mountain,
    When the wild thyrsus is shaken,   85
    And with heads crownèd with ivy,
        We are thine, O Dionysus!
        To the Bacchus! To the Bacchus!
    For we bear triumphing God's son
    Dionysus, and from Phrygia,   90
    From the high hills to the wide ways
    Where in Hellas there is dancing
        Lead him, Thunder his name.

    Sudden and swift there came travail,
        When the wings of fire smote her,   95
        And by Love's descent blasted,
    Ere he was formed the womb cast him,
        And the Mother's soul went out
        In the swoop of God's lightning.
    But the Great Father received him,   100
    And he lay hid, and was folded
    In the chambers of creation.
    With a gold clasp he had bound him
    In his thigh, secret from Hera;

    And he bore him when the seasons   105
    Were fulfill'd, hornèd, a Bull-god;
    And with serpents for a garland
    He is crown'd: whence do the Mænads
    With the creatures of the wildwood

Weave them crowns for their hair.

Nurse of the Maid that bore him,
City of Thebes, let ivy,
Briony, briony with tendrils,
Berry and bloom adorn thee!
Come with an oaken spear to the rout,
Come with a spear of pinewood!
Round your limbs be a fawn-skin thrown,
Dappled and tufted with tassels of wool!
Cleanse your souls with the proud, riotous thyrsus,
And arise! Round you the earth all will be dancing,
Bromius* leads you, ye know not where,
Over the hills, to the hills and away!
There be the wanderers,
From spindle, and from ingle-nook
Lash'd by thee, Dionysus.

Hall of the holy War-dance,
Cradle of Zeus, when round him,
Crying, a little one, the armour
Clashed, with a hollower boom from
Corybant's drum; three helmeted heads
Tossed in the Cretan cavern.*
Now that drum with an undertone
Beats to the lilt of the Lydian flute,
Softly blown for the night-orgies of Rhea;*
And a throb comes in the sweet songs of the Mænads;
Satyrs behind, in the wake by the tomb
Prance for his mother, the last of the choirs,
Rounding the mystery
When men, holding triennial feast,
Learn thy way, Dionysus.

Sweet my Belovèd who running over the mountaintops
Falls voluptuously, when Bacchanals hunt,
Nakèd, with only the pelt of fawns,
Rending the kid for the blood of the carnival,
Rushing to the East by the glimmering valley, when a trumpet calls,
Bromios, Evoi!
Flowing with milk is the plain, with wine-wells, flowing with bees'
ambrosia.
And as smoke rising from frankincense

121 Another name for Dionysus.
131 This detail from the story of the birth of Zeus in a cavern in Crete is sometimes rendered "three-crested helmet." Its meaning is not known.
134 Mother of Zeus.

The High Priest uplifts   150
   Tawny flare of a pine-torch,
   Then with thyrsus enkindled,
By leaping, and dancing, he is shepherd to the rovers,
      And shouts loud in exultance,
And his locks, showering, are blown by the nightwind.   155
Preluding sweet song by a passionate cry,
   "Ho!" he cries, "to the Bacchus!
      Ho! to the Bacchus!"
   Tmolus, peak with the golden falls,
   Sing to the Lord Dionysus,   160
Sing him with humming and drone of drums,
Glory to the glorious, the Leader of joyance!
   Call, as ye called on the mountains of Phrygia!
      Flute of the haunting melody
      Breathe, and ye cymbals of ecstasy,   165
         Be clashed in measure
For feet that roam to the hills, to the hills!
As the hoofs of a foal when his mother is pasturing,
So will your feet be afire with glee of the springtime.

                    (*Enter* TEIRESIAS, *led*)   170

TEIRESIAS   Who stands before the gate? Bid Cadmus come,
   Agenor's son, of Sidon, who hath built
   Our Theban city all compact of towers.
   Go, say Teiresias seeks him; well he knows
   What I, an old man with my elder, swore: 175
   To raise the fiery thyrsus, our loins girt
   With fawn-skins, and our heads with ivy crowned.

                    (*Enter* CADMUS)

CADMUS   O welcome, friend! While yet within I knew
   That voice of understanding. Here am I   180
   Arrayed in livery of the god. He is
   My daughter's son; then who so fit as we
   To do him honour, as our strength avails?
   But where to dance? and where to rest? and where
   To toss a hoary head? Let age lead age;   185
   Lead me, Teiresias: wisdom is of thee.
   For night nor day I shall not weary be,
   Beating the thyrsus on the earth. Oh sweet
   Oblivion of old age.
TEIRESIAS   I too, like thee,   190
   Am in my prime, impatient for the dance.
CADMUS   Shall we then to the mountain, charioting?
TEIRESIAS   We do him wrong to seek for chariot-wheels.
CADMUS   We are old; yet I will lead thee like a child.
TEIRESIAS   Without our labour God will lead us on.   195
CADMUS   Is there no other who will dance for him?

TEIRESIAS   We only are sound of mind: the rest are mad.

CADMUS   The way is long; but clasp thy hand in mine.

TEIRESIAS   There then. . . . My hand, to be thy yokefellow.

CADMUS   Far be it from me, who am man, to scorn a god.   200

TEIRESIAS   We chop no logic with the powers that be.
     No argument can filch our heritage,
  Religion, that is old as time; no sage,
  Set on a pinnacle above his peers.
  Will any say I shame my hoary hair   205
  When out I go a-dancing, ivy-crowned?
  The god has set no bourn; he chose not youth
  To dance for him; he looks to young and old
  For common service; and there is no place
  For magic numbers at his festival.   210

CADMUS   Teiresias, since for thee the light is dark,
  I am seer and interpreter for thee
  For Pentheus now with urgent stride comes near,
  Successor to my throne, Echion's son,
  Like one possessed. Wild words are in his mouth.   215
  (*Enter the young king* PENTHEUS *in fury. A reckless, sensual character, of
       brilliant eloquence, in fact rather like Alcibiades**)

PENTHEUS   And if I leave the land awhile, must I
  Return to this new pestilence? Our homes
  Deserted, and our women running wild   220
  On wooded hills, veiling their wantonness
  With false religion for a foundling god,
  Dionysus, or whatever name it be!
  And in their midst, for sacrament, is set
  The wassail-bowl. Yea, there be solitudes   225
  Among the hills, for deeds of shame! So much
  For Mænads, incense-bearers! Love, I say,
  Not Bacchus! Aphrodite leads the rout.
    I have captured some. Their hands are manacled,
  My servants hold them in the common jail,   230
  And I will hunt down from the mountain-side
  The truants: Ino, and Autonoë,
  And Queen Agave, mother to my flesh.
  Once let me take them in my fowling-nets
  Of steel, we'll have no more of devilry!   235
    They tell me that there is a Stranger come,
  Some false Enchanter from the Lydian hills,
  His perfumed hair in yellow ringlets hung,
  His eyes as dark as wine, and in their deeps
  The lure of Aphrodite. He by day   240
  And in the gracious night is ministrant
  To women in their flower. Once in my toils,

[217] A handsome, brilliant, and unscrupulous Athenian general and statesman.

Farewell to thyrsus-beat! A headless corpse,
I think, will toss its yellow hair no more!
    His message is: Dionysus is divine, 245
The groin of Zeus was cradle to the Babe
That was by torches of the lightning burnt
With Semele, when she lied of her love-child.
What strangling would avenge such blasphemy
From that imposter, be he who he may? (*These words evoke a strange silence*) 250
    But what is here? The prince of augury
Teiresias, in a dappled fawn-skin clad?
My mother's father—O a sight for mirth!—
Goes revelling with the thyrsus. Sire, for shame!
Folly sits ill upon thy hoary hair. 255
Come, and shake off the ivy. Get thy hand
Free of the thyrsus, for my mother's sake!
    This is thy work, Teiresias! A new god,
New auspices, and new burnt-offering
Would bring new profits for thine augury! 260
But for thy grey old age, thy lot were chains
Moping, with all thy Mænads in a ring,
For these foul sacraments. Once let the grape
Bring merriment to women,—I ask no more—
Nothing is wholesome in your mysteries. 265

CHORUS   Blaspheme not! Stranger, dost thou not fear God,
And Cadmus, once the Sower of Dragon-seed?*
Son of Echion, shame not all thy line!

TEIRESIAS   In masters of persuasion to speak well
Is no great matter, once the sails are set. 270
Thy tongue runs light, as though thy heart were sound,
Yet in thy words is no sincerity;
And bold adventurers of nimble tongue
Ruin the city, if they be not wise.
    And as for this young god, whom thou dost scorn, 275
I have no words to tell how great he is
In Hellas. Vain, presumptuous youth, there be
Two gods pre-eminent: Demeter first,
Our Mother Earth, whichever name we will,
Dispenses all dry grain for nourishment. 280
He that came after, Semele's son, fulfilled
The perfect round, and for refreshment gave
The grape, that brings to miserable men
Rest, when their veins are with the vintage flown,
And sleep, and dear relief from daily pain. 285
He is god, he is drink-offering to all gods,
And by his grace all blessings flow to men.

---

267 By divine direction Cadmus slew a dragon and sowed its teeth as seed. His harvest was a troup of giant
    warriors, one of whom was Echion, the father of Pentheus.

A silly tale, say you, that in the groin
Of Zeus they wrapt him? Learn the parable.
When from the thunder-blast the Father bore   290
His infant to Olympus, Hera sought
To hurl him from the heights of heaven; but Zeus
Hoodwinked her in the high celestial way.
With ether from the groinèd arcs of fire
That roof the world, he made a changeling,   295
That Hera's wrath might vent itself in vain.
And with the passing of long ages, men
Figured the groin of Zeus, changing the name
From groins of heaven, and wove a tale withal.
   A prophet is our god. His ecstasy   300
Is instinct with strange visions, when the wine
Enters our veins with power; his votaries speak
In oracles. Even in the pomp of war
He hath his portion. Men-at-arms have fled
In sudden fear or ever a spear was thrown   305
For the weird madness that he sent on them.
One day upon the cliffs of Delphi, thou
Shalt see his leaping torch set the twin peaks
Ablaze; and his triumphal progress pass
Through Hellas. Then take heed. Boast not that thou   310
Art sovereign, lest in seeming so to be
Thy fantasy mislead thee. Rather seem
Wise. Give him hospitality. Pour out
Libation, revel, crown thy head with flowers.
   Dionysus will not make your women chaste   315
In love, for chastity is of the heart.
Go, seek it there, for none can ravish it
Eternally. In the wine-festival
She that is chaste will keep her body pure.
   Dost thou not glory when the multitude   320
Attend thee in the gates, to hail the name
Of Pentheus? What if he delights in praise?
So I and Cadmus, whom thou dost deride,
Will thatch our heads with ivy, for the dance,
Grey-headed team, but dancers, none the less.   325
I will not, for thy favour, fight with God.
Thou stricken one, no herbs can make thee whole,
And not without them is thy mind diseased.

CHORUS   Most reverend prophet, Phœbus is not shamed
   By one who worships Bromius, the great God.   330

CADMUS   My son, Teiresias counsels well. Abide
   With us. Pass not the bounds of public peace,
   For all thy wisdom is a wandering light.
   What if he be no god? Then have thy way,

But call him God. It is a noble lie 335
That Semele's love-child be acclaimed divine,
And honour all our lineage. Bear in mind
Actæon,* and how pitiably he died
For his vain vaunting that he could outspeed
The Huntress in her valleys. Rabid hounds 340
That were his nurslings tore him limb from limb.
Let not the like befall thee. Here be crowns
Of ivy. Come, be of our company!

PENTHEUS   I tell thee, touch me not! Back to the rout!
Wipe not thy filthy madness on my head! 345
And as for thy seducer, he shall rue
His doctrine. Who will go for me? Make haste!
The Siege Prophetic where his auspices
Are vended, root it up with trident's prongs,
And hew it all to wreckage on the ground, 350
And fling his chaplets to the wind and storm!
These are the wounds will cut him to the heart.
   Go up and down the city! Run to earth
The womanish alien whose infection breeds
Among our wives, and lures them from the hearth; 355
And if ye take him, bring him here in chains
For death by stoning. Bitter to him be
The day he came to Thebes for festival.

TEIRESIAS   Unhappy man, what hast thou said? Before
Thou wert deluded: this is madness now. 360
   Come, Cadmus, let us go, and pray for him,
Though he be savage; and for all the land
Pray, lest some visitation come on them
Undreamt of. Take the thyrsus, follow me.
Hold me; I will hold thee; for two old men 365
Need not fall down. The Bacchus, son of Zeus,
Requires our faithful service. Let us go.
May Pentheus, name of grief, bring us no grief.
I speak not as a prophet, but as man
Whose ears have heard the fool blaspheming God. (*They go off together*) 370

CHORUS   There is One ruling in heaven,
        There is One radiant on earth,
        When her wings hover on the deep.
        (Shall a king dare to offend?)
        Be ye still! Holiness hears! 375
        He hath blasphemed the divine Child
        Who is thronèd and anointed
        In the fragrance of the vine-bloom;
      The Enchanter: by the largess of his hand

---

338 Actaeon was another of Cadmus' grandsons; while hunting, he inadvertently saw Artemis bathing,
was changed by her into a stag and was pursued and killed by his own dogs.

Are the feet light in the dance,   380
    And the heart laughs to the flute.
If a god drink or a mortal
When the wine gleams in the chalice,
When the rose crowns thee, or ivy,
There is rest there from remembrance,   385
There is sleep flows from the wine-bowl to fold thee.

For the vain boast of the fool,
And the tongue breaking the rein
Will at last come to despair.
But a heart dwelling at peace   390
Is a still port in the storm,
And a house builded to stand firm,
When the wild weather will shake thee.
For we walk not in the darkness;
There are watchers where the stars kindle their fires.   395
    How unwise then are the wise,
    And the man eager to know
If he pass that which is lawful
In the high perilous adventure
Will despise earth and her gladness.   400
    And I hold such in derision;
    They are spell-bound and mislighted by Reason.

    O Wind, bear me to Cyprus,
    Where sea-born Aphrodite,
    And Loves haunting about her steps,   405
    Weave their spells to beguile me.
Paphos, down by the estuary
Where the Nile with a rainless flood
Waters land of the stranger.
Bear me where for a Muses' bower   410
Thessaly keeps in beauty enshrined
    Solemn slopes of Olympus.
O there spirit me, Bromius, Bromius,
Thou Torch-bearer of Mænads!
For there is Frolic,   415
And there Witchery,
And there is freedom for the sacred orgies.

The Bacchus, the Divine Child
Takes delight in the banquet,
He loves Peace and her infant Wealth;   420
Peace that Mother of Boyhood
His good pleasure to every man,
Be he rich or of low degree,

Gave heart's ease in the wine-cup,
Hating those that frown on the feast.   425
Vessels of joy be raised in the night,
    Days be served by his altar.
Be heart-free of the arrogant fellowship,
    The vainglorious wisemen.
        And humbly offer   430
        In simplicity
    The faith of poor men,
        And the old observance.

———————

(*Enter a* MESSENGER, *leading Dionysus, manacled*)

MESSENGER   King Pentheus, here am I. I have fulfilled   435
The chase whereon thou sentst me, not in vain.
This gentle creature of the wild forebore
To flee, but gave his hands of his own will,
And grew not pale, nor lost his wine-dark bloom.
Smiling he gave himself, as though for love,   440
And freed my task from all indignity.
I was ashamed, and said, "Not by my will
"I lead thee, but by his whom I obey"
And all the Mænads that in thy dark keep
The gaolers held, and manacled for shame,   445
Are free to frolic in the vale. The height
Is jubilant, and resounds with Bromios' name.
The shackles from their feet fell off; the keys
Unlocked the doors, moved by no mortal hand.
In this man's wake are many wonders done   450
In Thebes. Let be: the rest is in thy hand.
PENTHEUS   Let him go free. Once in my snaring-net
He is not so nimble to escape my will. . . .
        (*Sneering, yet his senses dazzled by the Stranger's beauty*)
    Thy body hath its beauty, not ill-made,   455
O Stranger, for the quest of women's flesh,
For which thou art in Thebes. No wrestler's hair
Framed such a face in flowing locks, to wake
Desire. Far from the sun love's labour kept
That skin so white, in the cool cloister's shade.   460
If we would hunt with Love we must be fair.
    Come, tell me first thy name and all thy race.
DIONYSUS   A simple tale; it is soon told. Maybe
Thou hast heard of Tmolus, where the crocus blows?
PENTHEUS   The range that girds Sardis with a ring-wall?   465
DIONYSUS   I come from Tmolus. I was Lydian born.
PENTHEUS   Whence hast thou mysteries to reveal to men?
DIONYSUS   Dionysus breathed on me, the son of Zeus.

PENTHEUS	Some foreign Zeus, a breeder of young gods?	
DIONYSUS	Zeus, that was Semele's bridegroom here in Thebes.	470
PENTHEUS	Came he by night, or in the sight of men?	
DIONYSUS	He saw me, and I saw, and was ordained.	
PENTHEUS	What is the ritual of thine ordinance?	
DIONYSUS	Only the mystic sees beyond the veil.	
PENTHEUS	A cunning feint, that I might long to know!	475
DIONYSUS	The rites abhor the irreligious soul.	
PENTHEUS	Thou hast seen God in his person as he is?	
DIONYSUS	As he would seem. For I command him not.	
PENTHEUS	Again the subtle swerve. Thy words are void.	
DIONYSUS	One shall be proven void whose words are wise.	480
PENTHEUS	And is this way the first he hath essayed?	
DIONYSUS	Barbarians all are dancing in his name.	
PENTHEUS	Since they are witless where the Greeks are wise.	
DIONYSUS	They are wiser here. Their ways are not as yours.	
PENTHEUS	Hold ye these ceremonies by night or day?	485
DIONYSUS	Chiefly by night, for her solemnity.	
PENTHEUS	The dark for women is craft and rottenness.	
DIONYSUS	Seek it by day, and evil may be found.	
PENTHEUS	Thou darkenest counsel. Thou shalt rue the day.	
DIONYSUS	And thou shalt rue thy brutal blasphemy.	490
PENTHEUS	(*Jocular*) 'Tis a bold Bacchus, not devoid of wit.	
DIONYSUS	What are these terrors that thou hast prepared?	
PENTHEUS	First I will cut this lovely tress away.	
DIONYSUS	My holy tress? I cherish it for God.	
PENTHEUS	Surrender now the thyrsus to my hand.	495
DIONYSUS	Deprive me. In his service it is borne.	
PENTHEUS	In darkness of the dungeon thou shalt lie.	
DIONYSUS	The god himself will free me, when I choose.	
PENTHEUS	Go call him with thy Mænads for a choir!	
DIONYSUS	He is present now and sees what I endure.	500
PENTHEUS	Where is he? For mine eyes can see him not.	
DIONYSUS	Beside me. The unholy see not God.	
PENTHEUS	Seize him! He mocks at Thebes, he mocks at me!	
DIONYSUS	The Holy bids the unholy bind me not.	
PENTHEUS	I bid them bind, and I am sovereign here.	505
DIONYSUS	What is thy life? What art thou? Who art thou?	
PENTHEUS	Pentheus, Echion's son, Agave's child.	
DIONYSUS	Thy name is of the family of grief.*	
PENTHEUS	Begone! and tether him in the stable, near	
	The manger, in the gloom of glooms! There weave	510
	Thy mystic round! His train, his ministers	
	Of evil, sell them in the slave-market!	
	Or take their timbrels and their cymbals! Now	

---

508 Pentheus' name, from *penthos,* suggests mourning.

These thrumming hands shall serve me at the loom.

DIONYSUS   So be it. I go. But what is sin remains   515
Sin; and the price shall be required of thee
By one whom thou deniest. He it is
That suffereth wrong when I am led in chains.

(DIONYSUS *is led off by guards.* PENTHEUS *goes*)

CHORUS   Fair above all waters   520
The august Maid of the Well.
Acheloüs for an issue*
Had the Well sacred to Dirce.
Did her breast rock a little one,
Who was snatch'd out of the wildfire?   525
When the Father to the portals
Of his thigh with prophecy called him:
"Dithyramb, I thus reveal thee
"To the womb of Man ascending.
"Dithyramb; so will the Thebans   530
"In supreme Mystery hail thee!"
But alas! for holy Dirce
She hath chased away the orgies,
And for all the bliss I brought her
She denies me, she repels me!   535
But a time comes for repentance;
She will yet taste of the vine-bloom;
She will yet weave me a dance to speed me.
Dreadful wrath of Pentheus!
From the old Dragon he came,   540
When the grim sheaves were embattled
In the harvest of the Men-at-arms.
He is no man who is sprung
From Echion, but a true son
Of the Earth-born, and Gigantic   545
In his challenge to the Godhead.
Will he hang a holy maiden
Who is ministrant to Bacchus?
For with violence he assailed me,
And the High Priest is a captive   550
In a dark and dismal dungeon.
Dionysus, wilt thou hear me?
(For perchance he treads a measure
And a gold thyrsus is glancing
In the high peace of Olympus)   555
When the last throes are upon me
Will he stoop down to defend a servant?

---

522 Acheloüs was the father of all rivers.

Is it Nysa,* and the forest
　　Where the wild things are aware?
Is it peaks yellow with crocus   560
　　Where his feet dance in the dawn?
Is it haply on Olympus
Where the leaves whisper of Orpheus?
For the time was when a harp sighed,
And the wild beasts were enchanted,   565
And the trees danced in the greenwood.
　　　Thou art blest, Pieria,*
For Evan glories to seek thee,
For the worship of the gorges
　　Where the swift Axios breaks.   570
He will dance over the torrent
When the choir sweeps to the South-west;
　　For the Great Reveller unseen
Bears the cup that hath healed unrest.
Now the Thessalian chivalry   575
Pour to him for vials of grace
　　Crystal beauty of water.

DIONYSUS (*Within*) Io!
　Bacchanals, hail! and again, hail!
　　Io, Bacchus! Io, Bacchus!   580
CHORUS Where is he? Vanishing voice of a benison!
　Where is my Lover who bade me hail?
DIONYSUS (*Within*) Io! Io! it is I: hail!
　Semele's son, the Divine Child.
CHORUS Io! Io! come to me! come to me!   585
　　Come with a rare hilarity,
　　Reveller, O Bromios, Bromios!
DIONYSUS (*Within*) Heave in convulsion, my Lady of Earthquaking!
CHORUS Ah! Ah!
　—Palace of Pentheus, rocking and wavering   590
　　Thou shalt fall eternally!
　—It is the Lord! It is Dionysus!
　—Blessèd his name!
　　　—Blessèd for aye.
　—See how a tremor is shaking the capitals!   595
　　Pillars are tottering! Listen to Bromios
　　　Shouting triumph through the halls!
DIONYSUS (*Within*) Kindle the lightning, the torch of the Thunderer!
　Fire, ah fire the palace of Pentheus!
CHORUS Ah! Ah!   600
　See how wildfire spreads that aureole

---

558 An unknown sacred fountain.

567 This and the following are rivers and streams which Dionysus had to cross in his passage from east to
west.

That around Semele's tomb halloweth the ground,
Semele once for love withering to ashes
  In God's lightning.
(*Trembling*) Terrible, fiery God of the Bacchanals!   605
Shudder before him: he ruins the house,
  Adown, adown with loud confusion
Shattering all with the blast of Zeus!
     (DIONYSUS *appears*)

DIONYSUS Mænads from the hills of Asia, what bewilderment of fear 610
Struck you down upon your faces? Heard ye Bromius in his might
Shatter the house to its foundations? Lift your hearts, be not afraid!
Let the trembling flesh triumphant rise and answer to my call!

CHORUS Light of lights! O mighty Prophet of the Dionysiac choir!
O sweet visitant with comfort for the desolate of soul!   615

DIONYSUS Did a wild despair possess you when the marshals of the king
Led me hence? And did ye mourn me, hid in Pentheus' gloomy cell?

CHORUS Who was left to be my guardian if the darkness closed on thee?
Tell me, how hast thou escaped him, when the tyrant held thee fast?

DIONYSUS I myself was my deliverer, with no striving nor distress. 620

CHORUS Though thy hands were bound behind thee in the clutch of cruel
               rope?

DIONYSUS Nay, with fancy there I mocked him. When he fondly thought
               to bind,
Never he touched, and never he held me, puffed up with the wind of 625
               dreams.
Lo! a Bull was at the manger, in the confines of my cell.
Round his hocks he slung the nooses, making fast the cloven hooves,
Breathing hard: with rage and anguish sweat was dripping from his brow;
Clenched his teeth, his lips were bruisèd. I the while was standing by, 630
And with tranquil eyes beheld him. Then with might the Bacchus came,
Shook the house, and lit the hovering fenfire on my mother's tomb.
Here he dashed, and there, distracted; called the seneschals to bring
Water-pots, and draw Acheloüs; all the household toiled in vain.
Soon he raised the loud alarum, cried that I had broken bounds, 635
Left his labour, scoured the palace, up and down, with sabre drawn.
Then the Bacchus (though I saw not, I but guess what he devised)
To the grand court sent a phantom. Pentheus with his iron blade
Made a pass, and stabbed the shining airy shape, as though he slew.
Then the Bacchus came with earthquake, and more terrible by far 640
Shook, and laid the house in ruins, all along the pillared hall.
Bitter his wrath to see my bondage. Pentheus then refused the fight,
Wearied out; for shall a mortal fling his challenge to the gods?
He had dared, and he was vanquished. I with quiet step withdrew,
And I came to you, despising all the arrogance of kings.   645
  Hark! Was it the creak of buskins, as he crossed the court within?
Soon he will be here. What language can he find for such a pass?
Light of heart shall I receive him, though he breathe the blast of war,

Since the dignity of patience is the birthright of the wise.

(*Enter* PENTHEUS)   650

PENTHEUS   We are abused! The stranger is gone free,
Whom we had held under constraint of chains.

Eà! Eà!*

He is there! How now? When thou hast taken leave,
Art thou so bold to meet me face to face?   655

DIONYSUS   No further! Bid thy wrath walk quietly.

PENTHEUS   Who was it burst the confines of thy cell?

DIONYSUS   Surely I spoke of him? Hast thou not heard?

PENTHEUS   Of whom? Thou art ever weaving some new tale.

DIONYSUS   He came, that gave to men the clustered vine.   660

(PENTHEUS *mutters a curse*)

DIONYSUS   Well hast thou cursed the holy gift of God.

PENTHEUS   Close down every portcullis in the wall!

DIONYSUS   What fence can stay the feet that are divine?

PENTHEUS   Ah wise, too wise, save where it profits thee!   665

DIONYSUS   Where wisdom most avails, there am I wise.
But first give audience: one attends thee here
Who from the mountain hath some news for thee.
We will abide thy pleasure, never fear.

(*Enter* MESSENGER, *a shepherd lad with the awkward beauty of youth*)   670

MESSENGER   Pentheus, thou sovereign of this Theban land,
But now I left Cithæron, on whose head
Shower chaste crystals of the incessant snow.

PENTHEUS   And what might bring thee with such eager speed?

MESSENGER   Mine eyes have seen the Mænads, whose white limbs   675
Flew swift as spears in throbbing ecstasy
Out of the land. I come to tell, O King
(Let all give ear), of more than miracles.
But first I ask how it may please thy grace:
Whether I shall speak boldly without fear,   680
Or tack to leeward; for, my lord, I dread
Thy sudden rage: thou art too much a king.

PENTHEUS   Speak on, for I will give thee sanctuary.
It is not just men who need fear my rage.
For every horror in thy tale, the more   685
Bitterly their seducer shall repent.

MESSENGER   Our flocks and herds were on the height, scaling
The free horizon, when the early sun
Sent forth his rays to comfort. And, behold!
Three choirs of Mænads, and three priestesses,—   690
Autonoë and thy mother Agave led
Two choirs, and in the third was Ino queen.
They slept with limbs at ease. One leant her back
Against an olive; one on the oak-leaves

653 An exclamation of surprise.

That strew the ground had thrown a careless head,
Yet with all modesty; not as thou say'st,
Drunken with wine, and with the haunting flute;
None sought for love sequestered in the shade.
   Thy Mother first uprising, in their midst
Woke the wild cry, and from their eyelids shook   700
Sleep, for she heard the lowing of hornèd kine.
And roused from their heavy bewilderment,
They darted up, and rank to rank they stood—
Young women and old and yet unmarried maids;
Arrayed upon their shoulders their wild hair,   705
And where the knots were loosened, they looped up
Their stippled fawnskins, and for curious belts
Girt them about with snakes of flickering tongue.
Here some young mother, whose sweet babe at home
Forsaken lies, had snatched a tender fawn   710
From the gazelles; and one a lion-cub,
And suckled her wild nursling at her breast,
Decking it with a chain of ivy-buds,
Or leaves of curly oak, or briony-bloom.
One with a thyrsus smote upon the rock,   715
And water spouted like a mountain-spring;
One pierced the ground with a long fennel-stalk,
And God sent bubbling up a well of wine;
Or thirsting for a creamy draught, they stooped,
Pressing their finger-tips into the moss,   720
And nests of milk were there; the thyrsus-shaft,
Among its ivy, dropped with honey-dew.
   We herds and shepherds gathered to the tryst,
Each with a tale to tell more wonderful
Than other. Then uprose a vagabond,   725
A saucy fellow of the streets, and said,
"O ye that move in the high solitude
"Of mountain-tops, is it your will to chase
"Agave, mother of Pentheus, from the rout,
"And gain a king's reward?" And we acclaimed   730
His counsel. Crouching in the brushwood, we
Waylaid the Mænads. At the appointed hour
They raised the sacred spear. "Iacchus,* hail!"
A thousand voices cried; and a breeze ran
Over the hill; the leafy revellers woke,   735
And all the wild was lilting in the dance.
   It chanced I saw Agave sweeping by
Where I lay hid, and out I flashed on her,
Leaving my shelter vacant. Loud she cried,
"O follow, follow, ye swift hounds! These men   740

733 Another name for Dionysus.

"Are on the trail! The hunt is up! To me!
"To arms! and couch the thyrsus for the charge!"
   We scattered then, and saved our limbs untorn,
So foiled, they swooped upon the browsing herd,
With never a blade of steel; yet there we saw   745
A comely heifer lowing in their hands,
Then torn in two; some fell upon the calves.
A fragment here of ribs, and forefeet there,
Tossed to and fro, or on the olives hung
That dripped with clotted gore. The lordly bulls,   750
Vaunting ere now, with fury in their horns,
Were grappled by ten thousand maidens' hands,
And thrown. More swiftly were their bones laid bare
Than close the eyelids on thy royal eyes.
Away they sped like birds, flushed from the fields   755
Low-lying, by Asopus, harvesters,
That peck the kernels from the earèd grain,
To Hysiæ, to Erythræ, villages
About Cithæron's roots, as mailèd foes
Descend for devastation far and wide;   760
Ravished the children from the hearth, and high
Mounted them on their shoulders. Safe they rode
Unbound, and fell not to the dusty plain.
No bronze! no iron! Flames were in their hair,
Yet they were not consumed. And when the folk,   765
In anger at their wrongs, rallied to arms,
We witnessed a great miracle, O king!
For never a Mænad heeded the sharp spear,
That glanced aside, while the frail thyrsus drew
Blood; and the ranks were broken; men-at-arms,   770
Routed by women! Surely God was there.
Then, as in changes of the dance, the Maids
Returned again to their mysterious wells,
And bathed; the serpents licked the drops of blood,
And cleansed the radiant cheeks with flickering tongue. 775
   Whoever be this god, let him be free
Of Thebes, my master. Great in all beside
Is he; and this they tell me, by his grace
Man got the vine to help him of his pain.
And where there is no wine, no love can be,   780
Nor balm for aching hearts, nor any joy.
CHORUS   I tremble to speak freely to a king.
   Yet must I speak no less. Great is my lord
   Bacchus; no other god more great than he.
PENTHEUS   The riot of Mænad like a forest-fire   785
   Advances: foul ignominy to Greece!

No time for scruple. To the Electran Gate,*
Herald, and muster all the shielded men,
And lancers that bestride the mettled steed,
And targeteers, and archers all that twang   790
The bow-string, that we may march out to war
With Mænads! It is outrage beyond dreams
That women thus should trample on men's pride.
DIONYSUS   Thou wilt not hearken, Pentheus, to my word,
Yet still, for all I suffer at thy hands,   795
I warn thee: venture not on war with God.
Abide in peace; for Bromius will not see
His Mænads hunted from their hills of joy.
PENTHEUS   Look to thyself! Thou art my prisoner still.
Wilt thou have life from me, or chastisement?   800
DIONYSUS   Kick not against the pricks, but rather burn
Sacrifice, being a mortal matched with God.
PENTHEUS   I offer women's blood for sacrifice
With noise and tumult on Cithæron's wolds.
DIONYSUS   Your ranks will break and scatter, with what shame!   805
When the light thyrsus routs the shield of brass!
PENTHEUS   O who will rid me of this stranger's tongue,
Doing or suffering, never yet at peace!
DIONYSUS   Still there is time, my friend, to make all well. . . .
PENTHEUS   How well? By serving those who are my slaves?   810
DIONYSUS   I, with no force, will bring your women home.
PENTHEUS   What would he have? Some other crafty snare?
DIONYSUS   If by my craft I seek to save thy soul?
PENTHEUS   A plot, to charter riot for all time!
DIONYSUS   I have indeed a charter, made with God.   815
PENTHEUS   My arms!—And give me respite from thy tongue!
DIONYSUS (*Sweeping into one all these conflicting emotions*)   Ah! . . .
Dost thou desire to see them on their hills?
PENTHEUS   Ten thousand pieces I would give to see.
DIONYSUS   Why hast thou fallen into such strong desire?   820
PENTHEUS   It would be grief to see them drunk with wine.
DIONYSUS   Yet thou art eager for the grievous sight?
PENTHEUS   Among the olives, silently, to see . . .
DIONYSUS   But if thou hidest they will find the trail.
PENTHEUS   Nay, I will brave them. That was nobly said.   825
DIONYSUS   Is it thy will to venture on that way?
PENTHEUS   Lead me. I am impatient to be gone.
DIONYSUS   Then clothe thy body in long linen folds.
PENTHEUS   And be a woman, who am such a man?
DIONYSUS   But if a man intrude he is destroyed.   830

[787] The gate guarding the southern entrance to Thebes, where the roads from Plataea and Mount Cithaeron
came in.

PENTHEUS (*Slyly*)   Stranger, thy craft is not of yesterday.

DIONYSUS   Dionysus nurtured me in all his wiles.

PENTHEUS   How best can thy deep counsel be fulfilled?

DIONYSUS   I will array thee for the spectacle.

PENTHEUS   In women's raiment? I recoil with shame.   835

DIONYSUS   Then thou art weary of thy desire to see.

PENTHEUS   Tell me, what raiment shall my body wear?

DIONYSUS   Long love-locks shall be hung upon thy head.

PENTHEUS   And so adorned, what shall my garments be?

DIONYSUS   A trailing robe; a fillet on thy hair.   840

PENTHEUS   Is there some emblem thou wilt bid me wear?

DIONYSUS   Thyrsus, and fawn-skin, stippled with white wool.

PENTHEUS   I cannot bear to go in women's weeds.

DIONYSUS   In battle thou shalt wear a robe of blood.

PENTHEUS   True. It is wiser to find vantage-ground.   845

DIONYSUS   Than hunt for evil in an evil chase.

PENTHEUS   How can I pass through Thebes and be unseen?

DIONYSUS   By some deserted way, with me for guide.

PENTHEUS   So I be not discovered to the foe . . .
I will go back . . . and think what I shall do.   850

DIONYSUS   Choose then thy way; there is no flaw in mine.

PENTHEUS   Well, I might go. . . . Either with armèd men,
Or I will be won over to thy way. . . . (*He goes into the palace*)

DIONYSUS   Women, the man is in the fowler's snare,
Mænads await him: he goes forth to die.   855
    I call on thee, Dionysus: thou art near.
Grant us revenge! Disorder first his brain
With giddy fantasy; for he would spurn
A woman's raiment had he health of mind.
It will be merry in the streets of Thebes   860
To lead the fool that blustered of his power,
How fallen! in a woman's trumpery clad!
I go to find the robes he shall put on
For his long journey, where by a mother's hand
The victim shall be slain, and at the last   865
Shall see Dionysus in his majesty.
No god so dreadful, none so sweet as he. (*He follows* PENTHEUS. *During
                the choral interval the* MESSENGER *goes*)

CHORUS   O to dance through a livelong night,
        White feet on the mountains!   870
    Revel, and fling my throat to the wind,
    Wet with flurries of the drifting dew!
    So the fawn from the hunters fled
    Leaps on grass with a fresh delight,
    Clear at last of the beaters' ring   875
        She frolics out and away
    Past the bounds and the woven snare.

Though disquiet of baying hounds,
  Keeping pace with cries of the hunt,
Urge her feet to be stormy-swift,
    Light she flies, and afar
Runs by the river in joy of the wild
    To haunts remote from man
Shadowing the babes that hide in the woodland.

  Nothing of delight nor of sacred lore
    Passeth a joy that the gods have given,
      When on the head of foes
  We hold triumphant hands of power.
      There is delight, there is desire.

  Slow to move is the wrath of God,
      But sure in its vengeance,
  Visiting all presumptuous men,
  Such as worship their own conceit,
  Magnifying the gods no more.
  Pride of reason hath made them mad.
  Stealthy, held on the leash of God,
      The feet of Time in the end
  Track the impious. Seek not thou
  More to know than the faith of old;
  Seek no greater rule for the soul;
  Say not here is a hard belief.
      Only God can avenge
  If there be haply a Power unseen.
      Then through the ages keep
Ceremony Nature gave to her children.

  Nothing of delight nor of sacred lore
    Passeth a joy that the gods have given,
      When on the head of foes
  We hold triumphant hands of power.
      There is delight, there is desire.

        (*Rocking, with a humming undertone*)
  Happy he who hath found in harbour
  Lull of the waves, the bosom of quietness.
  Happy he that hath done with striving,
  Done with the fret and the struggle for vanity.
  Some are kings and the rest are humble.
  Hopes there be ten thousand thousand,
      Some that ripen to harvest,
    And some dreams that are still-born
    And long since have departed.

Happier he who lives for the day,
　　Finding God, to enjoy him.

(Enter DIONYSUS)

DIONYSUS　Ho! thou that art athirst for hidden things,
Intruder where none dare intrude, come out!
Pentheus, I call, parade before the house,
Thou masker in the Bacchanalian choir,
Spy on thy mother, and my mysteries. . . .
　　Is this some princess of old Cadmus' line?

(Enter PENTHEUS)

PENTHEUS　Nay, but I see twin suns, an ancient Thebes
Twofold, twin fortresses with seven gates.*
It seems as though a Bull were leading me,
And horns are on his head. Was there a time
Thou wert not man? For very Bull art thou.

DIONYSUS　God is our escort, under truce, who was
Estranged. The scales are fallen from thine eyes.

PENTHEUS　And what of me? Is it not Ino's mien?
Or like Agave? Am I not her child?

DIONYSUS　I seem to see them when I look on thee.
But stay, this lovely tress has fallen awry
That under the neat fillet was confined.

PENTHEUS　It was dishevelled when with beck and bow
I tossed my head in Bacchic ecstasy.

DIONYSUS　I am thy tiring-woman to array
The locks that are disordered. Pray, be still.

PENTHEUS　Do thou adorn me. I am in thy hands.

DIONYSUS　Thy belt is loosened, and the linen folds
Fall not about thy feet in order due.

PENTHEUS　By the right foot, methinks, they fall awry,
But on the left they keep the ankle's line.

DIONYSUS　Ah! there will be no other friend like me
When thou hast seen the Mænads' chastity.

PENTHEUS　If I would be a Mænad in all things,
Which hand must wield the thyrsus in the dance?

DIONYSUS　Raise it with thy right hand and thy right foot
In time. I praise thee for thy change of heart.

PENTHEUS　Can I pluck up Cithæron, raising it
With all its Mænads high above my head?

DIONYSUS　The will is power. In that old heart of thine
Was nothing sound. But now thy heart is whole.

PENTHEUS　Shall we take crowbars, or with shoulders bowed
Uproot the mountain with our naked hands?

DIONYSUS　And bid the Nymphs go homeless, and destroy
The Throne, where men have heard the pipes of Pan?

925

930

935

940

945

950

955

960

965

---

932 Pentheus is seeing double, a symptom of his madness at this point.

PENTHEUS   Well said. We fight not women by our strength
    Of arm. (*Cunningly*) We hide among the olive trees.
DIONYSUS   Thou shalt be hidden as befits the spy
    Who comes to lie in ambush for the god.
PENTHEUS   I hold them in my hand, like fledgling birds   970
    Contained in the dear shelter of the nest.
DIONYSUS   Such is thy mission. Thou wilt capture them
    Maybe, unless they capture thee before.
PENTHEUS   Lead me through Thebes by all the public ways!
    No other man hath dared a feat like mine.   975
DIONYSUS   Alone thou sufferest for this land, alone.
    For thee remains the conflict that is due.
        I bless thy going out. The homeward way
    Not I . . .
PENTHEUS   My mother's hand shall speed me home.   980
DIONYSUS   A sign to all.
PENTHEUS   This end have I desired.
DIONYSUS   Her hands shall bear thee . . .
PENTHEUS   Gently charioted.
DIONYSUS   A mother's hands . . .   985
PENTHEUS   Caress me by the way.
DIONYSUS   Such a caress . . .
PENTHEUS   Fulfils my heart's desire.
DIONYSUS   Too sharp of wit, thou art gone to sharper pain!
    Thou art gone where thy renown shall vault to heaven.   990
    Stretch out thy hands, Agave! Stretch your hands,
    Daughters of Cadmus! Youth in all his pride
    I bring to judgment, where with Bromius I
    Pronounce his doom. Let silence speak the rest.
CHORUS   Ravenous dogs of hell, harry and drive him on!   995
    Merrily goes the dance on yon mountain-side!
            Let one heart be whetted.
    Let the bedizened fool awake lust of blood
    In mad eyes that gleam on some beacon-height.
    From some eyrie where she stands sentinel   1000
            A mother will see her son,
    And cry View-halloo, rallying all the hunt:
            "Who is it ventures here?
    "What spy dares to watch on the inviolate hill-top,
    "Come with unhallowed feet? Who was a mother to him?"   1005
            Surely no flesh of man
    Could whelp such a brood, but some fierce lioness,
    Or Gorgon that haunts the waste Libyan sand.
    Come down in full panoply! come Justice, clear as day!
    With bright sword to pierce through and through him,   1010
    The impious tyrannous son of Echion, from fangs
            Of the old Dragon born!

Who with rebellious pride cruelly turned to scorn
 Bromios' holy rite, Semele's holy tomb.
            He goes out to battle;   1015
Folly with pride and pomp has marched out to war,
To win mighty spoils from the Unconquerable.
But no man escapes when Death holds his court,
            There is the sinner arraigned.
The contrite of heart alone dwell at peace.   1020
            Zealous am I for truth;
But though questing far precious to me is a quiet
Happiness, that supreme Grace of humility won.
            Night and day, so content
I serve God with mirth, and seek all piety,   1025
And ask not to pass the bourn set by God.
Come down in full panoply! Come Justice, clear as day,
With bright sword to pierce through and through him,
The impious tyrannous son of Echion, from fangs
            Of the old Dragon born!   1030

Appear, Mystic Bull, Snake with the hundred heads,
Or come down in flame, Lion of tawny fire.
O come, Bacchus, come and make fast the snare!
We hunt down the huntsman! Merrily goes the dance!
For now he is fallen among the Mænads, sharp-set for blood.   1035

———————

(*Enter* MESSENGER)

MESSENGER   O house of the Sidonian Senator*
  How thy felicity is passed away!
  Thou Dragon-seed of Ophis, battle-line
  That Cadmus reaped from earth! though but a slave   1040
  I weep for thee; for if a slave be true
  He takes a master's sorrow for his own.
CHORUS   What of the revel? Give us of thy news.
MESSENGER   Pentheus, the great Echion's son, is dead.
 CHORUS   O King Bromios!   1045
                A Great God art thou!
MESSENGER   Woman, what hast thou said? Wilt thou make bold
  To glory in my great Lord's calamity?
CHORUS   I sing joy in strange orisons! I no more
      Here in an alien land cower in fear of chains!   1050
MESSENGER   Think you there is no man in Thebes?
CHORUS   My liege
   Is Dionysus, is Dionysus! Wherefore no
            Vassal of Thebes am I!

1037 The House of Cadmus. Cadmus was a Sidonian, or Phoenician.

MESSENGER   I might forgive; but when the deed is done   1055
    It is unlovely to insult the dead.
CHORUS   Sing me the song of death! tell me the pains he bore!
    Bitter, ah, bitter the end of proud, godless kings!
MESSENGER   Beyond the hamlets of our Theban land
    We had gone out to where Asopos rolls;   1060
    Pentheus and I, his follower, and our Guide,
    The Stranger, marshal of this embassy.
    Cithæron was before us. On the ascent
    We choose a grassy slope where the footfall
    Was like our voices, silent. There we saw   1065
    And were not seen. Below was a deep cleft
    Scooped from the cliffs, darkling with the great pines,
    And fresh with dew. Mænads were sitting there,
    Their hands employed in happy pastimes. One
    Garlands her thyrsus where the ivy-trails   1070
    Had slipped, and some, as colts make holiday,
    Quit of the wicked yoke at evening, sang,
    In antiphone, a Bacchic roundelay.
        Pentheus, the doomed, seeing no drunken rout,
    Said, "Stranger, where we stand, I see but ill   1075
    "These maskers at their revel. If I could climb
    "Rocks, or bestride the mane of some tall pine,
    "Then would I rightly see the masquerade."
    I saw the Stranger, saw the awful deed.
    He took a pine-tree by the skiey crest,   1080
    And bent it down and down to dusty earth,
    Arching it like a bow, or pictured wheel
    Traced by a carpenter. No hand of man
    Could bend the giant of the mountains. There
    He set my master in the pine-branches,   1085
    And let the trunk recoil into the air,
    But slowly, careful lest his man be thrown;
    And straight and stark it rose in the stark sky,
    And Pentheus rode aloft. Then was he seen
    More than he saw. In the dim distance he   1090
    Rode, and the Stranger vanished in thin air,
    And out of heaven a voice (surely it was
    Dionysus calling): "Damsels, rise! I bring
    "To judgment him to whom my orgies were
    "A mockery! Now avenge me on his head!"   1095
    And with the voice a star of dreadful fire
    Lightened and shot between the earth and sky.
    Hushed was the air; the forest glade had hushed
    Its leaves; there was no cry of beast or bird.
    Hardly aware, the Mænads stood awhile   1100

Alert; this way and that they flashed their eyes;
And then again the voice, the battle-cry
Clear, and a rush like pigeons on the wing
Beating upwind; with rhythmic feet in time
His mother Agave and her sisters ran,   1105
And all the Mænads: over the cornices
Of snow and ice they leapt in ecstasy.
And when they saw my master on the pine
They brought huge craggy boulders to the assault,
A rock was their siege-tower to storm the pine,   1110
And their artillery was the olive-boughs
For spears, and many a thyrsus hurtled by
Pentheus, unhappy target; all in vain.
He sat with this one bulwark, the great height
That baffled zeal, between him and despair.   1115
They sang the thunder-spell, and with oak-wands
Made thunderous, strove to pluck up by the spurs
The giant pine, with never a blade of steel;
But when they saw their labour spent in vain
Agave cried: "Compass it in a ring,   1120
"Grasp ye the trunk, my Mænads! Take by storm
"That rider! Let us not return to God
"And say our hunt was vain!" Ten thousand hands
Grappled the pine and plucked it from the mould,
And headlong from his lofty seat he fell   1125
Among the boulders, with ten thousand groans.
So Pentheus fell, and knew that death was near.
His mother, priestess of the sacrifice,
Struck; and he tore the fillet from his hair;
And tenderly caressed her cheek, and pled: 1130
"It is I, Mother! it is I, thy son,
"Pentheus, the infant of Echion's halls!
"Pity me, Mother, and for all my sins,
"Mother, forgive, and slay not thine own son!"
Foam was upon her lips, her eye-balls rolled.   1135
Bacchus had all her heart, far from the old
Sweet memories; and she heeded not his prayer.
She knelt on him; her fingers clenched on his;
And wrenched an arm out of the socket. God
Gave more than mortal power to her weak hands.   1140
On the other side was Ino. So they broke
His body. Then Autonoë and the rout
Swept up. There rose a medley of weird sound.
He groaned while life was in him; they for joy
Sang Alalai!*   1145
                    A Mænad snatched an arm,

1145 A war cry.

And one his buskined feet; the ribs were bare
And grinning white. From bloody hand to hand
The flesh of Pentheus, like a ball, was thrown.
   Deep in the forest's heart the fragments lie 1150
Or on the edge of the sheer precipice,
A long quest for the searchers . . .
                        But the head
His mother claimed for hers, her lion's head,
Spoil from the mountain; on her thyrsus-point 1155
She bears her trophy in triumphal march
Over Cithæron, all her dances done.
Sorrow for spoil she brings, triumphant still
To hang upon the gates of Thebes, and calls
Dionysus, Hunter, Comrade, Conqueror! 1160
To whom she bears the conquest of her tears.
   Where Queen Agave walks I will not stay,
But leave the path of grief, ere she return.
   Nothing is fairer than the contrite heart
That worships God; and not unwise is he 1165
Who garners wealth that bears such rich return.
CHORUS   Bacchanals, call his name
      Glorious!
  Sing for a fallen foe
     Thanksgiving. 1170
The son of the Dragon, devoted, processionally
   Trailing his rich embroideries went,
     And bearing the holy thyrsus,
       Ritual robes of Death.
The Bull was hierophant to go before. 1175
      Rejoice, Theban Maids!
You hands have brought the far-renownèd Conqueror
     Groans, and the revel of tears.
   Mother, I wish him joy of that hand's caress;
     Dripping with blood of a son. 1180
—Who comes with eager feet? Her eyes are wild.
It is Agave, mother of Pentheus. Come,
Receive the pageant of the Lord of Joy. (*The* MESSENGER *retires*)

              (*Enter* AGAVE)
AGAVE   Mænads of far-away! 1185
CHORUS   Who is it calleth me?
AGAVE   Fresh from the hills we bring
  The head of a lion to hang on the lintel.
   Blessèd the hunt to-day!
CHORUS   I greet thee in name of one sovereign Lord. 1190
AGAVE   No ropes had I to take the spoil,

A mountain-whelp in the prime of his valour.
    So thine eyes may see.
CHORUS   Was it the wilderness?
AGAVE   Cithæron. . . .   1195
CHORUS   Cithæron?
AGAVE   Slew him for sacrifice.
CHORUS   And who the smiter?
AGAVE   I was the first to smite.
    Ye choirs triumphal, hymn to Agave's name!   1200
CHORUS   Thy comrades?
AGAVE   The daughters. . . .
CHORUS   The daughters?
AGAVE (*Shrieking*)   Of Cadmus . . .
    I was the first, the first to lay hold on him.   1205
    Blessing attend my chase! . . . Prithee to feast with me!
CHORUS   Where is the feast for thee?
AGAVE   He is a tender thing. . . .
    Touch him! the down on his lip is of gossamer,
    Flowery-soft his hair.   1210
CHORUS   Such hair seems to know the kind hand of man.
AGAVE   Our Bacchus is
    A hunter bold.
    With cunning sleight he had slipped on the quarry
    All the Mænad-band.   1215
CHORUS   Hot on the trail is he.
AGAVE   Ye praise me?
CHORUS   We praise thee.
AGAVE   Verily Thebes will ring . . .
CHORUS   And thy son Pentheus . . .   1220
AGAVE   Praise to his mother will bring,
    Who down the mountain came with a lion for spoil.
CHORUS   Beyond hope . . .
AGAVE   Beyond dreams . . .
CHORUS   Thy gladness?   1225
AGAVE   My glory!
    Warrior, warrior I!
    Carry my trophy high! Blazon my deed afar!
CHORUS   Let all the townsfolk see, unhappy one,
    The spoils of triumph that thou bringest home.   1230
AGAVE   O ye that dwell beneath the towered rock
    That crowns the land of Thebes, approach and see.
    When Cadmus' daughters go a-hunting, they
    Seek no Thessalian spear with barbèd head,
    No nets: the finger-tips of their white hands   1235
    Are all their weapons. Go to! vaunt no more!
    Trouble no furnace for the tempered blade!

We with our hands have taken him! Our hands
Spoiled his young valour, tore him limb from limb.
Where is my agèd father? Where my son   1240
Pentheus? Go, bid him bring a ladder with rungs
Strongly dovetailed, and scale the pediment,
And nail this head upon the architrave,
This lion's head that I went out to slay,
                              (*Enter* CADMUS)   1245

CADMUS   Follow me, servants, to the outer court.
   Bear what remains of Pentheus on the bier
   That after all the labour of my quest
   I now bring home. For on Cithæron's wolds
   Each fragment singly lay, and far apart,   1250
   And all were buried in the trackless wood.
   For some one told me of my daughter's deed
   When I with old Teiresias from the rout
   Was come within the city wall. I turned,
   And sought the wild again, and found him dead   1255
   Upon the mountain, by the Mænads slain.
   Autonoë wandered there, over the heath,
   Who was Actæon's mother, pitiful,
   Scourged by her madness; Ino wandered there;
   But no Agave; to the town, they said,   1260
   Her frenzy swept her; and they told me true.
   I see her here, though fain I would not see.

AGAVE   Father, behold the boast of thine old age!
   The daughters of thy loins excel in strength
   All women sprung of mortal seed; and I   1265
   Excel them all. I left the ignoble loom
   For a great destiny. The jungle called:
   I went a-hunting; in my arms I bear
   The prize of valour. On thy palace-gate
   It shall be hung. So take it in thy arms,   1270
   My father; bid thy compeers celebrate
   My chase with feasting. Blessings on thy head,
   Blessings have fallen by my feat-of-arms!

CADMUS   Oh grief not to be seen! Infinite grief!
   What ravage these unhappy hands have wrought!   1275
   Woe for thy grief, and after, woe for mine!
   Not unprovoked, but with excess of pain
   Bromius destroyed us, choosing us for kin.

AGAVE   How crabbed is old age in men! Its eyes
   Will still be frowning. Would my son had come   1280
   Laden with spoils when he went out to ride
   From Thebes with his companions, as became
   His mother's child. But he is only bold

To fight with God. Father, wilt thou rebuke
My son? Where is he? Who will call him here 1285
To bear his part in my felicity?
CADMUS   Alas! alas! when she awakes to truth,
What grief must come! And yet thus to remain!
Could it be ever so, thy state would be
Not fortunate, maybe, yet without pain. 1290
AGAVE   Is it not glorious? What is here for pain?
CADMUS   First lift thine eyes upon the height of heaven.
AGAVE   And what is there that thou wouldst have me see?
CADMUS   Is it the same heaven as it was before?
AGAVE   It seems more limpid, more ethereal. 1295
CADMUS   And is the strangeness still upon thy soul?
AGAVE   That word is strange to me. I am become
Not as I was, but, somehow, sane again.
CADMUS   Is thy mind clear to hear and understand?
AGAVE   I cannot now recall what I have been. 1300
CADMUS   Who took thee to his house to be thy bride?
AGAVE   Echion, of the dragon-seed, they say.
CADMUS   What child was born therein to him and thee?
AGAVE   Pentheus, the offspring of his love and mine.
CADMUS   Whose is that Head thou holdest in thine arms? 1305
AGAVE   A lion's. For the hunters told me so.
CADMUS   Look. For the looking is but little toil.
AGAVE   Ah! what is here? What is it in my hands?
CADMUS   Let thy gaze dwell on it. Look closer still.
AGAVE   It is the utmost life can hold for me. 1310
CADMUS   Is it so like a lion in thine eyes?
AGAVE   No, it is Pentheus' head who was my son.
CADMUS   He was bewailed ere yet thou wert aware.
AGAVE   Who slew him? And how came he to my arms?
CADMUS   Unhappy truth! this is no time for thee. 1315
AGAVE   Speak! My heart throbs in pain to be relieved.
CADMUS   By thee and by thy sisters he was slain.
AGAVE   Where did he die? At home? Or tell me where.
CADMUS   Where died Actæon, hunted by his hounds.
AGAVE   What was his errand on Cithæron's wolds? 1320
CADMUS   To stay the rout and bandy words with God.
AGAVE   And me? What power swept us to the hills?
CADMUS   Madness; it came and swept our women away.
AGAVE   Dionysus hath destroyed us. Now I know.
CADMUS   Since we had flouted his divinity. 1325
AGAVE   Where is the body of my belovèd child?
CADMUS   With pains I gathered all that here is laid.
AGAVE   Is every limb in linkèd order set?
CADMUS   No, no! Stretch not thy hand to touch thy dead!
AGAVE   Then take the head, my father, and restore 1330

His form who suffered thrice our human pain.
Surely the curse was mine, for mine the sin!
What part had Pentheus in my blasphemy?

CADMUS   He was like thee: he would not worship God.
He hath entangled us in common doom,   1335
Himself and you; so all our house is dead;
And me, who, with no sons, behold my heir
The infant of thy womb, to whom we looked
For succour in distress, gone to his death,
In shame and agony. Thou, child of my child,   1340
Wert pillar of my roof, to shelter me
In my old age, with reverence. No man dared
Insult me, when he saw thy countenance
In wrath, for thou wouldst have requital due.
Now I am outcast from my ancestral halls,   1345
Cadmus the Great, who sowed the dragon-seed
And reaped the harvest of the men-at-arms.
O well-belovèd, though thou art no more
Thou art among my dearest, O my son.
Never again wilt thou caress my beard   1350
And say, "My mother's father," O my son;
"Who wrongs thee? Who dishonours thine old age?
"Who vexes thee with words that give thee pain?
"Speak, Father, I will chasten him for thee."
Now am I derelict, and thou art forlorn,   1355
Sorrowful mother, sisterhood forlorn!
Let any man who scorns the powers of heaven
Look on this death, and tremble, and believe.

CHORUS   Sacred is grief; but this child of thy child,
Though it be grief to thee, was justly slain.   1360

AGAVE   Father, thou seest all my glory turned
To tears. Suffer me to lament my son.
Tell me, how can I cherish him, and lay
His body to my heart? What dirge will serve
To mourn for these thy broken limbs, my son?   1365
O dearest face! O cheek with softest down
Of youth, I give my veil to cover thee. . . .
But for these mangled limbs deformed with blood,
Where shall I find the robes for them? What hands
Will give thee human tribute, O my son?   1370
Why do I shrink? Why fear to touch my child?
Go forth, unhappy hand, and take thy dead.
Take him, ah, take him! Straighten all his limbs,
And set the head upon the strong young neck;
With thy right hand lift up this shattered side.   1375
Nay, I will take each fragment in my hands
And kiss the flesh I suckled at my breast!

This was his arm, his fingers that entwined
My fingers, like the ivy with the bay.
Lie there, the strong hand of my warrior son.   1380
Lie there, the feet, the little stumbling feet
I guided. Who has led you such a way?
Kiss me, sweet lips, again . . . O women, death
Is creeping over them. His radiant skin
Grows wan. Beauty revisits not his face!   1385
Away! away! for I can bear no more
To look upon him! Pain has mastered me.
I will but make his grave, and then to die.

       (Thunder-music. Dionysus is discovered in a glow of light)

DIONYSUS   Thou shalt not make his grave. Depart from hence,*   1390
Agave, for his blood is on thy hands.
The unclean shall not defile the sepulchre
Of him that they have slain. My ministers
Attend you to the Theban marches. Go,
Fulfil your mourning in an alien land,   1395
Thou and thy sisters. I am Semele's babe,
Dionysus, son of God, whom ye despised.
Thou, Cadmus, husbandman of dragon-seed,
Shalt wear the diadem in barbaric realms.
So speaks the oracle. And when thy time   1400
Is come, thyself a dragon, and with thee
Thy dragon-mate, the immortal consort given
To thee, O mortal, for thy prowess in war,
Harmonia, Ares' daughter, charioted
By victims from the altar, shall descend   1405
On Hellas, and with hosts innumerable
Destroy; but when ye sack the Delphian shrine
Woe for your homecoming! Ares at last
Will take thee and Harmonia to your rest,
The Blessèd Isles shall be your safe abode.   1410
   Hearken to me, who am no son of man,
But son of Zeus. Had ye with contrite hearts
Received me when ye would not, ye might then
Have found your peace in God, your great ally.

CADMUS   Have pity on us, Dionysus: we have sinned.   1415
DIONYSUS   Too late. For ye were tried, and knew me not.
CADMUS   True. But the chastisement exceeds the sin.
DIONYSUS   Nay, but the sin was man's insult to God.
CADMUS   But God should have no passions, like a man.
DIONYSUS   Zeus hath ordained my vengeance long ago.   1420
AGAVE   Ah! Father, our exile was foreordained!
DIONYSUS   Why then delay to bow your heads to fate?

1390 Dionysus' disposition of the characters. Cadmus and his wife Harmonia are to be changed into ser-
    pents or dragons, in which form Cadmus is to lead a horde of barbarians in an invasion of Greece.

CADMUS   Surrender hope, my child? No hope remains
         For thee and all thy sisterhood of grief;
         No hope for me, thy father: an old man   1425
         I go to a strange land; and at the last
         Descend on Hellas with my motley horde,
         Fierce, like a dragon, with my dragon-mate,
         Harmonia, Ares' daughter, and my bride
         Immortal: so the oracle hath decreed,   1430
         Against our ancient altars and our tombs,
         With serried spears. Nor shall I find surcease
         Of sorrow, not when Acheron bears my sail
         On its dark bosom to the silent deep.

AGAVE   Father, I shall be homesick for thy love.   1435

CADMUS   My child, why wilt thou hold me, as a swan
         Shelters her dying one with white arching wings?

AGAVE   Where shall I turn when I am driven from home?

CADMUS   Ah! little one, there is no help in me.

AGAVE   Farewell to the house! farewell to the land!   1410
             And a long farewell to the joy that is fled
                 From my bridal halls!

CADMUS   Daughter, away! In Autonoë's hall
             Thy sisters await thee.

AGAVE   For a father I weep.   1445

CADMUS   I weep for a child,
         And at parting my tears for your sisters flowed.

AGAVE   Awful rue, in dread visitation
         Dionysus the King hath sent thee,
             And all of thy line.   1450

DIONYSUS   Rue for the wrongs that in Thebes ye had wrought me,
         For a desolate shrine, and a name unsung.

AGAVE   Bless me, my Father!

CADMUS   My blessings on thee,
         Though, child, it is hard for thee to be blessèd!   1455

AGAVE   Let the marshals advance; my companions wait
         In the halls, my sad sisters in exile;
             And lead me, O where
         Never Cithæron comes looming above,
         Never Cithæron comes watching again.   1460
         There let my heart have rest of the thyrsus;
             For we go no more to the revel.

CHORUS   How veiled are the lineaments of God!
         Where shall a man seek
         These glimpses that pass?   1465
         Many a hope is spent in the darkness;
         Out of the hopeless
         He hath built us a way.
             And so our story is ended.

Comic actors made up as an old woman and a man. The man has a padded tunic, phallus, and tights; both actors are masked. Clay, 4th century B.C. *Martin v. Wagner-Museum, University of Wurzburg*

Aristophanes

Aristophanes (c.450–c.385 B.C.) *was the most important writer of that form of comic drama known in antiquity as "Old Comedy." Conservative and highly critical by temperament, he ranged widely over the political, social, and literary abuses of his time, often combining such topical matter with fantasy to produce comic actions rich in satiric and poetic values. Altogether, he wrote forty plays, of which eleven are extant; perhaps* THE BIRDS *and* LYSISTRATA *best illustrate his work in Old Comedy. Toward the end of his career he modified this form in favor of a more tightly organized action in plays like the* PLUTUS *(388 B.C.) to produce our only extant examples of Middle Comedy.*

LYSISTRATA *was written shortly after the disastrous Sicilian expedition and not long before the revolt of the Four Hundred. Coming as it did in the middle of the Peloponnesian War, it represents a remarkable flash of verve and wit in a declining Athenian culture.*

Chronology

*c.*450 B.C. Probable year of his birth. Probably born in Kydathenaeon, a town in Attica, the son of Philippus and Zenodora.

427 Presented his first comedy, the lost *Banqueters.*

425 Produced *The Acharnians.*

424 Produced *The Knights.*

423 Produced *The Clouds.*

422 Produced *The Wasps.*

421 Produced *The Peace.*

414 Produced *The Birds.*

411 Produced *Lysistrata* and *Thesmophoriazusae.*

405 Produced *The Frogs.*

404 Old Comedy gives way to Middle Comedy; Sparta defeats Athens and assumes leadership of Greece.

392 Produced *The Ecclusiazusae,* his earliest extant Middle Comedy.

388 Produced *Plutus.*

*c.*385 Probable year of his death.

Selected Bibliography

Croiset, M., *Aristophanes and the Political Parties at Athens,* London, 1909.

Ehrenberg, Victor, *The People of Aristophanes: A Sociology of Old Attic Comedy,* Oxford, 1951.

Hugill, W. M., *Panhellenism in Aristophanes,* Chicago, 1936.

Lord, L. E., *Aristophanes: His Plays and Influence,* Boston, 1925.

Murray, Gilbert, *Aristophanes and the War Party,* London, 1919.

———, *Aristophanes: A Study,* New York, 1933.

Norwood, Gilbert, *Greek Comedy,* London, 1931.

Whitman, Cedric, *Aristophanes and the Comic Hero,* Cambridge, Mass., 1964.

LYSISTRATA

by Aristophanes

An English version by Dudley Fitts

Characters

LYSISTRATA

KALONIKE

MYRRHINE

LAMPITO

CHORUS

MAGISTRATE

KINESIAS

SPARTAN HERALD

SPARTAN AMBASSADOR

A SENTRY

ATHENIAN DRUNKARD

The supernumeraries include the BABY SON *of Kinesias;* STRATYLLIS, *a member of the hemichorus of Old Women; various individual speakers, both Spartan and Athenian.*
Until the exodos, *the* CHORUS *is divided into two hemichori: the first, of Old Men; the second, of Old Women. Each of these has its* CHORAGOS. *In the* exodos, *the hemichori return as Athenians and Spartans.*

Athens. First, a public square; later, beneath the walls of the Acropolis; later, a courtyard within the Acropolis. Time: early in 411 B.C.

Athens; a public square; early morning; LYSISTRATA *sola*

LYSISTRATA   If someone had invited them to a festival—
Bacchus's, say, or Pan's, or Aphrodite's, or
that Genetyllis business*—, you couldn't get through the streets,
what with the drums and the dancing. But now,
not a woman in sight!   5
                              Except—oh, yes!
                                        (*Enter* KALONIKE)
Here's one, at last. Good
morning, Kalonike.
KALONIKE   Good morning, Lysistrata.   10
                                        Darling,

---

³ References to cults of love and wine.

don't frown so! You'll ruin your face!

LYSISTRATA   Never mind my face.
Kalonike,
the way we women behave! Really, I don't blame the men   15
for what they say about us.

KALONIKE   No; I imagine they're right.

LYSISTRATA   For example: I call a meeting
to think out a most important matter—and what happens?
The women all stay in bed!   20

KALONIKE   Oh, they'll be along.
It's hard to get away, you know: a husband, a cook,
a child . . . Home life can be *so* demanding!

LYSISTRATA   What I have in mind is even more demanding.

KALONIKE   Tell me: what is it?   25

LYSISTRATA   Something big.

KALONIKE   Goodness! *How* big?

LYSISTRATA   Big enough for all of us.

KALONIKE   But we're not all here!

LYSISTRATA   We would be, if *that's* what was up!   30
                             No, Kalonike,
this is something I've been turning over for nights;
and, I may say, sleepless nights.

KALONIKE   Can't be so hard, then,
if you've spent so much time on it.   35

LYSISTRATA   Hard or not,
it comes to this: Only we women can save Greece!

KALONIKE   Only we women? Poor Greece!

LYSISTRATA   Just the same,
it's up to us. First, we must liquidate   40
the Peloponnesians—

KALONIKE   Fun, fun!

LYSISTRATA   —and then the Boeotians.

KALONIKE   Oh! But not those heavenly eels!*

LYSISTRATA   You needn't worry.   45
Athens shall have her sea food. —But here's the point:
If we can get the women from those places
to join us women here, why, we can save
all Greece!

KALONIKE   But dearest Lysistrata!   50
How can women do a thing so austere, so
political? We belong at home. Our only armor's
our transparent saffron dresses and
our pretty little shoes!

LYSISTRATA   That's it exactly.   55
Those transparent saffron dresses, those little shoes—
well, there we are!

44 Boeotia was famous for its sea food, especially its eels.

KALONIKE   Oh?

LYSISTRATA   Not a single man would lift
his spear—   60

KALONIKE   I'll get my dress from the dyer's tomorrow!

LYSISTRATA   —or need a shield—

KALONIKE   The sweetest little negligée—

LYSISTRATA   —or bring out his sword.

KALONIKE   I know where I can buy   65
the dreamiest sandals!

LYSISTRATA   Well, so you see. Now, shouldn't
the women have come?

KALONIKE   Come? they should have *flown*!

LYSISTRATA   Athenians are always late.   70
                              But imagine!
There's no one here from the South Shore.

KALONIKE   They go to work early,
I can swear to that.

LYSISTRATA   And nobody from Acharnai.   75
They should have been here hours ago!

KALONIKE   Well, you'll get
that awful Theagenes woman: she's been having
her fortune told at Hecate's shrine.*
                              But look!   80
Someone at last! Can you see who they are?
                    (*Enter* MYRRHINE *and other women*)

LYSISTRATA   People from the suburbs.

KALONIKE   Yes! The entire
membership of the Suburban League!   85

MYRRHINE   Sorry to be late, Lysistrata.
                              Oh, come,
don't scowl so! Say something!

LYSISTRATA   My dear Myrrhine,
what is there to say? After all,   90
you've been pretty casual about the whole thing.

MYRRHINE   Couldn't find
my girdle in the dark, that's all.
                              But what *is*
'the whole thing'?   95

LYSISTRATA   Wait for the rest of them.

KALONIKE   I suppose so. But, look!
Here's Lampito!
                    (*Enter* LAMPITO *with women from Sparta*)

LYSISTRATA   Darling Lampito,   100
how pretty you are today! What a nice color!

---

79 Theagenes was notoriously superstitious; his practice of never leaving home without consulting Hecate
  is here transferred to his wife.

Goodness, you look as though you could strangle a bull!

LAMPITO   Ah think Ah could! It's the work-out
in the gym every day; and, of co'se that dance of ahs
where y' kick yo' own tail.*   105

LYSISTRATA   What lovely breasts!

LAMPITO   Lawdy, when y' touch me lahk that,
Ah feel lahk a heifer at the altar!

LYSISTRATA   And this young lady?
Where is she from?   110

LAMPITO   Boeotia. Social-Register type.

LYSISTRATA   Good morning, Boeotian. You're as pretty as green grass.

KALONIKE   And if you look,
you'll find that the lawn has just been cut.

LYSISTRATA   And this lady?   115

LAMPITO   From Corinth. But a good woman.

LYSISTRATA   Well, in Corinth
anything's possible.

LAMPITO   But let's get to work. Which one of you
called this meeting, and why?   120

LYSISTRATA   *I* did.

LAMPITO   Well, then:
what's up?

MYRRHINE   Yes, what *is* 'the whole thing,' after all?

LYSISTRATA   I'll tell you. —But first, one question.   125

MYRRHINE   Ask away!

LYSISTRATA   It's your husbands. Fathers of your children. Doesn't it bother
you
that they're always off with the Army? I'll stake my life,
not one of you has a man in the house this minute!   130

KALONIKE   Mine's been in Thrace the last five months, keeping an eye
on that General.*

MYRRHINE   Mine's been in Pylos for seven.

LAMPITO   And mahn,
whenever he gets a *dis*charge, he goes raht back   135
with that li'l ole speah of his, and enlists again!

LYSISTRATA   And not the ghost of a lover to be found!
From the very day the war began—
                              those Milesians!
I could skin them alive!   140
                    —I've not seen so much, even,
as one of those devices they call Widow's Delight.
But there! What's important is: I've found a way
to end the war, are you with me?

105 Among the physical exercises practised by Greek girls was the strenuous *bibasis*, a dance in which the
    dancer kicked her buttocks with her heels.
132 A certain Eukrates about whom nothing is known.

MYRRHINE   I should *say* so!   145
Even if I have to pawn my best dress and
drink up the proceeds.*
KALONIKE   Me, too! Even if they split me
right up the middle, like a flounder.
LAMPITO   Ah'm shorely with you.   150
Ah'd crawl up Taygetos* on mah knees
if that'd bring peace.
LYSISTRATA Then here it is.
Women! Sisters!
If we really want our men to make an armistice,   155
we must be ready to give up—
MYRRHINE   Give up what?
Quick, tell us!
LYSISTRATA   But *will* you?
MYRRHINE   We will, even if it kills us.   160
LYSISTRATA Then we must give up sleeping with our men. (*Long silence*)
Oh? So now you're sorry? Won't look at me?
Doubtful? Pale? All teary-eyed?
                                  But come: be frank with me,
as I've certainly been with you. Will you do it?   165
MYRRHINE   I couldn't. No.
Let the war go on.
KALONIKE   Nor I. Let the war go on.
LYSISTRATA You, you little flounder,
ready to be split up the middle?   170
KALONIKE   Lysistrata, no!
I'd walk through fire for you—you *know* I would!—, but don't
ask us to give up *that*! Why, there's nothing like it!
LYSISTRATA And you?
BOEOTIAN   No. I must say *I'd* rather walk through fire.   175
LYSISTRATA You little salamanders!
No wonder poets write tragedies about women.
All we want's a quick tumble!
                                  But you from Sparta:
if you stand by me, we may win yet! Will you?   180
It means so much!
LAMPITO   Ah sweah, it means *too* much!
By the Two Goddesses,* it does! Asking a girl
to sleep—Heaven knows how long!—in a great big bed
with nobody there but herself! But Ah'll stay with you!   185
Peace comes first!
LYSISTRATA   Spoken like a true Spartan!

---

147 Athenian women were frequently satirized for heavy drinking.
151 A rugged mountain range in the Peloponnesus.
183 Demeter and Persephone; a woman's oath.

KALONIKE But, if—
    oh dear!
       —if we give up what you tell us to,   190
will there *be* any peace?

LYSISTRATA   Why, mercy, of course there will!
We'll just sit snug in our very thinnest gowns,
perfumed and powdered from top to bottom, and those men
simply won't stand still! And when we say No,   195
they'll go out of their minds! And there's your peace.
You can take my word for it.

LAMPITO   Ah seem to remember
that Colonel Menelaus threw his sword away
when he saw Helen's breast all bare.   200

KALONIKE   But, goodness me!
What if they just get up and leave us?

LYSISTRATA   Well,
we'd have to fall back on ourselves, of course.
But they won't.   205

KALONIKE What if they drag us into the bedroom?

LYSISTRATA   Hang on to the door.

KALONIKE What if they slap us?

LYSISTRATA   If they do, you'd better give in.
But be sulky about it. Do I have to teach you how?   210
You know there's no fun for men when they have to force you.
There are millions of ways of getting them to see reason.
Don't you worry: a man
doesn't like it unless the girl co-operates.

KALONIKE I suppose so. Oh, all right! We'll go along!   215

LAMPITO Ah imagine us Spahtans can arrange a peace. But you
Athenians! Why, you're just war-mongerers!

LYSISTRATA   Leave that to me.
I know how to make them listen.

LAMPITO   Ah don't see how.   220
After all, they've got their boats; and there's lots of money
piled up in the Acropolis.

LYSISTRATA   The Acropolis? Darling,
we're taking over the Acropolis today!
That's the older women's job. All the rest of us   225
are going to the Citadel to sacrifice—you understand me?
And once there, we're in for good!

LAMPITO   Whee! Up the rebels!
Ah can see you're a good strat*ee*gist.

LYSISTRATA   Well, then, Lampito,   230
let's take the oath.

LAMPITO   Say it. We'll sweah.

LYSISTRATA   This is it.

—But Lord! Where's our Inner Guard? Never mind.
                                        —You see this   235
shield? Put it down there. Now bring me the victim's entrails.

KALONIKE But the oath?

LYSISTRATA   You remember how in Aeschylus' *Seven**
they killed a sheep and swore on a shield? Well, then?

KALONIKE But I don't see how you can swear for peace on a shield.   240

LYSISTRATA What else do you suggest?

KALONIKE   Why not a white horse?
We could swear by that.

LYSISTRATA   And where will you get a white horse?

KALONIKE I never thought of that. *What* can we do?   245

MYRRHINE   I have it!
Let's set this big black wine-bowl on the ground
and pour in a gallon or so of Thasian,* and swear
not to add one drop of water.

LAMPITO   Ah lahk *that* oath!   250

LYSISTRATA Bring the bowl and the wine-jug.

KALONIKE   Oh, what a simply *huge* one!

LYSISTRATA Set it down; and, women, place your hands on the gift-offering.

O Goddess of Persuasion! And thou, O Loving-cup!
Look upon this our sacrifice, and   255
be gracious!

KALONIKE It spills out like blood. How red and pretty it is!

LAMPITO And Ah must say it smells good.

MYRRHINE   Let me swear first!

KALONIKE No, by Aphrodite, let's toss for it!   260

LYSISTRATA Lampito: all of you women: come, touch the bowl,
and repeat after me:
I WILL HAVE NOTHING TO DO WITH MY HUSBAND
    OR MY LOVER

KALONIKE *I will have nothing to do with my husband or my lover*   265

LYSISTRATA THOUGH HE COME TO ME IN PITIABLE
    CONDITION

KALONIKE *Though he come to me in pitiable condition*
(Oh, Lysistrata! This is killing me!)

LYSISTRATA I WILL STAY IN MY HOUSE UNTOUCHABLE   270

KALONIKE *I will stay in my house untouchable*

LYSISTRATA IN MY THINNEST SAFFRON SILK

KALONIKE *In my thinnest saffron silk*

LYSISTRATA AND MAKE HIM LONG FOR ME.

KALONIKE *And make him long for me.*   275

LYSISTRATA I WILL NOT GIVE MYSELF

KALONIKE *I will not give myself*

238 *Seven Against Thebes.*
248 A popular wine from Thasos.

248 ARISTOPHANES

LYSISTRATA   AND IF HE CONSTRAINS ME
KALONIKE   *And if he constrains me*
LYSISTRATA   I WILL BE AS COLD AS ICE AND NEVER MOVE   280
KALONIKE   *I will be as cold as ice and never move*
LYSISTRATA   I WILL NOT LIFT MY SLIPPERS TOWARD THE
      CEILING
KALONIKE   *I will not lift my slippers toward the ceiling*
LYSISTRATA   OR CROUCH ON ALL FOURS LIKE THE LIONESS   285
      IN THE CARVING
KALONIKE   *Or crouch on all fours like the lioness in the carving*
LYSISTRATA   AND IF I KEEP THIS OATH LET ME DRINK FROM
      THIS BOWL
KALONIKE   *And if I keep this oath let me drink from this bowl*   290
LYSISTRATA   IF NOT, LET MY OWN BOWL BE FILLED WITH
      WATER.
KALONIKE   *If not, let my own bowl be filled with water.*
LYSISTRATA   You have all sworn?
MYRRHINE   We have.   295
LYSISTRATA   Then thus
      I sacrifice the victim. (*Drinks largely*)
KALONIKE   Save some for us!
      Here's to you, darling, and to you, and to you! It's all
      for us women. (*Loud cries off-stage*)   300
LAMPITO   What's all *that* whoozy-goozy?
LYSISTRATA   Just what I told you.
      The older women have taken the Acropolis. Now you, Lampito,
      rush back to Sparta. We'll take care of things here. And
      be sure you get organized!   305
                              The rest of you girls,
      up to the Citadel: and mind you push in the bolts.
KALONIKE   But the men? Won't they be after us?
LYSISTRATA   Just you leave
      the men to me. There's not fire enough in the world   310
      to make me open *my* door.
KALONIKE   I hope so, by Aphrodite!
      At any rate,
      let's remember the League's reputation for hanging on! (*Exeunt*)

_____

                  The hillside just under the Acropolis   315
            (*Enter* CHORUS OF OLD MEN *with burning torches and braziers;
                        much puffing and coughing*)
MALE CHORAGOS   Easy, Drakes, old friend! Don't skin your shoulders
      with those damnable big olive-branches. What a job!
OLD MEN (*Strophe 1*)   Forward, forward, comrades! Whew!   320
      The things that old age does to you!
      Neighbor Strymodoros, would you have thought it?

We've caught it—
                    And from women, too!
Women that used to board with us, bed with us—   325
Now, by the gods, they've got ahead of us,
Taken the Acropolis (Heaven knows why!),
Profaned the sacred statuar-y,
                    And barred the doors,
                    The aggravating whores!   330
MALE CHORAGOS   Come, Philourgos, quick, pile your brushwood
next to the wall there.
                    These traitors to Athens and to us,
we'll fry each last one of them! And the very first
will be old Lykon's wife.*   335
OLD MEN (*Antistrophe 1*)   By Demeter I swear it—(ouch!),
    I'll not perform the Kleomenes-crouch!
    How he looked—and a good soldier, too—
        When out he flew,
                    that filthy pouch   340
    Of a body of his all stinking and shaggy,
    Bare as an eel, except for the bag he
    Covered his rear with. Lord, what a mess!
    Never a bath in six years, I'd guess!
                    Unhappy Sparta,   345
                    With such a martyr!*
MALE CHORAGOS   What a siege, friends! Seventeen ranks strong
we stood at the Gate, and never a chance for a nap.
And all because of women, whom the gods hate
(and so does Euripides).   350
                    It's enough to make a veteran
turn in his medals from Marathon!
OLD MEN (*Strophe 2*)   Forward, men! Just up the hillside,
    And we're there!
    Keep to the path! A yoke of oxen   355
        Wouldn't care
            To haul this lumber. Mind the fire,
            Or it'll die before we're higher!
                    Puff! Puff!
            This smoke will strangle me, sure enough!   360
(*Antistrophe 2*)   Holy Heracles, I'm blinded,
    Sure as fate!
    It's Lemnos-fire we've been toting;*
        And isn't it great
            To be singed by this infernal flame?   365
            (Laches, remember the Goddess: for shame!)

335 Rhodia, a famous belle of the day.

346 Kleomenes, a King of Sparta, had captured the Acropolis but had been forced to give it up.

363 *I.e.* volcanic; Mount Moschylus on the island of Lemnos was the site of Vulcan's forge.

Woof! Woof!

    A few steps more, and we're under the roof!

MALE CHORAGOS It catches! It's blazing!

Down with your loads!   370

We'll sizzle 'em now,

By all the gods!

Vine-branches here, quick!

Light 'em up,

And in through the gate with 'em!   375

If that doesn't stop

Their nonsense—well,

We'll smoke 'em to Hell.

Ker*shoo*!

(What we really need   380

Is a grad-u-ate,

Top of his class,

From Samos Military State.*

A*choo*!)

Come, do   385

Your duty, you!

Pour out your braziers,

Embers ablaze!

But first, Gentlemen, allow me to raise

The paean: 390

              Lady

Victory, now

Assist thine adherents

Here below!

Down with women!   395

Up with men!

*lo triumphe!**

OLD MEN Amen!

(*Enter* CHORUS OF OLD WOMEN *on the walls of the Acropolis, carrying jars*

    of water to extinguish the fire set by the CHORUS OF OLD MEN)   400

FEMALE CHORAGOS Fire, fire!

Quickly, quickly, women, if we're to save ourselves!

OLD WOMEN (*Strophe*) Nikodike, run!

    Or Kalyke's done

To a turn, and poor Kratylla's   405

Smoked like a ham.

           Damn

These men and their wars,

Their hateful ways!

I nearly died before I got to the place   410

Where we fill our jars:

383 At this time Samos was the headquarters of Athenian military activities.

397 A ritual cry of triumph.

Slaves pushing and jostling—
Such a hustling
I never saw in all my days!
(*Antistrophe*) But here's water at last. 415
Sisters, make haste
And slosh it down on them,
The silly old wrecks!

Sex

Almighty! What they want's 420
A hot bath? Send it down!
And thou, Athena of Athens town,
Assist us in drowning their wheezy taunts!
O Trito-born!* Helmet of Gold!
Help us to cripple their backs, the old 425
Fools with their semi-incendiary brawn!

(*The* OLD MEN *capture a woman,* STRATYLLIS)

STRATYLLIS Let me go! Let me go!

FEMALE CHORAGOS   You walking corpses,
have you no shame? 430

MALE CHORAGOS   I wouldn't have believed it!
An army of women in the Acropolis!

FEMALE CHORAGOS So we scare you, do we? Grandpa, you've seen
only our pickets yet!

MALE CHORAGOS   Hey, Phaidrias! 435
Help me with the necks of these jabbering hens!

FEMALE CHORAGOS Down with your pots, girls! We'll need both hands
if these antiques attack us.

MALE CHORAGOS   Want your face kicked in?

FEMALE CHORAGOS Want to try my teeth? 440

MALE CHORAGOS   Look out! I've got a stick!

FEMALE CHORAGOS You lay a half-inch of your stick on Stratyllis,
and you'll never stick again!

MALE CHORAGOS   Fall apart!

FEMALE CHORAGOS   I'll chew your guts! 445

MALE CHORAGOS   Euripides! Master!
How well you knew women!

FEMALE CHORAGOS   Listen to him! Rhodippe,
up with the pots!

MALE CHORAGOS   Demolition of God, 450
what good are your pots?

FEMALE CHORAGOS   You refugee from the tomb,
what good is your fire?

MALE CHORAGOS   Good enough to make a pyre
to barbecue you! 455

FEMALE CHORAGOS We'll squizzle your kindling!

MALE CHORAGOS You think so?

---

424 A name for Athena, who according to some versions of her story was born at Lake Tritonis in Libya.

FEMALE CHORAGOS	Yah! Just hang around a while!	
MALE CHORAGOS	Want a touch of my torch?	
FEMALE CHORAGOS	Your torch needs a bath.	460
MALE CHORAGOS	How about you?	
FEMALE CHORAGOS	Soap for a senile bridegroom!	
MALE CHORAGOS	Senile? Hold your trap!	
FEMALE CHORAGOS	Just *you* try to hold it!	
MALE CHORAGOS	The yammer of women!	465
FEMALE CHORAGOS	The yatter of men!	

But you'll never sit in the jury-box again.

MALE CHORAGOS   Gentlemen, I beg you, burn off that woman's hair!
FEMALE CHORAGOS   Let it come down! (*They empty their pots on the men*)

MALE CHORAGOS	What a way to drown!	470
FEMALE CHORAGOS	Hot, hey?	
MALE CHORAGOS	Say,	

enough!

| FEMALE CHORAGOS | Dandruff | |

needs watering. I'll make you   475
nice and fresh.

MALE CHORAGOS   For God's sake, you
sluts, hold off!

(*Enter a* MAGISTRATE *accompanied by four constables*)

MAGISTRATE   These degenerate women! What a racket of little drums,   480
what a yapping for Adonis on every house-top!
It's like the time in the Assembly when I was listening
to a speech—out of order, as usual—by that fool
Demostratos,* all about troops for Sicily,*
that kind of nonsense—   485
                    and there was his wife
trotting around in circles howling
Alas for Adonis!—
                    and Demostratos insisting
we must draft every last Zakynthian that can walk—   490
and his wife up there on the roof,
drunk as an owl, yowling
Oh weep for Adonis!—
                    and that damned ox Demostratos
mooing away through the rumpus. That's what we get   495
for putting up with this wretched woman-business!

MALE CHORAGOS   Sir, you haven't heard the half of it. They laughed at us!
Insulted us! They took pitchers of water
and nearly drowned us! We're still wringing out our clothes,

------

484 (*a*) A well known demagogue; (*b*) the speech alludes to the festival in honor of Adonis which four
    years earlier had coincided with the decision to undertake the disastrous Sicilian expedition. It was
    believed that the women's madness in lamenting Adonis had influenced the decision.

for all the world like unhousebroken brats. 500

MAGISTRATE And a good thing, by Poseidon!
Whose fault is it if these women-folk of ours
get out of hand? We coddle them,
we teach them to be wasteful and loose. You'll see a husband
go into a jeweler's. 'Look,' he'll say, 505
'jeweler,' he'll say, 'you remember that gold choker
'you made for my wife? Well, she went to a dance last night
'and broke the clasp. Now, I've got to go to Salamis,
'and can't be bothered. Run over to my house tonight,
'will you, and see if you can put it together for her.' 510
Or another one
goes to a cobbler—a good strong workman, too,
with an awl that was never meant for child's play. 'Here,'
he'll tell him, 'one of my wife's shoes is pinching
'her little toe. Could you come up about noon 515
'and stretch it out for her?'
                                          Well, what do you expect?
Look at me, for example. I'm a Public Officer,
and it's one of my duties to pay off the sailors.
And where's the money? Up there in the Acropolis! 520
And those blasted women slam the door in my face!
But what are we waiting for?
                                          —Look here, constable,
stop sniffing around for a tavern, and get us
some crowbars. We'll force their gates! As a matter of fact, 525
I'll do a little forcing myself.

(*Enter* LYSISTRATA, *above, with* MYRRHINE, KALONIKE, *and the* BOEOTIAN)

LYSISTRATA   No need of forcing.
Here I am, of my own accord. And all this talk
about locked doors—! We don't need locked doors, 530
but just the least bit of common sense.

MAGISTRATE Is that so, ma'am!
                                —Where's my constable?
                                                          —Constable,
arrest that woman, and tie her hands behind her. 535

LYSISTRATA If he touches me, I swear by Artemis
there'll be one scamp dropped from the public pay-roll tomorrow!

MAGISTRATE Well, constable? You're not afraid, I suppose? Grab her,
two of you, around the middle!

KALONIKE   No, by Pandrosos!* 540
Lay a hand on her, and I'll jump on you so hard
your guts will come out the back door!

MAGISTRATE   That's what *you* think!
Where's the sergeant?—Here, you: tie up that trollop first,
the one with the pretty talk! 545

---

540 One of the daughters of the founder of Athens; a woman's oath.

MYRRHINE   By the Moon-Goddess!*
  Just you try it, and you'd better call a surgeon!
MAGISTRATE   Another one!
                         Officer, seize that woman!
                                       I swear   550
  I'll put an end to this riot!
BOEOTIAN   By the Taurian,*
  one inch closer and you won't have a hair on your head!
MAGISTRATE   Lord, what a mess! And my constables seem to have left me.
  But—women get the best of us? By God, no!   555
                                   —Scythians!*
  Close ranks and forward march!
LYSISTRATA   'Forward,' indeed!
  By the Two Goddesses, what's the sense in *that*?
  They're up against four companies of women   560
  armed from top to bottom.
MAGISTRATE   Forward, my Scythians!
LYSISTRATA   Forward, yourselves, dear comrades!
  You grainlettucebeanseedmarket girls!
  You garlicandonionbreadbakery girls!   565
  Give it to 'em! Knock 'em down! Scratch 'em!
  Tell 'em what you think of 'em! (*General mêlée; the Scythians yield*)
                         —Ah, that's enough!
  Sound a retreat: good soldiers don't rob the dead!
MAGISTRATE   A nice day *this* has been for the police!   570
LYSISTRATA   Well, there you are.—Did you really think we women
  would be driven like slaves? Maybe now you'll admit
  that a woman knows something about glory.
MAGISTRATE   Glory enough.
  especially glory in bottles! Dear Lord Apollo!   575
MALE CHORAGOS   Your Honor, there's no use talking to them. Words
  mean nothing whatever to wild animals like these.
  Think of the sousing they gave us! and the water
  was not, I believe, of the purest.
FEMALE CHORAGOS   You shouldn't have come after us. And if you try it again, 580
  you'll be one eye short!—Although, as a matter of fact,
  what I like best is just to stay at home and read,
  like a sweet little bride: never hurting a soul, no,
  never going out. But if you *must* shake hornets' nests,
  look out for the hornets!   585
OLD MEN (*Strophe*)   Good God, what can we do?
         What are we coming to?
  These women! Who could bear it? But, for that matter, who
         Will find

---

⁵⁴⁶ Artemis.
⁵⁵² Again, Artemis, who was worshipped at Taurica Chersonesos.
⁵⁵⁶ Athen's finest archers.

What they had in mind 590
When they seized Cranaos' city
And held it (more's the pity!)
Against us men of Athens, and our police force, too?

MALE CHORAGOS We might question them, I suppose. But I warn you, sir,
don't believe anything you hear! It would be un-Athenian 595
not to get to the bottom of this plot.

MAGISTRATE   Very well.
My first question is this: Why, so help you God,
did you bar the gates of the Acropolis?

LYSISTRATA   Why? 600
To keep the money, of course. No money, no war.

MAGISTRATE You think that money's the cause of war?

LYSISTRATA   I do.
Money brought about the Peisandros business*
and all the other attacks on the State. Well and good! 605
They'll not get another cent here!

MAGISTRATE   And what will you do?

LYSISTRATA What a question! From now on, we intend
to control the Treasury.

MAGISTRATE   Control the Treasury! 610

LYSISTRATA Why not? Does that seem strange? After all,
we control our household budgets.

MAGISTRATE   But that's different!

LYSISTRATA "Different"? What do you mean?

MAGISTRATE   I mean simply this: 615
it's the Treasury that pays for National Defense.

LYSISTRATA Unnecessary. We propose to abolish war!

MAGISTRATE Good God.—And National Security?

LYSISTRATA   Leave that to us.

MAGISTRATE You? 620

LYSISTRATA   Us.

MAGISTRATE   We're done for, then!

LYSISTRATA   Never mind.
We women will save you in spite of yourselves.

MAGISTRATE   What nonsense! 625

LYSISTRATA If you like. But you must accept it, like it or not.

MAGISTRATE Why, this is downright subversion!

LYSISTRATA   Maybe it is.
But we're going to save you, Judge.

MAGISTRATE   I don't *want* to be saved! 630

LYSISTRATA Tut. The death-wish. All the more reason.

MAGISTRATE   But the idea
of women bothering themselves about peace and war!

LYSISTRATA Will you listen to me?

604 A politician, who, even as Aristophanes was completing this play, was bringing about the revolution
of the Four Hundred, which overthrew Athenian democracy.

MAGISTRATE   Yes. But be brief, or I'll—   635

LYSISTRATA This is no time for stupid threats.

MAGISTRATE   By the gods,
I'm losing my mind!

AN OLD WOMAN   That's nice. If you do, remember
you've less to lose than *we* have.   <inline_sidenote>640</inline_sidenote>

MAGISTRATE   Quiet, you old buzzard!
Now, Lysistrata: tell me what you're thinking.

LYSISTRATA Glad to.
                    Ever since this war began
we women have been watching you men, agreeing with you,   645
keeping our thoughts to ourselves. That doesn't mean
we were happy: we weren't, for we saw how things were going;
but we'd listen to your at dinner
arguing this way and that.
                        —Oh you, and your big   650
Top Secrets!—
                    And then we'd grin like little patriots
(though goodness knows we didn't feel like grinning) and ask you:
"Dear, did the Armistice come up in Assembly today?"
And you'd say, "None of your business! Pipe down!," you'd say.   655
And so we would.

AN OLD WOMAN   *I* wouldn't have, by God!

MAGISTRATE You'd have taken a beating, then!
                                —Please go on.

LYSISTRATA Well, we'd be quiet. But then, you know, all at once   660
you men would think up something worse than ever.
Even *I* could see it was fatal. And, "Darling," I'd say,
"have you gone completely mad?" And my husband would look at me
and say, "Wife, you've got your weaving to attend to.
"Mind your tongue, if you don't want a slap. 'War's   665
"'a man's affair!'"*

MAGISTRATE   Good words, and well pronounced!

LYSISTRATA You're a fool if you think so.
                              It was hard enough
to put up with all this banquet-hall strategy.   670
But then we'd hear you out in the public square:
"Nobody left for the draft-quota here in Athens?"
you'd say; and, "No," someone else would say, "not a man!"
And so we women decided to rescue Greece.
You might as well listen to us now: you'll have to, later.   675

MAGISTRATE *You* rescue Greece? Absurd!

LYSISTRATA   You're the absurd one!

MAGISTRATE You expect me to take orders from a woman?

LYSISTRATA Heavens, if that's what's bothering you, take my veil,
here, and my girdle, and my market-basket. Go home   680

666 Quoted from Hector's farewell to Andromache, *Iliad,* VI, 492.

to your weaving and your cooking! I tell you, "War's
a woman's affair!"

FEMALE CHORAGOS   Down with your pitchers, comrades,
but keep them close at hand. It's time for a rally!

OLD WOMEN (*Antistrophe*)   Dance, girls, dance for peace!   685
    Who cares if our knees
Wobble and creak? Shall we not dance for such allies as these?
    Their wit! their grace! their beauty!
    It's a municipal duty
To dance them luck and happiness who risk their all for Greece!   690

FEMALE CHORAGOS   Women, remember your grandmothers! Remember, you
                        were born
among brambles and nettles! Dance for victory!

LYSISTRATA   O Eros, god of delight! O Aphrodite! Cyprian!
Drench us now with the savor of love!   695
Let these men, getting wind of us, dream such joy
that they'll tail us through all the provinces of Hellas!

MAGISTRATE   And if we do?

LYSISTRATA   Well, for one thing, we shan't have to watch
                                  you   700
going to market, a spear in one hand, and heavens knows
what in the other.

FEMALE CHORAGOS   Nicely said, by Aphrodite!

LYSISTRATA   As things stand now, you're neither men nor women.
Armor clanking with kitchen pans and pots—   705
you sound like a pack of Corybantes!*

MAGISTRATE   A man must do what a man must do.

LYSISTRATA   So I'm told.
But to see a General, complete with Gorgon-shield,
jingling along the dock to buy a couple of herrings!   710

FEMALE CHORAGOS   *I* saw a Captain the other day—lovely fellow he was,
nice curly hair—sitting on his horse; and—can you believe it?—
he'd just bought some soup, and was pouring it into his helmet!
And there was a soldier from Thrace
swishing his lance like something out of Euripides,   715
and the poor fruit-store woman got so scared
that she ran away and let him have his figs free!

MAGISTRATE   All this is beside the point.
                    Will you be so kind
as to tell me how you mean to save Greece?   720

LYSISTRATA   Of course!
Nothing could be simpler.

MAGISTRATE   I assure you, I'm all ears.

LYSISTRATA   Do you know anything about weaving?
Say the yarn gets tangled: we thread it   725
this way and that through the skein, up and down,

706 Wild and frenzied dancers; attendants of the goddess Cybele.

until it's free. And it's like that with war.
We'll send our envoys
up and down, this way and that, all over Greece,
until it's finished. 730

MAGISTRATE Yarn? Thread? Skein?
Are you out of your mind? I tell you,
war is a serious business.

LYSISTRATA So serious
that I'd like to go on talking about weaving. 735

MAGISTRATE All right. Go ahead.

LYSISTRATA The first thing we have to do
is to wash our yarn, get the dirt out of it.
You see? Isn't there too much dirt here in Athens?
You must wash those men away. 740
Then our spoiled wool—
that's like your job-hunters, out for a life
of no work and big pay. Back to the basket,
citizens or not, allies or not,
or friendly immigrants! 745
And your colonies?
Hanks of wool lost in various places. Pull them
together, weave them into one great whole,
and our voters are clothed for ever.

MAGISTRATE It would take a woman 750
to reduce state questions to a matter of carding and weaving!

LYSISTRATA You fool! Who were the mothers whose sons sailed off
to fight for Athens in Sicily?

MAGISTRATE Enough!
I beg you, do not call back those memories. 755

LYSISTRATA And then,
instead of the love that every woman needs,
we have only our single beds, where we can dream
of our husbands off with the Army.
Bad enough for wives! 760
But what about our girls, getting older every day,
and older, and no kisses?

MAGISTRATE Men get older, too.

LYSISTRATA Not in the same sense.
A soldier's discharged, 765
and he may be bald and toothless, yet he'll find
a pretty young thing to go to bed with.
But a woman!
Her beauty is gone with the first grey hair.
She can spend her time 770
consulting the oracles and the fortune-tellers,
but they'll never send her a husband.

MAGISTRATE Still, if a man can rise to the occasion—

LYSISTRATA (*Furiously*)   Rise? Rise, yourself!
Go invest in a coffin!   775
                            You've money enough.
                                                    I'll bake you
a cake for the Underworld.*
                            And here's your funeral
wreath! (*She pours water upon him*)   780
MYRRHINE   And here's another! (*More water*)
KALONIKE   And here's
my contribution! (*More water*)
LYSISTRATA   What are you waiting for?
All aboard Styx Ferry!*   785
                            Charon's calling for you!
It's sailing-time:don't disrupt the schedule!
MAGISTRATE   The insolence of women! And to me!
No, by God, I'll go back to court and show
the rest of the Bench the things that might happen to them!   790
                    (*Exit* MAGISTRATE)
LYSISTRATA   Really, I suppose we should have laid out his corpse
on the doorstep, in the usual way.
                            But never mind!
We'll give him the rites of the dead tomorrow morning!   795
          (*Exit* LYSISTRATA *with* MYRRHINE *and* KALONIKE)
OLD MEN (*Strophe 1*)   Sons of Liberty, strip off your clothes for action! Men
                                                    arise!
Shall we stand here limp and useless while old Cleisthenes' allies*
Prod a herd of furious grandmas to attempt to bring to pass   800
A female restoration of the Reign of Hippias?*
            Forbid it, gods misogynist!
            Return our Treasury, at least!
We must clothe ourselves and feed ourselves to face these civic rages,
And who can do a single thing if they cut off our wages?   805
MALE CHORAGOS   Gentlemen, we are disgraced forever if we allow
these madwomen to jabber about spears and shields
and make friends with the Spartans. What's a Spartan? a wild
wolf's a safer companion any day! No, their plan's
to bring back Dictatorship; and we won't stand for that!   810
From now on, let's go armed, each one of us
a new Aristogeiton!*
                    And to begin with,

778 A honey cake was usually placed in the hand of the dead to be given to Cerberus, the three-headed dog
    guarding the gates of Hades.
785 The Styx was the river over which Charon ferried the souls of the dead.
799 An Athenian of notorious ambisexual tendencies.
801 Hippias was the last of the Athenian tyrants. He had ruled with his brother Hipparchos until the
    latter's death at the hands of the patriots Aristogeiton and Harmonius; Hippias was killed later at
    Marathon.
812 See note to line 801.

I propose to poke a number of teeth
down the gullet of that harridan over there.   815
OLD WOMEN (*Antistrophe 1*)   Hold your tongues, you senile bravoes, or,
    I swear, when you get home
Your own mothers wouldn't know you! Strip for action, ladies, come!
I bore the holy vessels in my eighth year,* and at ten
I was pounding out the barley for Athena Goddess;* then   820
            They elected me Little Bear
            For Artemis at Brauron Fair;*
I'd been made a Basket-Carrier by the time I came of age:*
So trust me to advise you in this feminist rampage!

FEMALE CHORAGOS   As a woman, I pay my taxes to the State,   825
    though I pay them in baby boys. What do you contribute,
you impotent horrors? Nothing but waste:
our treasury, the so-called Glory of the Persian Wars,
gone! rifled! parceled out for privilege! And you
have the insolence to control public policy,   830
leading us all to disaster!
                  No, don't answer back
unless you want the heel of my slipper
slap against that ugly jaw of yours!

OLD MEN (*Strophe 2*)   What impudence!   835
        What malevolence!
        Comrades, make haste,
All those of you who still are sensitive below the waist!
        Off with your clothes, men!
        Nobody knows when   840
           We'll put them back on.
           Remember Leipsydrion!*
        We may be old,
        But let's be bold!

MALE CHORAGOS   Give them an inch, and we're done for! We'll have them   845
launching boats next and planning naval strategy.
Or perhaps they fancy themselves as cavalry!
That's fair enough: women know how to ride,
they're good in the saddle. Just think of Mikon's paintings,*
all those Amazons wrestling with men! No, it's time   850
to bridle these wild mares!

---

819 Four girls of high birth between the ages of seven and eleven were appointed to service in the Temple
  of Athena in the Acropolis.
820 At ten a girl of aristocratic family was eligible to be Mill-maid and to grind the sacred grain of Athena.
822 Brauron was a town on the coast of Attica where a ceremony to Artemis was celebrated in which a
  little girl impersonated a bear.
823 Girls carried baskets containing precious objects sacred to Athena.
842 After the patriots had killed Hipparchos (see line 801 note), they fled and fortified themselves in
  Leipsydrion. After a heroic defense they were forced to surrender.
849 Mikon was one of the many painters who dealt with the invasion of Attica by the Amazons, a fabulous
  race of warrior-women.

OLD WOMEN (*Antistrophe 2*)   Hold on, or
     You *are* done for,
     By the Two Goddesses above!
Strip, strip, my women: we've got the veterans on the move!   855
     Tangle with me, Gramps,
     And you'll have cramps
      For the rest of your days!
      No more beans! No more cheese!
     My two legs   860
     Will scramble your eggs!
FEMALE CHORAGOS   If Lampito stands by me, and that elegant
     Theban girl, Ismenia—what good are *you*?
                          Pass your laws!
Laws upon laws, you decrepit legislators!   865
At the worst you're just a nuisance, rationing Boeotian eels
on the Feast of Hecate, making our girls go without!
That was statesmanship! And we'll have to put up with it
until some patriot slits your silly old gizzards! (*Exeunt omnes*)

       The scene shifts to a court within the Acropolis   870
           (*Re-enter* LYSISTRATA)
FEMALE CHORAGOS   But Lysistrata! Leader! Why such a grim face?
LYSISTRATA   Oh the behavior of these idiotic women!
     There's something about the female temperament
     that I can't bear!   875
FEMALE CHORAGOS   What in the world do you mean?
LYSISTRATA   Exactly what I say.
FEMALE CHORAGOS   What dreadful thing has happened?
     Come, tell us: we're all your friends.
LYSISTRATA   It isn't easy   880
     to say it; yet, God knows, we can't hush it up.
FEMALE CHORAGOS   Well, then? Out with it!
LYSISTRATA   To put it bluntly,
     we're desperate for men.
FEMALE CHORAGOS   Almighty God!   885
LYSISTRATA   Why bring God into it?—No, it's just as I say.
     I can't manage them any longer: they've gone man-crazy,
     they're all trying to get out.
                Why, look:
one of them was sneaking out the back door   890
over there by Pan's cave;* another
was sliding down the walls with rope and tackle;
another was climbing aboard a sparrow,* ready to take off
for the nearest brothel—I dragged *her* back by the hair!

---

[891] A grotto on the north side of the Acropolis.
[893] A bird sacred to Aphrodite, it had been harnessed to the goddess' car.

They're all finding some reason to leave.

Look there!

There goes another one.

—Just a minute, you!

Where are you off to so fast?

FIRST WOMAN   I've got to get home! 900

I've a lot of Milesian wool, and the worms are spoiling it.

LYSISTRATA Oh bother you and your worms! Get back inside!

FIRST WOMAN I'll be back right away, I swear I will!

I just want to get it stretched out on my bed.

LYSISTRATA You'll do no such thing. You'll stay right here. 905

FIRST WOMAN   And my wool?

You want it ruined?

LYSISTRATA   Yes, for all I care.

SECOND WOMAN Oh dear! My lovely new flax from Amorgos—*

I left it at home, all uncarded! 910

LYSISTRATA   Another one!

And all she wants is someone to card her flax.

Get back in there!

SECOND WOMAN   But I swear by the Moon-Goddess,

the minute I get it done, I'll be back! 915

LYSISTRATA   I say No!

If you, why not all the other women as well?

THIRD WOMAN O Lady Eileithyia!* Radiant goddess! Thou

intercessor for women in childbirth! Stay, I pray thee,

oh stay this parturition! Shall I pollute 920

a sacred spot?

LYSISTRATA   And what's the matter with *you*?

THIRD WOMAN I'm having a baby—any minute now!

LYSISTRATA But you weren't pregnant yesterday.

THIRD WOMAN   Well, I am today! 925

Let me go home for a midwife, Lysistrata:

there's not much time.

LYSISTRATA   I never heard such nonsense.

What's that bulging under your cloak?

THIRD WOMAN   A little baby boy. 930

LYSISTRATA It certainly isn't. But it's something hollow,

like a basin or— Why, it's the helmet of Athena!

And you said you were having a baby!

THIRD WOMAN   Well, I am! So there!

LYSISTRATA Then why the helmet? 935

THIRD WOMAN   I was afraid that my pains

might begin here in the Acropolis; and I wanted

to drop my chick into it, just as the dear doves do.

---

909 An island in the Aegean famed for its flax.

918 The goddess invoked by women at childbirth. It was unlawful to bear children on the Acropolis because it was holy ground.

LYSISTRATA 263

LYSISTRATA Lies! Evasions!—But at least one thing's clear:
you can't leave the place before your purification.   940

THIRD WOMAN But I can't stay here in the Acropolis! Last night I dreamed
of a snake.*

FIRST WOMAN And those horrible owls, the noise they make!*
I can't get a bit of sleep; I'm just about dead.

LYSISTRATA You useless girls, that's enough: Let's have no more lying.   945
Of course you want your men. But don't you imagine
that they want you just as much? I'll give you my word,
their nights must be pretty hard.

                        Just stick it out!
A little patience, that's all, and our battle's won.   950
I have heard an Oracle. Should you like to hear it?

FIRST WOMAN An Oracle? Yes, tell us!

LYSISTRATA   Quiet, then.—Here
is what it said:
IF EVER THE SWALLOWS, ESCHEWING HOOPOE-BIRDS,   955
SHALL CONSPIRE TOGETHER TO DENY THEM ALL ACCESS,
THEIR GRIEF IS FOREVER OVER.
                            These are the words
from the Shrine itself.
              AYE, AND ZEUS WILL REDRESS   960
THEIR WRONGS, AND SET THE LOWER ABOVE THE HIGHER.

FIRST WOMAN Does that mean we'll be on top?

LYSISTRATA   BUT IF THEY RETIRE,
EACH SWALLOW HER OWN WAY, FROM THIS HOLY PLACE,
LET THE WORLD PROCLAIM NO BIRD OF SORRIER GRACE   965
THAN THE SWALLOW.

FIRST WOMAN   I swear, *that* Oracle makes sense!

LYSISTRATA Now, then, by all the gods,
let's show that we're bigger than these annoyances.
Back to your places! Let's not disgrace the Oracle. (*Exeunt* LYSISTRATA   970
    and the dissident women; the CHORUSES *renew their conflict*)

OLD MEN (*Strophe*) I know a little story that I learned way back in school
Goes like this:
Once upon a time there was a young man—and no fool—
Named Melanion;* and his   975
One aversi-on was marriage. He loathed the very thought!
So he ran off to the hills, and in a special grot
Raised a dog, and spent his days
Hunting rabbits. And it says
That he never never never did come home.   980
It might be called a refuge *from* the womb.

---

942 The sacred snake of the Acropolis. It was never seen but was believed to guard the holy ground.

943 Owls were sacred to Athena.

975 Melanion was the suitor of Atalanta, who hated men. The Chorus of Men have made him a hater of
women.

All right,
        all right,
                all right!
We're as pure as young Melanion, and we hate the very sight   985
Of you sluts!

A MAN   How about a kiss, old woman?

A WOMAN   Here's an onion in your eye!

A MAN   A kick in the guts, then?

A WOMAN   Try, old bristle-tail, just try!   990

A MAN   Yet they say Myronides*
        On hands and knees
        Looked just as shaggy fore and aft as I!

OLD WOMEN (*Antistrophe*)   Well, *I* know a little story, and it's just as good
                                                                as yours.   995

Goes like this:
Once there was a man named Timon*—a rough diamond, of course,
And that whiskery face of his
Looked like murder in the shrubbery. By God, he was a son
Of the Furies, let me tell you! And what did he do but run   1000
From the world and all its ways,
Cursing mankind! And it says
That his choicest execrations as of then
Were leveled almost wholly at *old* men.
All right,   1005
        all right,
                all right!
But there's one thing about Timon: he could always stand the sight
Of us "sluts"!

A WOMAN   How about a crack in the jaw, Pop?   1010

A MAN   I can take it, Ma—no fear!

A WOMAN   How about a kick in the face?

A MAN   You'd show your venerable rear.

A WOMAN   I may be old;
        But I've been told   1015
        That I've nothing to worry about down there!

(*Re-enter* LYSISTRATA)

LYSISTRATA   Oh, quick, girls, quick! Come here!

FEMALE CHORAGOS   What is it?

LYSISTRATA   A man!   1020
        A man simply bulging with love!
                                O Cyprian Queen,
        O Paphian, O Cythereian! Hear us and aid us!

FEMALE CHORAGOS   Where is this enemy?

991 A famous Athenian general.
997 A famous Athenian misanthrope.

LYSISTRATA   Over there, by Demeter's shrine. 1025

FEMALE CHORAGOS Damned if he isn't. But who *is* he?

MYRRHINE   My husband.
Kinesias.

LYSISTRATA Oh then, get busy! Tease him! Undermine him!
Wreck him! Give him everything—kissing, tickling, nudging,   1030
whatever you generally torture him with—: give him everything
except what we swore on the wine we would not give.

MYRRHINE Trust me!

LYSISTRATA   I do. But I'll help you get him started.
The rest of you women, stay back.   1035

                    (*Enter* KINESIAS)

KINESIAS   Oh God! Oh my God!
I'm stiff for lack of exercise. All I can do to stand up!

LYSISTRATA Halt! Who are you, approaching our lines?

KINESIAS   Me? I.   1040

LYSISTRATA A man?

KINESIAS   You have eyes, haven't you?

LYSISTRATA   Go away.

KINESIAS Who says so?

LYSISTRATA   Officer of the Day.   1045

KINESIAS   Officer, I beg you,
by all the gods at once, bring Myrrhine out!

LYSISTRATA Myrrhine? And who, my good sir, are you?

KINESIAS Kinesias. Last name's Pennison. Her husband.

LYSISTRATA Oh, of course. I beg your pardon. We're glad to see you.   1050
We've heard so much about you. Dearest Myrrhine
is always talking about "Kinesias"—never nibbles an egg
or an apple without saying
"Here's to Kinesias!"

KINESIAS   Do you really mean it?   1055

LYSISTRATA   I do.
When we're discussing men, she always says,
"Well, after all, there's nobody like Kinesias!"

KINESIAS Good God.—Well, then, please send her down here.

LYSISTRATA And what do *I* get out of it?   1060

KINESIAS   A standing promise.

LYSISTRATA I'll take it up with her. (*Exit* LYSISTRATA)

KINESIAS   But be quick about it!
Lord, what's life without a wife? Can't eat. Can't sleep.
Every time I go home, the place is so empty, so   1065
insufferably sad! Love's killing me! Oh,
hurry!

          (*Enter* MANES, *a slave, with Kinesias' baby; the voice of* MYRRHINE
                          is heard off-stage)

MYRRHINE But of course I love him! Adore him!—But no,   1070
he hates love. No. I won't go down.

(Enter MYRRHINE, above)

KINESIAS   Myrrhine!
   Darlingest little Myrrhine! Come down quick!

MYRRHINE   Certainly not.   1075

KINESIAS   Not? But why, Myrrhine?

MYRRHINE   Why? You don't need me.

KINESIAS   Need you? My God, *look* at me!

MYRRHINE   So long! (*Turns to go*)

KINESIAS   Myrrhine, Myrrhine, Myrrhine!   1080
   If not for my sake, for our child! (*Pinches* BABY)
              —All right, you: pipe up!

BABY   Mummie! Mummie! Mummie!

KINESIAS   You hear that?
   Pitiful, I call it. Six days now   1085
   with never a bath; no food; enough to break your heart!

MYRRHINE   My darlingest child! What a father *you* acquired!

KINESIAS   At least come down for his sake!

MYRRHINE   I suppose I must.
   Oh, this mother business!* (*Exit*)   1090

KINESIAS   How pretty she is! And younger!
   She's so much nicer when she's bothered!

           (MYRRHINE *enters, below*)

MYRRHINE   Dearest child,
   you're as sweet as your father's horrid. Give me a kiss.   1095

KINESIAS   Now you see how wrong it was to get involved
   in this sceming League of women. All this agony
   for nothing!

MYRRHINE   Keep your hands to yourself!

KINESIAS   But our house   1100
   going to rack and ruin?

MYRRHINE   *I* don't care.

KINESIAS   And your knitting
   all torn to pieces by the chickens? Don't you care?

MYRRHINE   Not at all.   1105

KINESIAS   And our vows to Aphrodite?
   Oh, *won't* you come back?

MYRRHINE   No.—At least, not until you men
   make a treaty to end the war.

KINESIAS   Why, if that's all you want,   1110
   by God, we'll make your treaty!

MYRRHINE   Oh? Very well.
   When you've done that, I'll come home. But meanwhile,
   I've sworn an oath.

KINESIAS   Don't worry.—Now, let's have fun.   1115

MYRRHINE   No! Stop it! I said no!
            —Although, of course,

---

¹⁰⁹⁰ A line that parodies Euripides' *Iphigenia at Aulis*, 917.

I *do* love you.

KINESIAS   I know you do. Darling Myrrhine:
come, shall we?   1120

MYRRHINE   Are you out of your mind? In front of the child?

KINESIAS Take him home, Manes. (*Exit* MANES *with baby*)
                                        There. He's gone.
                                                          Come on!
There's nothing to stop us now.   1125

MYRRHINE   You devil! But where?

KINESIAS In Pan's cave. What could be snugger than that?

MYRRHINE But my purification before I go back to the Citadel?

KINESIAS There's always the Klepsydra.*

MYRRHINE   And my oath?   1130

KINESIAS   Leave the oath to me.
After all, I'm the man.

MYRRHINE   Well . . . if you say so!
                                        I'll go find a bed.

KINESIAS Oh, bother a bed! The ground's good enough for me!   1135

MYRRHINE No. You're a bad man, but you deserve something better than
                                        dirt. (*Exit* MYRRHINE)

KINESIAS What a love she is! And how thoughtful!
                    (*Re-enter* MYRRHINE)

MYRRHINE   Here's your bed.   1140
Now let me get my clothes off.
                          But, good horrors!
We haven't a mattress!

KINESIAS   Oh, forget the mattress!

MYRRHINE   No.   1145
Just lying on blankets? Too sordid!

KINESIAS   Give me a kiss.

MYRRHINE Just a second. (*Exit* MYRRHINE)

KINESIAS   I swear, I'll explode!
                    (*Re-enter* MYRRHINE)   1150

MYRRHINE   Here's your mattress.
Go to bed now. I'll just take my dress off.
                          But look—
where's our pillow?

KINESIAS   I don't need a pillow!   1155

MYRRHINE   Well, *I* do. (*Exit* MYRRHINE)

KINESIAS I don't suppose even Heracles
would stand for this!
                    (*Re-enter* MYRRHINE)

MYRRHINE   There we are. Ups-a-daisy!   1160

KINESIAS So we are. Well, come to bed.

MYRRHINE   But I wonder:
is everything ready now?

1129 A sacred spring near Pan's cave.

KINESIAS   I can swear to that. Come, darling!
MYRRHINE   Just getting out of my girdle.   1165
                              But remember, now,
     what you promised about the treaty!
KINESIAS   I'll remember.
MYRRHINE   But no coverlet!
KINESIAS   Damn it, I'll be   1170
     your coverlet!
MYRRHINE   Be right back. (*Exit* MYRRHINE)
KINESIAS   This girl and her coverlets
     will be the death of me.
                              (*Re-enter* MYRRHINE)   1175
MYRRHINE   Here we are. Up you go!
KINESIAS   Up? I've been up for ages!
MYRRHINE   Some perfume?
KINESIAS   No, by Apollo!
MYRRHINE   Yes, by Aphrodite!   1180
     I don't care whether you want it or not. (*Exit* MYRRHINE)
KINESIAS   For love's sake, hurry!
                         (*Re-enter* MYRRHINE)
MYRRHINE   Here, in your hand. Rub it right in.
KINESIAS   Never cared for perfume.   1185
     And this is particularly strong. Still, here goes!
MYRRHINE   What a nitwit I am! I brought you the Rhodian bottle!*
KINESIAS   Forget it.
MYRRHINE   No trouble at all. You just wait here. (*Exit* MYRRHINE)
KINESIAS   God damn the man who invented perfume!   1190
                         (*Re-enter* MYRRHINE)
MYRRHINE   At last! The right bottle!
KINESIAS   I've got the rightest
     bottle of all, and it's right here waiting for you.
     Darling, forget everything else. Do come to bed!   1195
MYRRHINE   Just let me get my shoes off.
                              —And, by the way,
     you'll vote for the treaty?
KINESIAS   I'll think about it. (MYRRHINE *runs away*)
     There! That's done it! Off she runs,   1200
     with never a thought for the way I'm feeling. I must
     have *some*one, or I'll go mad! Myrrhine
     has just about ruined me.
                         And you, strutting little soldier:
     what about you? There's nothing for it, I guess,   1205
     but an expedition to old Dog-fox's* bordello.
OLD MEN   She's left you in a sorry state:
              You have my sympathy.

1187 *I.e.* from Rhodes.
1206 A nickname for a famous procurer.

What upright citizen could bear
      Your pain? I swear, not I!   1210
Just the look of you, with never a woman
To come to your aid! It isn't human!

KINESIAS   The agony!

MALE CHORAGOS   Well, why not?
          She has you on the spot!   1215

FEMALE CHORAGOS A lovelier girl never breathed, you old sot!

KINESIAS A lovelier girl? Zeus! Zeus!
          Produce a hurricane
      To hoist these lovely girls aloft
          And drop them down again   1220
Bump on our lances! Then they'd know
What they do that makes men suffer so. (*Exit* KINESIAS)

(*Enter a* SPARTAN HERALD)

HERALD Gentlemen, Ah beg you will be so kind
as to direct me to the Central Committee.   1225
Ah have a communication.
          (*Re-enter* MAGISTRATE)

MAGISTRATE   Are you a man,
or a fertility symbol?

HERALD   Ah refuse to answer that question!   1230
Ah'm a certified herald from Spahta, and Ah've come
to talk about an ahmistice.

MAGISTRATE   Then why
that spear under your cloak?

HERALD   Ah have no speah!   1235

MAGISTRATE You don't walk naturally, with your tunic
poked out so. You have a tumor, maybe,
or a hernia?

HERALD   No, by Castor!*

MAGISTRATE   Well,   1240
something's wrong, I can see that. And I don't like it.

HERALD Colonel, Ah resent this.

MAGISTRATE   So I see. But what *is* it?

HERALD   A scroll
with a message from Spahta.   1245

MAGISTRATE   Oh. I've heard about these scrolls.
Well, then, man, speak out: How are things in Sparta?

HERALD Hard, Colonel, hard! We're at a standstill.
Can't seem to think of anything but women.

MAGISTRATE How curious! Tell me, do you Spartans think   1250
that maybe Pan's to blame?

1239 One of Sparta's protective spirits.

HERALD Pan? No. Lampito and her little naked friends.
They won't let a man come near them.

MAGISTRATE How are you handling it?

HERALD   Losing our minds,   1255
if you want to know, and walking around hunched over
like men carrying candles in a gale.
The women have sworn they'll have nothing to do with us
until we get a treaty.

MAGISTRATE   Yes, I know.   1260
It's a general uprising, sir, in all parts of Greece.
But as for the answer—
                          Sir: go back to Sparta
and have them send us your Armistice Commission.
I'll arrange things in Athens.   1265
                          And I may say
that my standing is good enough to make them listen.

HERALD A man after mah own heart! Sir, Ah thank you! (*Exit* HERALD)

———————————

OLD MEN (*Strophe*) Oh these women! Where will you find
               A slavering beast that's more unkind?   1270
                  Where a hotter fire?
               Give me a panther, any day!
               He's not so merciless as they,
                  And panthers don't conspire!

OLD WOMEN (*Antistrophe*) We may be hard, you silly old ass,   1275
               But who brought you to this stupid pass?
                  You're the ones to blame.
               Fighting with us, your oldest friends,
               Simply to serve your selfish ends—
                  Really, you have no shame!   1280

MALE CHORAGOS No, I'm through with women for ever!*

FEMALE CHORAGOS   If you say so.
Still, you might put some clothes on. You look too absurd
standing around naked. Come, get into this cloak.

MALE CHORAGOS Thank you; you're right. I merely took it off   1285
because I was in such a temper.

FEMALE CHORAGOS   That's much better
Now you resemble a man again.
                              Why have you been so horrid?
And look: there's some sort of insect in your eye!   1290
Shall I take it out?

MALE CHORAGOS   An insect, is it? So that's
what's been bothering me! Lord, yes: take it out!

FEMALE CHORAGOS You might be more polite.

1281 Parodies lines in Euripides' *Hippolytus*.

What an enormous gnat!

MALE CHORAGOS You've saved my life.

That gnat was drilling an artesian well
in my left eye.

FEMALE CHORAGOS Let me wipe 1300
those tears away!—And now: one little kiss?

MALE CHORAGOS Over my dead body!

FEMALE CHORAGOS You're so difficult!

MALE CHORAGOS These impossible women! How they do get around us!
The poet was right: Can't live with them, or without them! 1305
But let's be friends.
And to celebrate, you might lead off with an Ode.

OLD WOMEN (*Strophe*) Let it never be said
 That my tongue is malicious:
 Both by word and by deed 1310
I would set an example that's noble and gracious.
 We've had sorrow and care
 Till we're sick of the tune.
 Is there anyone here
 Who would like a small loan? 1315
 My purse is crammed,
 As you'll soon find;
And you needn't pay me back if the Peace gets signed!
 I've invited to lunch
 Some Karystian rips—* 1320
 An esurient bunch,
But I've ordered a menu to water their lips!
 I can still make soup
 And slaughter a pig.
 You're all coming, I hope? 1325
 But a bath first, I beg!
 Walk right up
 As though you owned the place,
And you'll get the front door slammed to in your face!

 (*Enter* SPARTAN AMBASSADOR, *with entourage*) 1330

MALE CHORAGOS The Commission has arrived from Sparta.
 How oddly
they're walking!
 Gentlemen, welcome to Athens!
How is life in Laconia? 1335

AMBASSADOR Need we discuss that?
Simply use your eyes.

1320 The Karystians were allies of Athens at this time, but were disdained for their primitive manners
 and loose morals.

OLD MEN	The poor man's right: *What* a sight!	

AMBASSADOR Words fail me. 1340
But come, gentlemen, call in your Commissioners,
and let's get down to a Peace.

MALE CHORAGOS The state we're in! Can't bear
a stitch below the waist. It's a kind of pelvic
paralysis. 1345

AN ATHENIAN Won't somebody call Lysistrata?
She has the answer.

A SPARTAN Yes, there, look at him.
Same thing. Seh, do y'all feel a certain strain 1350
early in the morning?

ATHENIAN I do, sir. It's worse than a strain.
A few more days, and there's nothing for us but Cleisthenes,
that broken blossom!

MALE CHORAGOS But you'd better get dressed again. 1355
You know these prudes who go around Athens with chisels,
looking for prominent statues.*

ATHENIAN Sir, you are right.

SPARTAN He certainly is! Ah'll put mah own clothes back on.

(Enter ATHENIAN COMMISSIONERS*)* 1360

AN ATHENIAN They're no better off than we are!

—Greetings, Laconians!

SPARTAN *(To one of his own group)* Colonel, we got dressed just in time.

Ah sweah,
if they'd seen us the way we were, there'd have been a new war 1365
between the states.

ATHENIAN Call the meeting to order.

Now, Laconians,
what's your proposal?

AMBASSADOR We'd lahk to consider peace. 1370

ATHENIAN Good. That's on our minds, too.

—Summon Lysistrata.

We'll never get anywhere without her.

AMBASSADOR Lysistrata?
Summon Lysis-*any*body!* Only, summon! 1375

MALE CHORAGOS No need to summon:
here she is, herself.

(Enter LYSISTRATA*)*
Lysistrata! Lion of women!
This is your hour to be 1380
hard and yielding, outspoken and sly, austere and
gentle. You see here

1357 That is, statues with prominent male sexual organs, or *phalloi*.

1375 Lysistrata's name means "dissolver of armies."

the best brains of Hellas (confused, I admit,
by your devious charming) met as one man
to turn the future over to you.   1385
LYSISTRATA   That's fair enough,
unless you men take it into your heads
to turn to each other instead of to me. But I'd know
soon enough if you did!
                          —Where is that goddess of Peace?   1390
Go, some of you: bring her here. (*Exeunt two* SERVANTS)
                          And now,
summon the Spartan Commission. Treat them courteously:
our husbands have been lax in that respect.
Take them by the hand, women,   1395
or by anything else, if they seem unwilling.
                                    —Spartans:
you stand here. Athenians: on this side. Now listen to me.
    (*Re-enter* SERVANTS, *staggering under the weight of a more than life-size
        statue of a naked woman: this is* PEACE)   1400
I'm only a woman, I know; but I've a mind,
and I can distinguish between sense and foolishness.
I owe the first to my father; the rest
to the local politicians.* So much for that.
Now, then.   1405
What I have to say concerns both sides in this war.
We are all Greeks.
Must I remind you of Thermopylae? of Olympia?
of Delphi? names deep in all our hearts?
And yet you men go raiding through the country,   1410
Greek killing Greek, storming down Greek cities—
and all the time the Barbarian across the sea
is waiting for his chance.—That's my first point.
AN ATHENIAN   Lord! I can hardly contain myself!
LYSISTRATA   And you Spartans: 1415
Was it so long ago that Pericleides
came here to beg our help?* I can see him still,
his white face, his sombre gown. And what did he want?
An army from Athens! Messenia
was at your heels, and the sea-god splitting your shores.   1420
Well, Kimon and his men,
four thousand infantry, marched out of here to save you.
What thanks do we get? You come back to murder us.
ATHENIAN   Can't trust a Spartan, Lysistrata!
A SPARTAN   Ah admit it.   1425
When Ah look at those legs, Ah sweah Ah can't trust mahself!

1404 The preceding four lines were probably quoted from Euripides' *Melanippe the Wise* (*cf.* fragment 483, Nanck).

1417 In 464 B.C. during a revolt in Sparta, when an earthquake had just severely damaged the city.

LYSISTRATA   And you, men of Athens:
you might remember that bad time when we were down,
and an army came from Sparta
and sent Hippias and the Thessalians   1430
whimpering back to the hills. That was Sparta,
and only Sparta; without Sparta, we'd now be
cringing helots, not walking about like free men!
        (*From this point, the male responses are less to* LYSISTRATA *than to the*
                                statue of PEACE)   1435
A SPARTAN   An eloquent speech!
AN ATHENIAN   An elegant construction!
LYSISTRATA   Why are we fighting each other? Why not make peace?
AMBASSADOR   Spahta is ready, ma'am,
so long as we get that place back.   1440
LYSISTRATA   Place? What place?
AMBASSADOR   Ah refer to Pylos.*
MAGISTRATE   Not while I'm alive, by God!
LYSISTRATA   You'd better give in.
MAGISTRATE   But—what were we fighting about?   1445
LYSISTRATA   Lots of places left.
MAGISTRATE   All right. Well, then:
Hog Island first, and that gulf behind there, and the land between
the Legs of Megara.
AMBASSADOR   Mah government objects.   1450
LYSISTRATA   Over-ruled. Why fuss about a pair of legs? (*General assent;*
                    the statue of PEACE *is removed*)
AN ATHENIAN   Let's take off our clothes and plow our fields.
A SPARTAN   Ah'll fertilize mahn first, by the Heavenly Twins!
LYSISTRATA   And so you shall,   1455
once we have peace. If you are serious,
go, both of you, and talk with your allies.
ATHENIAN   Too much talk already. We'll stand together!
We've only one end in view. All that we want
is our women: and I speak for our allies.   1460
AMBASSADOR   Mah government concurs.
ATHENIAN   So does Karystos.
LYSISTRATA   Good.—But before you come inside
to join your wives at supper, you must perform
the usual lustration. Then we'll open   1465
our baskets for you, and all that we have is yours.
But you must promise upright good behavior
from this day on. Then each man home with his woman!
ATHENIAN   Let's get it over with!
SPARTAN   Lead on: Ah follow!   1470
ATHENIAN   Quick as a cat can wink! (*Exeunt all but the* CHORUSES)
OLD WOMEN (*Antistrophe*)   Embroideries and

1442 A lost possession. For the moment political and sexual desires become confused.

Twinkling ornaments and
Pretty dresses—I hand
Them all over to you, and with never a qualm.   1475
They'll be nice for your daughters
On festival days
When the girls bring the Goddess
The ritual prize.
Come in, one and all: 1480
Take what you will.
I've nothing here so tightly corked that you can't make it spill!
You may search my house,
But you'll not find
The least thing of use,   1485
Unless your two eyes are keener than mine.
Your numberless brats
Are half starved? and your slaves?
Courage, grandpa! I've lots
Of grain left, and big loaves.   1490
I'll fill your guts,
I'll go the whole hog;
But if you come too close to me, remember: 'ware the dog!

(*Exeunt* CHORUSES)

———————

(*An* ATHENIAN DRUNKARD *approaches the gate and is halted by a* SENTRY)   1495
DRUNKARD   Open. The. Door.
SENTRY   Now, friend, just shove along!
So you want to sit down! If it weren't such an old joke,
I'd tickle your tail with this torch. Just the sort of thing
that this kind of audience appreciates.   1500
DRUNKARD   I. Stay. Right. Here.
SENTRY   Oh, all right. But you'll see some funny sights!
DRUNKARD   Bring. Them. On.
SENTRY   No, what am I thinking of?
The gentlemen from Sparta are just coming back from supper.   1505
Get out of here, or I'll scalp you! (*Exit* DRUNKARD)
(*The general company re-enters; the two* CHORUSES *now represent* SPARTANS
and ATHENIANS)
MAGISTRATE   I must say,
I've never tasted a better meal. And those Laconians!   1510
They're gentlemen, by the Lord! Just goes to show:
a drink to the wise is sufficient. And why not?
A sober man's an ass.
Men of Athens, mark my words: the only efficient
Ambassador's a drunk Ambassador. Is that clear?   1515
Look: we go to Sparta,
and when we get there we're dead sober. The result?

Everyone cackling at everyone else. They make speeches;
and even if we understand, we get it all wrong
when we file our reports in Athens. But today—!   1520
Everybody's happy. Couldn't tell the difference
between *Drink to Me Only* and
the *Spar Spangled Athens.*

                    What's a few lies,
washed down in good strong drink?   1525

                 (*Re-enter* DRUNKARD)

SENTRY   God almighty,
he's back again!

DRUNKARD   I. Resume. My. Place.

A SPARTAN (*To an* ATHENIAN) I beg you, seh,   1530
take your instrument in your hand and play for us.
Ah'm told
you understand the in*tric*acies of the floot?
Ah'd lahk to execute a song and dance
in honor of Athens,   1535
               and, of course, of Spahta.

(*The following song is a solo—an aria—accompanied by the flute. The* CHORUS
         OF SPARTANS *begins a slow dance*)

DRUNKARD   Toot. On. Your. Flute.

SPARTAN CHORAGOS Mnemosyne,*   1540
    Inspire once more the Grecian Muse
    To sing of glory glory glory without end.
    Sing Artemesion's shore,*
    Where Athens fluttered the Persian fleet—
    *Alalai,** that great   1545
    Victory! Sing Leonidas and his men,
    Those wild boars, sweat and blood
    Down in a red drench. Then, then
    The barbarians broke, though they had stood
    A myriad strong before!   1550
                O Artemis,
    Virgin Goddess, whose darts
    Flash in our forests: approve
    This pact of peace, and join our hearts,
    From this day on, in love.   1555
    Huntress, descend!

LYSISTRATA All that will come in time.

                  But now, Laconians,
take home your wives. Athenians, take yours.
Each man be kind to his woman; and you, women,   1560

1540 Goddess of memory and mother of the Muses.

1543 Where in 480 B.C. the Athenian fleet successfully engaged the Persians, while Leonidas and his Spartans
    were making their famous stand at Thermopylae.

1545 A war cry.

be equally kind. Never again, pray God,
shall we lose our way in such madness.
                              —And now
let's dance our joy! (*From this point the dance becomes general*)

CHORUS OF ATHENIANS   Dance! 1565

                    Dance!

                              Dance, you Graces!

      Artemis, dance!

                  Dance, Phoebus, Lord of dancing!

Dance, Dionysus, in a scurry of Maenads! 1570

                  Dance, Zeus Thunderer!

            Dance, Lady Hera,

      Queen of the Sky!

                        Dance, dance, all you gods!

Dance for the dearest, the bringer of peace, 1575

Deathless Aphrodite!

LYSISTRATA   Now let us have another song from Sparta.

CHORUS OF SPARTANS   From Taygetos' skyey summit,

            Laconian Muse, come down!

      Sing the glories of Apollo, 1580

            Regent of Amyclae Town.

                  Sing of Leda's Twins,

                  Those gallant sons,

                  On the banks of Eurotas—

                        *Alalai Evohe!** 1585

      Here's to our girls

            With their tangling curls,

                  Legs a-wriggle,

                  Bellies a-jiggle,

                        A riot of hair, 1590

                  A fury of feet,

      Evohe! Evohai! Evohe!

                        as they pass

            Dancing,

                  dancing,

                        dancing, 1595

                              to greet

      Athena of the House of Brass!*

1585 Now an orgiastic war cry.

1598 A famous temple on the acropolis of Sparta.

GREEK GODS: *A Brief Glossary*

ATHENA (Roman name—Minerva) One of the heavenly deities; virgin goddess of wisdom, skill, spinning and weaving, horticulture and agriculture. Her title Pallas refers to the Titan named Pallas whom she killed in the war between the gods and giants.

APHRODITE (Roman name—Venus) One of the heavenly deities; goddess of love and beauty. In one legend she was the daughter of Zeus and Dione; in another she supposedly arose from the foam of the sea at Cyprus.

APOLLO or **PHOEBUS APOLLO** One of the heavenly deities; son of Zeus and Leto and the twin brother of Artemis. He was the god of music, poetry, and healing; represented light and was often identified with the sun.

ARES (Roman name—Mars) One of the heavenly deities; son of Zeus and Hera. He was the god of war, violence, brutality, confusion and destruction.

ARTEMIS (Roman name—Diana) One of the heavenly deities; daughter of Zeus and Leto and the twin sister of Apollo. She was the virgin goddess of maidenly vigor, modesty and grace, and light, also the guardian and protector of wild beasts and mortals.

DIONYSUS (Roman name—Bacchus) One of the earthly deities; legendary son of Zeus and Semele. He was god of wine (its good and bad qualities) and fertility. Usually he was attended by Satyrs, Sileni, and groups of frenzied women.

EUMENIDES The lesser divinities of the underworld. A euphemistic name for the Erinyes in Greek mythology meaning "kindly ones." The female Erinyes were avengers of sin; children of night and darkness, they punished offenders in the afterworld. They were called Furiae or Dirae by the Romans.

FURIAE—see **EUMENIDES**

HEPHAESTUS (Roman name—Vulcan) One of the heavenly deities; son of Zeus and Hera. He was the god of fire and metallic arts; the blacksmith of the gods who built their dwellings and created their arms and armor.

HERA (Roman name—Juno) One of the heavenly deities; daughter of Cronus and Rhea and the wife and sister of Zeus. She was the queen of heaven, inferior only to Zeus; the goddess of virtuous womanhood, childbirth, and dignity.

HERMES (Roman name—Mercury) One of the heavenly deities; son of Zeus and Maia. He was the herald and messenger of the gods; also the protector of herdsmen, god of science, commerce, invention and the arts. The most serious of his duties was to conduct the souls of the dead.

HESTIA (Roman name—Vesta) One of the heavenly deities; first born daughter of Cronus and Rhea. She was the goddess of the hearth.

HYMEN Originally the name of a Greek marriage song, the name was later personified and Hymen became the god of marriage.

PALLAS—see **ATHENA**

PAN One of the lesser earthly deities; the god of pastures and flocks. He had the head and body of a man and the hindquarters of a goat.

PHOEBE The daughter of Uranus and Gaea; the mother of Leto and thus the grandmother of Artemis. In later writings the name Phoebe became synonymous with the moon.

PHOEBUS or **PHOEBUS APOLLO**—see **APOLLO**

POSEIDON (Roman name—Neptune) The chief god of water and ocean, and the brother of Zeus; he lived on Olympus whenever he liked. As ruler of the sea, he was able to shake his trident to control storms and earthquakes. He was also god of horses; in an affair with Medusa he bore the winged horse, Pegasus.

ZEPHYRUS One of the Winds (lesser divinities of heaven), a personification of Zephyr, the west wind, the mildest and gentlest of winds.

ZEUS (Roman name—Jupiter) One of the heavenly deities; son of Cronus and Rhea. He was the king of all the gods; also god of the sky, controlling rains, snows, tempests, heat, cold, thunder and lightning. By numerous paramours he was the father of Athena, the Horae, the Moirae, the Muses, the Graces; and such mortals as Hercules, Perseus, Castor, and Pollux.

2C2198